*The Italian-American Catalog*

# The Italian-
# American Catalog

*Edited by Joseph Giordano*

A DOLPHIN BOOK
*Doubleday & Company, Inc., Garden City, New York   1986*

# Acknowledgments

This book could not have been written without Murray Polner and Lakeville Press. Murray dreamed up the idea of a book about Italian-Americans and Lakeville Press agreed to copublish the book. At every stage of its life, Murray was at my side—encouraging, cajoling, demanding, rewriting and editing, serving as editor and friend.

I would also like to thank those writers and researchers who contributed to the work, most significantly Margi Saraco and Alex Polner, and Myra Alperson, who wrote many of the book's profiles. I was also helped by the following: Alberta Attanasio, Patricia L. Beemer, Valentino Belfiglio, Pasquale Bruno, Jr., the Center for Migration Studies and Diane Zimmerman, Ed Chasteen, Camille Cusumano, Donna Cusumano, Rose Feitelson, Jennifer Figurelli, Pamela De Figlio, I. Philip di Franco, Joseph DiGiuseppi, Doreen A. Dimitri, Richard Feminella, Marguerita Feitlowitz, Richard Gambino, Fred Gardaphe, Paul Giles, Lark Gould, Nancy Graff, William Gralnick, Rebecca Hirsch, Kevin Hortigan, Tom Johnson, Errol Laborde, Kathy Lamorte, Vincent Lampariello, Irving Levine, Theodora Luria, Jerre Mangione, Armand V. Mauro, Monica McGoldrick, Gary Mormino, Lorraine Mottola, Robert A. Orsi, Pamela Parlapiano, Ilene Perlman, *Il Progresso Italo-Americano,* and especially Paola Garofalo and Andrea Mantineo, Anne Marie Riccitelli, Gene Ruffini, Paul Sagsoorian, Joseph Sciorra, Umberto Sgherri, Anthony Sorrentino, David Szonyi, Clarke M. Thomas, and Ethel Wolvovitz. I also thank Julian Bach, my literary agent, and Doubleday editors Paul Aron, Alice Fasano, and Felecia Abbadessa. Finally, special thanks to my colleague and dearest friend, Irving Levine of The American Jewish Committee. His sensitivity and understanding of ethnicity was my inspiration.

*(continued on page vi)*

DESIGNED BY LAURENCE ALEXANDER

A Lakeville Press Book

*Library of Congress Cataloging in Publication Data*

Giordano, Joseph.
  The Italian-American catalog.

  "A Dolphin book."
  Bibliography: p. 245.
  1. Italian Americans.   I. Title.
E184.I8G55   1986      973'.0451      85-4556
ISBN 0-385-19375-0

To my wife, Mary Ann
   our children, David, Steven, Joseph, Peter, Thea,
      Chris, Dana, Angie, and Elena
   our families
   our heritage
   and the memory of Grace and Papa

*(Acknowledgments continued)*

For permission to reprint certain sections in this book, grateful acknowledgment is made to the people and publishers listed below. Effort has been made to obtain appropriate permission to reproduce the copyrighted material included in this book. If notified of errors or omissions, the editors and the publisher will make the necessary corrections in future editions.

Thanks to: *Attenzione* magazine for its graciousness in permitting republication of a number of its articles; the American Jewish Committee and the Anti-Defamation League; William Morris Agency, Inc., on behalf of Frank Capra, copyright © 1971, 1982, for permission to reprint from *The Name Above the Title,* by Frank Capra; Commission for Social Justice, Order Sons of Italy; the New York *News,* Inc., for "My Italian Mom," by Lorenzo Carcaterra, copyright © 1980, the New York *News,* Inc., reprinted by permission; Contemporary Books, Inc., for permission to reprint portions from Pasquale Bruno, Jr.'s *Pasta Tecnica;* Gale Research Company for excerpts from *Festivals Sourcebook,* edited by Paul Wasserman and Edmond L. Applebaum (copyright © 1984 by Paul Wasserman; reprinted by permission of Gale Research Company), second edition, Gale Research, 1984; The K. S. Giniger Company, Inc., for *The Cheese Handbook,* by Bruce Axler; Errol Laborde for "The Italians, St. Joseph's Is Their Day and the City Is Their Altar," in *New Orleans* magazine; the Library of Congress and the National Archives; Aldrich, Vermont, Public Library; Bettmann Archives; Culver Pictures, Inc; George Eastman House; Museum of the City of New York; National Baseball Hall of Fame and Museum; National Italian American Sports Hall of Fame; Western Reserve Historical Society; the New York Public Library; the National Italian-American Foundation; New Directions Publishing Corporation for Lawrence Ferlinghetti, *Landscapes of Living & Dying.* Copyright © 1977 by Lawrence Ferlinghetti, reprinted by permission of New Directions Publishing Corporation; Oceana Publications, Inc., for permission to reprint the chronology section from *The Italians in America, 1492–1972,* a chronology and fact book compiled and edited by Reverend Anthony F. LoGatto; the following restaurants for their recipes: Sal Anthony's Restaurant (New York City), Ennio & Michael Restaurant (New York City), Gargiulo's Restaurant (Brooklyn, New York), Mario's Restaurant (Bronx, New York), Restaurant Italia (Santa Monica, California); Schocken Books, Inc., for permission to reprint adaptation of rules of bocce from *The International Dictionary of Sports and Games* by J. A. Cuddon, copyright © 1979 by J. A. Cuddon, first published by Schocken Books, Inc., 1980; Marvin J. Cummins and the Social Science Institute of Washington University for the passage pertaining to the Hill; UNICO, National.

In addition, for the use of the January 7, 1974, cover of Man of the Year (John J. Sirica), thanks to Time Inc., copyright © 1973, all rights reserved, reprinted by permission of TIME. Thanks, too, to Doubleday & Company for permission to reprint segments from the following books: *Italian Cooking in the Grand Tradition,* by Jo Bettoja and Anna Maria Cornetto; *Off Center,* by Barbara Grizzuti Harrison; *The Immigrant Experience,* edited by Thomas Wheeler; *Blood of My Blood,* by Richard Gambino, and *The Things They Say Behind Your Back,* by William Helmreich.

# Contents

**Part One: FAMILY**     **1**

Introduction: L'Ordine della Famiglia     3
How Italian Is Your Family?     4
My Italian Mom     6
A Typical Italian-American Wedding     10
   My Grandmother Used to Say: Proverbs from the Old Country     12
How to Speak Without Words: The Art of Italian Gestures     13
Growing Up Italian Catholic     16
How to Protect Yourself from *Mal Ochio* (The Evil Eye)     20
Italian-American Women: Old Values, New Goals     21
   Women's Organizations     24
What Is Wrong with This Picture? Reflections on *The Godfather*     25
Imported from Italy     26
Taking Care of Mama and Papa     30
   Italian-American Homes for the Elderly     33
Preserving the Family Tradition     35

**Part Two: NEIGHBORHOOD**     **37**

Introduction: The Old Neighborhood     39
Italian-Americans in the United States     43
New York City     45
New Jersey     55
Hartford     57
Boston     59
Providence     65
Philadelphia     68
Pittsburgh     73
Chicago     75
St. Louis     78
New Orleans     81
San Francisco     89
Selected Guide to Italian Festivals in the United States     91

**Part Three: FOOD AND DRINK**     **93**

Introduction: The Family Dinner     95
Traditional Recipes     98
   *Pasta Fatta in Casa* Homemade Egg Pasta     98
   *Parmigiana di Melanzane* Eggplant Parmesan     100
   *Spaghetti all' Aglio, Olio, e Peperoncini* Spaghetti with Oil, Garlic, and
     Hot Red Pepper Flakes     101
   *Fettuccine di Casa* Our Fettucine     102
   *Peperoni della Nonna* Granny's Stuffed Peppers     103
   *Spaghetti alle Vongole* Spaghetti with Clam Sauce     104
   *Polenta al Pomodoro con Salsiccia* Polenta in Gravy     105
   *Cavatelli alla Conserva di Pomodoro* Cavatelli with Tomato Sauce     106

Fennel: Cure-all and Culinary Treat 107
  *Finocchio Stufato con Burro Salvia* Braised Fennel with Sage Butter 109
  *Crema di Finocchio* Cream of Fennel Soup 109
  *Finocchio Parmigiano* Baked Fennel Parmesan 110
  *Insalata di Finocchio e Crostacei* Fennel and Shellfish Salad 110
  *Pesce Spada con Finocchio Salsa* Swordfish with Fennel Sauce 111
Specialties of the House 112
  *Spiedini alla Romana* Mario's Restaurant 112
  *Fettuccine Verdi alla Gargiulo* Gargiulo's Restaurant 113
  *Spaghettini alla Puttanesca, Versione Bianca* Ennio & Michael Ristorante 114
  *Fusilli con Broccoli di Rapa* Sal Anthony's 114
  *Pasta al Pesce* Restaurant Italia 115
Desserts 116
  *Pignoli Cookies* 116
  Strufoli 117
Italian Cheeses 118
Italian Wines 120
Some of The Best Italian Cookbooks 122

**Part Four: CULTURE** **123**

Opera 125
Painting and Sculpture 131
Literature 132
  Books for Children 136
Popular Music 137
Film 141
Sports 157

**Part Five: HISTORY** **165**

The Italian Heritage 167
Historical Highlights: A Selective Chronology of Italians in America, 1492–1985 190
The Immigrant Experience 197
  Ellis Island 197
  The Trial of Sacco and Vanzetti 205
The Mafia: Setting the Myth Straight 207
Politics 210
Choosing a Dream: Italians in Hell's Kitchen 218

**Part Six: ITALY** **227**

In Search of My Sicilian Heritage 229
The Family Tree 237
Tracing Your Family Tree 241
Italian-American Cultural Organizations 243

**Selected Bibliography** **245**

# Foreword

This book is a celebration of Italian-American life. I wrote it because of my life and background.

My grandfather was born in Naples and came to this country in the late nineteenth century. For most of his life he was an impoverished, unskilled laborer. His son, my father, the oldest of eight children, was a journeyman steamfitter and, with my mother, raised three sons and a daughter. I was the first in my family to attend college.

In three generations, then, my family, like millions of other Italian-American families, has moved from poverty to working class to middle class—from the ethnic neighborhood to suburbia. Certainly, Italian-Americans can now be said to have made it.

But making it is only half the story. For the Italian-American, the issue of success is particularly complex, involving feelings and attitudes about personal identity and familial relationships.

The message we get from outside the family is to "be an individual," to "achieve," even if it is necessary to break away from the family, neighborhood, and the culture of our grandparents.

In the home, though, particularly in second- and third-generation families, we often get conflicting messages. In our family, my father would encourage me: "Get ahead, make something of yourself." But then there were the unspoken words that were in many ways more powerful: "Don't change. Stay close to home."

So what does it mean to be an Italian-American in an age of assimilation, in a time when we children and grandchildren of poor and illiterate immigrants are entering into mainstream America at an unprecedented rate?

This book is the answer to that question. It is about being Italian and American.

*The Italian-American Catalog* is my gift to you. It is to be enjoyed for the memories it may revive as well as used as a resource to help you choose those aspects of your heritage you wish to maintain, with hints on how to do it. For other Americans, this book offers a unique and informative look at the lives of my people.

*Joseph Giordano*

# Part One

# FAMILY

# Introduction:
# L'Ordine della Famiglia

What is the meaning of family for Italian-Americans? Are the third and fourth genera-tions more American than Italian? What values have they maintained? What values have been lost? How are family traditions passed on? Are Italian-Americans different from other ethnic families? How Italian is my family?

These questions are increasingly being raised by the grandchildren and great-grand-children of people who came to this country from Southern Italy at the turn of the century. Some are asking whether the Italian-American family can maintain its cohesive-ness while other families seem to be afflicted with higher rates of divorce, the problems of single parents, and the various social and economic stresses—from alcoholism and drug abuse to unemployment and inflation—faced by their members.

One thing is certain: there is no way to talk about Italian-Americans without also talking about the family, *la famiglia*, which is an inextricable part of the fabric of the Italian-American character.

As one writer put it, "The worst misfortune for Italians is to be without a family. Separation from one's family is tantamount to spiritual death." From its members, the family asks complete loyalty in exchange for unlimited support, security, and protection from a hostile world. The family is not just a means of helping a child to grow and to pass into adulthood and become independent, a launching pad to separate from; it involves the sort of close physical and emotional ties that last a lifetime.

Starting your own family and having children does not at all mean separating from the family into which you were born; rather it means bringing new people and resources into the family network. Given the durability of family ties, the family environment assumes overwhelming importance for good or ill; it can be nurturing and supportive or restric-tive and suffocating.

The radical influence of the Italian family has to be understood in the context of Italian history, particularly the experience of Southern Italians, the group from which by far the largest number of Italians who emigrated to America originated. Southern Italians have survived centuries of exploitation by foreign powers, the landed class, and corrupt rulers. At the mercy of wrenching poverty and recurrent national disasters, they learned there was only one institution on which they could depend—*la famiglia*.

The family demanded their loyalty; it got it because other institutions could not be trusted and so were treated with either contempt or indifference. As foreign rulers came and went, only those customs they brought that strengthened the family were main-tained. What was perceived as threatening to family life was ignored or resisted.

The mistrust of anyone outside the family was deeply imprinted and best expressed by the saying "You can trust members of your own family first; relatives second; Sicilians third; Italians fourth, and forget about the rest of them." Thus, the widespread poverty and social disorder in the south placed on the family the burden of sustaining the individual and of defending its members from external enemies. Strong family bonds were nothing less than a matter of survival.

The early immigrants from the *mezzogiorno* (the south) brought with them this idea of the family replanted in a new country, knowing it would again serve them well in dealing with a hostile environment. Insulating themselves within the family and neighborhood, they kept to *l'ordine della famiglia*—the unwritten but all-demanding complex code of duties and obligations regulating relationships within and outside of the family. "Family

3

first, individual needs second," clashed head on with American values of "be yourself, stand on your own two feet, don't depend on anyone."

For some, the tight-unit family was oppressive, holding them back, stifling their needs to express their individuality and to achieve success as American values defined it. They were ashamed, and some even hated their background. Some broke from the traditions; others repressed their desires and remained in the fold. Most, however, found some way to maintain close family ties while also moving into the mainstream. Over generations, then, the strength of *l'ordine della famiglia* has diminished as more Italian-Americans have become better educated and upwardly mobile.

Still, the change in the way the Italian-American family behaves has not been as rapid as one might think watching the changes in family life among other ethnic groups as they too have become Americanized and seen many of their members intermarry and even assimilate into the larger culture. The importance of family ties and loyalty is still taught early—and often—to Italian-American children. A seventy-year-old second-generation woman expressed it well: "I have always taught my children the most important thing is that they should love each other. If I gave them nothing else, that is one thing I drummed into their heads—*family.*"

How strongly these values will be expressed in the lives of the third and fourth generation is yet to be determined. They might provide a greater sense of security and identity; they might also be a source of conflict with spouses for whom individual growth is a more important value than family ties.

One thing is certain: *la via vecchia*—"the old way"—is still a powerful influence on family behavior. The census indicates that intact married-couple families are more prevalent among Italians than among the general population. In New York, for example, 85 percent of Italian families are headed by a married couple, compared to 78 percent of families in the overall state population. Similarly, the proportion of children under eighteen years living with both parents was higher, and the divorce rate lower, among Italians than in the general population.

The data also reveal that Italian families remain committed to elderly parents and other relatives. In New York, 95 percent of Italians sixty years of age and above live with their families, compared to about two thirds for the total population.

Clearly, then, the image of the close-knit, large, extended Italian-American family is a fact.

*Joseph Giordano*


# How Italian Is Your Family?

To what extent have you grown up with an Italian way of doing things?

While families and individuals differ widely on how they feel about being Italian, experts have identified some primary values and characteristics that are common in Italian-American families.

If you score 60 or above, it means that despite the number of generations in the United States and the dizzying changes in family life and values, your family is still very much the transmitter of Italian values and traditions.

Rate the following items according to how characteristic they were of your family while you were growing up and in your family life today.

1 Not Important

5 Very Important

| | *Your Family Growing Up* | *Your Family Today* |
|---|---|---|
| 1. Personal connections are the way to get things done. | 1 2 3 4 5 | 1 2 3 4 5 |
| 2. Grandparents are to be respected and their opinions valued. | 1 2 3 4 5 | 1 2 3 4 5 |
| 3. Mama and Papa's authority is never questioned. | 1 2 3 4 5 | 1 2 3 4 5 |
| 4. Men and women have separate and defined roles: men to protect; women to nurture. | 1 2 3 4 5 | 1 2 3 4 5 |
| 5. Family members are expected to take care of elderly parents and not put them in a nursing home. | 1 2 3 4 5 | 1 2 3 4 5 |
| 6. Old family members are respected for their wisdom. | 1 2 3 4 5 | 1 2 3 4 5 |
| 7. Family members live close to one another and have frequent contact. | 1 2 3 4 5 | 1 2 3 4 5 |
| 8. Touching, hugging, and kissing are ways of expressing affection. | 1 2 3 4 5 | 1 2 3 4 5 |
| 9. Secretive behavior is accepted as a way of relating. | 1 2 3 4 5 | 1 2 3 4 5 |
| 10. "Work hard, but also enjoy life" is a strong value. | 1 2 3 4 5 | 1 2 3 4 5 |
| 11. Caution in dealing with people and institutions outside of the family is the rule. | 1 2 3 4 5 | 1 2 3 4 5 |
| 12. Disobedience is not tolerated. | 1 2 3 4 5 | 1 2 3 4 5 |
| 13. Eating is regarded as a wonderful source of enjoyment and family connectedness. | 1 2 3 4 5 | 1 2 3 4 5 |
| 14. Physical discipline of children is seen at times to be appropriate. | 1 2 3 4 5 | 1 2 3 4 5 |
| 15. Loyalty to family is more valued than individuality. | 1 2 3 4 5 | 1 2 3 4 5 |
| 16. If one family member fails, it reflects poorly on the rest of the family. | 1 2 3 4 5 | 1 2 3 4 5 |
| 17. Right and wrong behavior is clearly defined. | 1 2 3 4 5 | 1 2 3 4 5 |
| 18. Religious beliefs are very important. | 1 2 3 4 5 | 1 2 3 4 5 |
| 19. You are expected not to do anything in public that would injure the image of the family or a member of the family. | 1 2 3 4 5 | 1 2 3 4 5 |
| 20. No matter how busy or successful you become, you are still expected to give time, money, or other assistance to family members who need it. | 1 2 3 4 5 | 1 2 3 4 5 |

*Monica McGoldrick and Joseph Giordano*

# My Italian Mom

One night late last month, the elders of my family decided that the time had come for me to take a wife. After all, they determined, I was twenty-five years old with a good job and no disabling diseases. The fact that, at the moment, I had no steady girlfriend did not faze them in the least.

For the curious among you, the elders consisted of my mother, a close family friend named Adalgisa Varuolo, and an aunt who corresponded with them directly from Central Headquarters in Southern Italy.

Through a mouthful of pasta, I asked, "Where is this wife of mine going to come from?"

"Simple," they answered, almost in unison, "Pompeii."

Of course, I thought, where else?

There is an orphanage in Pompeii, run by the good Sisters, to which my parents have donated enough money down through the years to have built a string of condominiums in Miami Beach. At this orphanage are hundreds of pretty, well-educated young women, all supposedly waiting patiently for the Good Lord to provide them with a willing husband. It was, said the elders, the only place left in this world where a man can be truly "sure" of the woman he marries. Against logic like that, who was I to argue?

Through the years, Americans have developed a romantic notion of what it must be like to have an Italian mother. They hear about the great food and the tender loving care, and they fall in love with the idea of being Italian. What they don't realize is that there's a lot more to being an Italian son than having a full stomach and clean socks. A lot more.

Before we can proceed to explain what it means to be an Italian son, however, we must first provide a definition of an Italian mother. To do this, we have to eliminate all second-generation Italian women. These are women who refer to themselves as Italian-Americans and speak only English. They do their shopping in malls, attend PTA meetings, and for the most part have forgotten or abandoned the old ways. Indeed, some of them recognize no difference between a mozzarella bought in a supermarket and one bought in an Italian deli. Obviously, they are not my idea of Italian mothers.

The true Italian mother is one who survived World War II, speaks little if any English, and does her shopping in stores where the owners speak her language. She is deeply religious, distrustful of strangers, and rebellious against anything new and modern. She does not drive, hates to travel, and owns no more than five dresses. And she is, sad to say, one of a dying breed.

My mother, Raffaela, is a perfect example of this kind of woman. She is fifty-eight years old, has been in this country twenty-six years, and knows only two words of English: "How much?" During the war she lost a husband, a son, and a brother. She remarried and came to this country, not expecting the American dream but a life of peace and tranquility, something she has not yet found. She is stubborn to the point of obstinance, says her rosary once a day, and never, never loses an argument. She is a *vera madre italiana.*

In order to live peacefully with this kind of a woman, you have to adjust. You must accept the fact that while you may grow and change, she never will. (Italian fathers learn this the hard way.) You realize from an early age that her laws are rigid and must be conformed with if you wish to keep your sanity. She is lord and master of her home, no matter what Papa may think.

Still, for those who persist in dreams of Italian sonhood, here are some of the things you should know:

6

## Sex

Italian mothers do not discuss sex with their sons. Ever. Nor, for that matter, do Italian fathers. It is a subject they are not comfortable with. Their parents never talked to them about sex, so why the hell should they talk to YOU about it. Yet, put five Italian mothers in a room together—without men—and the conversation might surprise you. Of course, once you enter the room they immediately go back to discussing the holiness of Padre Pio or how sad it is that cousin Gino died such an early death.

If sex is ever mentioned, it is always tied to a disease—if you do that, you get this, so don't do it. Or do you want to go blind? When I once, jokingly, mentioned to my parents that they both wore glasses, I was not spoken to for three days.

## Marriage

For an Italian mother, her son's marriage is both a happy and a traumatic event. She is losing a son and gaining, *dio mio,* a daughter-in-law. But no matter how good, kind, or considerate both your mother and your wife may be, the chances are that they are on a collision course. Sooner or later the fur will fly—and you are advised to remove yourself a safe distance.

Like all women, Italian mothers have certain prejudices. My mother would not be happy if I were to marry a Jewish woman ("They're not Catholic"), a French woman ("Too hot-blooded"), an Irish woman ("Are you kidding?"), or an American ("lazy and spoiled"). Even if she's Italian, she'd better be from the right part of Italy! Since my mother is from Ischia, an island that is a province of Naples, Sicilians are out ("They put raw meatballs in their sauce"). Northern Italians are dubious because "They're like Germans." If this all sounds confusing, it is. Any wonder why a lot of young Italian men enter the priesthood?

## Religion

In my parents' bedroom there is a statue of St. Anthony with a votive candle burning under it twenty-four hours a day. It was given to my mother by her mother-in-law (the only thing, she maintains, ever given to her by her mother-in-law that did not have a price tag on it) and will some day be handed down to me.

Surrounding St. Anthony is an all-star lineup of saints ranging from Jude, the patron of lost causes (for my father), to John the Apostle. There are also statues of Jesus and a cross on the wall. Is it any wonder that in my mother's bedroom you are overcome with an overwhelming desire to genuflect?

To an Italian mother, there is nothing like a nun. Show one to my mother and she immediately donates money. But as much as she loves nuns, that's how much she despises OTB parlors, because she believes they take money away from poor, hard-working families. Yet I'm sure that if nuns ran OTB parlors, my mother would be their best customer.

Italian mothers are firm believers in the powers of God and attend Mass not only on Sundays but on holidays, anniversaries of deaths, weddings—you name it. They're big on novenas, too. When you add it all up, one-third of an Italian mother's life is spent in church or on her way to church.

A few years ago, after sixteen years of Catholic-school training, from grammar school through college, I stopped going to Mass. I wanted to reevaluate my religion, examine it through reading and thought. I explained this to my mother, or at least tried to. She told me that if I stopped going to Mass, I would never amount to anything, that a dark cloud of evil would always follow me. I laughed.

There are generalizations that seem to fit all Italian mothers, especially mine.

• They are frugal. My mother has been known to walk ten blocks out of her way to save three cents on a head of lettuce. And they especially hate to throw things away. There is a blanket in my mother's closet that was used to keep me warm when I was a baby. Now twenty-five years later she uses it to iron clothes on. If you laugh at this, she throws one of her pearls of wisdom at you, such as "save the apple for when you're thirsty."

• They are clean. They are forever washing clothes and hanging them out to dry. After dinner in my house, we all march like POWs to the bathroom to wash hands and face. Or else.

• They are curious. Italian mothers are not used to television, not having had it in Italy. Consequently, after five minutes in front of the set they go sound asleep. However, as if by magic, they wake up five minutes before the end of the movie wanting to know everything that happened while they were sleeping. While you explain what happened, you miss the end of the movie.

• They are confident. My mother doesn't even know how to start a car, but the minute you put her in one to take her somewhere, you find yourself sitting next to Mario Andretti. She tells you how fast to go, when to stop, what to watch out for, and where to turn. And every Italian mother I know gets car-sick, usually one block before you reach your destination.

They spoil their grandchildren. Italian mothers are no different than anyone else; they let their grandchildren get away with murder. Of course, my mother does tend to get carried away. Last summer, during an afternoon cookout, my brother slapped his youngest daughter, Sandra. Next thing he knew, my mother was going after him with a broom handle.

You might be asking yourself, if Italian mothers are so much trouble, why not just move out? That is easier said than done. Italian mothers will use any trick, any ruse short of suicide, to keep their sons at home. I have thought—only *thought,* mind you—of moving out four times, and each time my mother has worked her wiles.

They use guilt like Roberto Duran uses a left hook. They tell you that by moving out you are nothing but an ungrateful, unloving son; that all the years of sacrifice were for nothing; that the reason they wake up racked with pain is because of all the clothes they have to wash. Your clothes.

Then they ask: who will cook . . . who will clean . . . are you turning into a bum? Meanwhile, your father is sneaking into your room and quietly unpacking your suitcase.

But of course the main reason Italian sons are usually slow to leave home is that they like it there. They like it that the meals are always on time and clothes are always clean. And deep down, maybe they just don't want to leave their mommies.

There is a lot more that goes into being an Italian son than what I have just mentioned. In fact, I have just skimmed the surface. There is so much more to tell, but I can't. I don't have the time. I have to be in Pompeii in the morning.

*Lorenzo Carcaterra*

# A Typical Italian-American Wedding

One of my fondest childhood memories of growing up in the forties was attending a family wedding. It was not just seeing my grandparents, uncles, aunts, and cousins (God knows, I saw them practically every weekend) but rather the special feeling of everyone wanting to share in a family celebration. Regardless of the arguments that occurred between and among family members, all was put aside, at least for the wedding. Everyone was going to have a good time.

In those days wedding receptions were usually held in the home, the church hall, or at an American Legion Club. Most working-class families could not afford to have the reception in a restaurant or hotel.

A wedding was a neighborhood event. The bride would walk down the stairs of her parents' home and neighbors would line up on each floor to throw pennies, candies, and rice. Women would lean out of their windows to wave to the bride or jokingly give some last advice to a nervous groom. It was rare for anyone outside of the family to be part of the wedding party. Female relatives who were dressmakers would make the gowns for the bride and her attendants. Everyone was invited to the reception and it seemed everyone came.

Families of the bride and groom prepared the food, and if the reception was to include a more elaborate meal, neighbors would join in and help. What became most popular, particularly among Southern Italian working-class families, was serving a variety of sandwiches with plenty of wine, beer, and music. At some receptions, the room became so congested that trays of food could not be passed to each table. And so, what became commonly known as the "football wedding" was created. The wrapped sandwiches were thrown to the guests. "Who wants a ham and cheese?" "Over here," several guests would shout, and the sandwiches flew over the heads of the crowd with the accuracy of a Joe Montana football pass. No wedding was complete without the trays of assorted cookies and pastries.

Friends who were musicians would provide the music. They always played "Travaglio e Sogno," a haunting song that no one ever knew the name of but always demanded with "Play that song, you know the one that goes 'da, dee, da, da, dum, dum—' " The playing of the tarantella would move everyone to dance. Entertainment was always provided by some budding Caruso or Sinatra. And there was always a ten-year-old cousin whose accordion repertoire consisted of one song—"Lady of Spain."

The evening would culminate with the giving of gifts to the newlyweds and the guests. The bride would wear a *borsa* (satin bag) on her arm in which the guests would place white envelopes with money. The guests received the little white sugared almonds in a white net bag.

Buried deep in the Italian-American psyche is the notion that marriage is not a release from the original family, but a joining, an expansion and embellishment of one family. Young couples struggle today trying to find a balance between autonomy and family loyalty.

Recently, one of my cousins, a successful lawyer, decided that she and her fiancé would have a small wedding ceremony with only the immediate family and close friends present. While not pleased with her decision, her parents did not object. However, when the couple returned from their honeymoon, the parents had rented an American Legion Hall, cooked the night before, and invited two hundred people to celebrate.

It was a wonderful post-wedding reception. The parents now felt that their daughter was "really" married.

*Joseph Giordano*

Italian-American wedding ca. 1920

# My Grandmother Used to Say:
# Proverbs from the Old Country

*Solo alla morte non c'è rimedio*
"Only death has no remedy"

*Chi va piano va sano e va lontano*
"He who proceeds slowly goes both safely and far"

*Chi va pian piano non arriva mai*
"He who takes his time never arrives"

*Chi ha la salute è ricco*
"He who has health has wealth"

*Una cena senza vino è come una famiglia senza figli*
"A dinner without wine is like a family without children"

*La migliore parola è quella che non si dice*
"The best word is that which is not spoken"

*Amici di tutti, amici di nessuno*
"A friend to all is a friend to none"

*Chi dorme non prende pesci*
"He who sleeps does not catch fish"

*Chi nasce tondo, non muore quadrato*
"He who is born round, does not die square"

*Un padre può mantenere dieci figli, ma dieci figli non possono mantenere un padre*
"A father can support ten children but ten children cannot support one father"

*Lavare la testa all'asino è perdere l'acqua e il sapone*
"Wash a jackass's head, and you are sure to lose both soap and water" or
"Don't cast pearls to swine"

*Le cose impossibili le facciamo subito, per i miracoli ci vuole un po' più tempo!*
"The impossible we do immediately, miracles take a little more time!"

"A proverb," said Cervantes, "is a short sentence based on long experience."

*Anthony Sorrentino*

# How to Speak Without Words:
# The Art of Italian Gestures

It is said that Italians from Southern Italy—especially Neapolitans and Sicilians—are capable of carrying out a conversation without saying a single word. While nonverbal ways of communicating are common to all Western societies, Italians have elaborated, refined, and stylized hundreds of gestures into an art.

Italians talking are often stereotypically depicted with wildly waving arms or other exaggerated contortions of the body. Nothing is further from the truth. Gestures convey a wide range of feelings, from poetic to intense anger. These messages, however, are best conveyed in an economical, subtle, flowing, almost imperceptible manner. A slowly raised chin means "I don't know" or, more often, "Perhaps I know, but I am not going to share it with you." The lifting of a single eyebrow signals to the other person that a discussion is at hand.

These ways of expressing oneself can still be observed today when Italians talk to each other, whether they live in Naples, Palermo, New York, or Chicago. Historians have noted that many gestures used today go back centuries and are identical to those carved in stone and etched on vases from ancient Rome and Greece.

But like any great traditional art, which is a refinement of what naturally flows out of the experience of a people, these gestures are easily understood, universal, and timeless. Here are some of the most popular.

*Joseph Giordano*

## THE KEY GESTURES

1. The Hand Purse—insistent query
2. The Chin Flick—disinterested/negative
3. The Teeth Flick—nothing/anger
4. The Eyelid Pull—be alert
5. The Forearm Jerk—sexual insult
6. The Ear Touch—affirmative/warning
7. The Horizontal Horn-sign—cuckold
8. The Nose Thumb—mockery
9. The Fingertips Kiss—praise and salutation

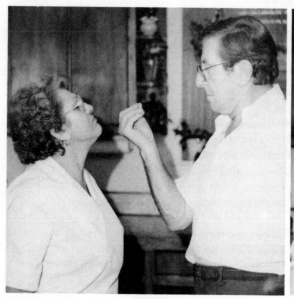
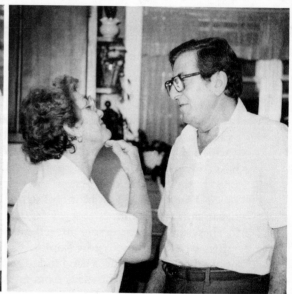

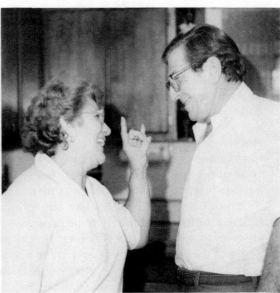

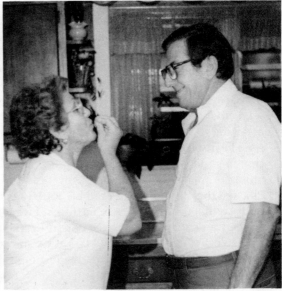

(Photos by Pamela Parlapiano)

# Growing Up Italian Catholic

It seemed that we were always lining up, on hot and humid days, with the coming darkness holding the secret promise of a breeze, to march in a procession. Ahead of us altar boys were holding the banners of the church societies, lurching about top-heavy in the hands of an old man or woman, and the band, a group of old men, half the sizes of their tubas and trombones, blasting away in their warm-up. Behind us, propped up on a flatbed truck and looking bigger than he or she ever did in the little wall niches in church, was the saint of the hour—St. Anthony, the Immaculate Conception, St. Francis—covered in ribbons and dollar bills. Then someone, one of the younger priests perhaps, would come dashing past and minutes later, in a ripple of excitement and with a sudden crash of the cymbals and the uneasy beginning of a Southern Italian marching dirge, we were on our way. We wound our way up and down every block of that Capuchin parish in the north Bronx. On the sidewalks, large women in big cotton dresses, vainly battling the heat, waved to their children in the procession; old men and women made the sign of the cross in apartment house windows; Italian-Americans stopped watering their lawns in honor of the passing divinity; and in the playgrounds, the games of basketball played by black kids from the projects went on as though we were invisible.

Our church was a Franciscan one and in all seasons the monks could be seen walking about the Bronx neighborhood in brown sandals and capes. Most of these men were Italian-Americans, born in places like Jersey City and Union City; but some came from Italy, because this was an Italian Capuchin province. These older monks fascinated me. My father told me stories about their special powers and histories: one was said to be an exorcist, another a visionary. They had names like Pacifico and Ludovico, and my contact with them was mainly as their altar boy at very early morning Masses. They were rough with me, knuckling me in the head with hard, callused knuckles, roughly adjusting my surplice, treating me in fact like a beloved but intractable barnyard animal; but they were also the ones to go and get me coffee and rolls on the mornings when I served the six o'clock Mass.

As a boy, I never waited in anxious guilt to be divinely punished for some small sexual transgression, a predicament that seems to have captured the imagination of many who remember growing up Catholic. I don't remember the Franciscans being at all interested in talking to us about sex. What I did wait around for, though, was a miracle. I wanted to see a heart bleed or a statue weep. I wanted to hear Saint Rocco's dog bark or to have the church suddenly, and for no natural reason, smell of roses. Or even a miracle more intimate and private: my father, a mystical Tuscan, had once gone to confession to Padre Pio, and the old monk had read his soul to its depths without my father uttering a word. Perhaps that could happen to me too, if I went to confession to a man like Padre Pacifico.

The foundation of the parish, or so I came to believe, was a group of old, old Italian women who came for the first Mass at six and stayed right through until the church doors had closed on the last casket of the morning. They always dressed in deep mourning and they were bent and small; as far as I knew, none of them ever died. They must have, of course; but the group never shrank and never got bigger. The explanation for this, I suppose, is that I could never distinguish any of them individually from any of the others, even though I saw them almost every day, and so it is possible that some died and others slid into the pews unnoticed to take their places. I do know that their sorrowful chanting got inside me and offered me, on some preconscious level, a stark and austere vision of reality, a human sense that is as old as the *Bhagavad Gita* or the laments of Homer, a conviction of human destiny as pain and the endurance of pain.

(Photo by Steven Marinelli)

Pain was also endured in the gym where, in keeping with the prevalent American Catholic spirituality of sport, and in disregard of widespread parental distaste for athletics, the younger Italian-American priests and some hard men from the parish put together a CYO and a Junior Holy Name. The men were all notable in the parish for working in Manhattan at jobs where they didn't noticeably sweat. They ran, with the strict moral control not usually associated with men with pencil mustaches, a weekly sports night and an annual sports event, which included as its central event, as might be expected, a boxing match, for which one of these men always managed to secure a regulation-size ring, complete with ropes and bell. I lasted a single round on one of these occasions, finally decked by a blow to my chest that I simply couldn't see coming.

In the summer, these men, the leaders of the Holy Name Society and the Saint Vincent DePaul Society, ran the gambling booth that was tucked away in the back of the parish bazaar. It was understood that they knew how to deal with the kinds of people who tended to come to a gambling booth. Out in front, the rest of the bazaar roared away in the night with the sound of a score of fortune wheels ticking away and of young men racing their cars back and forth in front of the girls. At least once a night, the young, soft-faced, gentle Italian-American priest who was said to have a way with boys like that was seen quietly leaning in the window of a souped-up Chevy telling someone to take it easy or go away.

The course of my own destiny, in the fantasy of my parents, ran through the squat, cream-colored brick building that hugged the side of the church. The nuns who taught us were members of an Italian-American order, brought especially to the neighborhood in the late 1940s by an Italian pastor, a smart and experienced man, who had no intention of having his people's children exposed to the prejudices of Irish-American nuns. This is not to say that our nuns were without prejudices. They were tough women, rough and determined in their labor of shaping the matter that came into their thick hands; they wore their crisp, clean-smelling habits like work clothes, and I remember them going about with their sleeves rolled up, though this could not have been. They favored the boys from the bad neighborhoods, with families unusually big for Italian-Americans and with pigeons on their roofs at home; perhaps they sensed in these kids a familiar ferocity and passion, for these nuns had a fierce and passionate faith that had nothing of the dainty piety of American Catholicism about it.

In the last days of grammar school, I got into a brutal fistfight with a boy who had bullied me for eight years. As the fight raged, some quisling went to call the nuns and the eighth-grade teacher came down to the gym. This particular nun had been trying to get me to assert myself, fearful that I was becoming too studious and withdrawn, too—she would never admit this—sacerdotal. My mother, who appeared on the scene in response to some obscure blood summons of her own, was about to plunge in and put an end to the shameful spectacle of her son in a public brawl. But the nun stopped her, one big woman stopping another. She said, "No, don't go in, I've been waiting for this for years," and she watched the fight for a little while longer with a real pedagogical satisfaction.

As an altar boy, I frequently had to absent myself from part of the morning's classes several days a week to serve at funerals, where my education continued. These were not quiet and dignified affairs. The old Italians in the neighborhood wanted to be sure that Jesus, Mary, and the saints heard what they were thinking and feeling, heard their sadness and got the message of their reproaches, for although death comes to all, still, in this case, St. Anthony could have done something. Throughout the Masses, people moaned and screamed and got up constantly to touch and talk to the casket. But the real time of sorrow came at the end of the Mass, as the priest and through him the rest of the world that was not related to the dead person said goodbye. After this, the family would be on their own for a time. Old women threw themselves onto the casket, trying to

(Photo by Pamela Parlapiano)

prevent it from leaving the church; men tore at the edges of their handkerchiefs with their teeth. Then the priest intoned what was really a farewell: "May the angels take you into paradise, may the martyrs welcome you on your way . . . may the choirs of angels welcome you, and with Lazarus, who once was poor, may you have everlasting rest." At this moment, the undertakers, dressed delicately in pinstripes, wearing gray gloves and walking with a stern and detached compassion, would appear from the shadows of the side aisles of the church and move toward the coffin. The priest and the altar boys, at least one of the boys inevitably in tears, never inured to this moment despite its familiarity, turned away. Strong hands would grasp the most distraught of the women. The coffin was wheeled out. And I went back to school.

The living were left to go their way, which they eventually did, in the company of friends and relatives, and with that mixture of gloom, incipient despair, and happiness that seemed to characterize these Italian-American people of the old north Bronx. The dead were not left behind in the cemetery either: with the Madonna and the saints, relatives and friends, the dead were included among the crowds of visitors to the clean kitchens of the Italian Bronx, dropping by—or summoned—to witness, to judge, and to protect. For these people did not go their way alone. Their deepest trust, despite constant avowals to the contrary, was in the communion of people, an intimacy of shared lives that simply did not know of distinctions between living and dead, sacred and profane.

*Robert A. Orsi*

# Joseph Cardinal Bernardin

The Cardinal of Chicago since December 1982 and the leader of the movement among Roman Catholic clergy to write the pastoral letter on nuclear warfare, Bernardin has often stated his aim of transforming the Catholic Church in America into a "peace church."

The son of immigrants—his father was a stonecutter from Northern Italy—he was born in Columbia, South Carolina, in 1928 and attended the University of South Carolina, initially as a premedical student. However, he decided to seek the priesthood instead, and completed studies in philosophy at St. Mary's Seminary in Baltimore in 1948. He was ordained after completing an M.A. in education at Catholic University in Washington, D.C.

Bernardin returned to South Carolina in 1952, rising through the ranks of the priesthood to become executive assistant to the bishop by 1964. Consecrated bishop two years later—at age thirty-eight, the youngest bishop in the U.S.—he went to Washington in 1968 as full-time general secretary of the National Conference of Catholic Bishops.

Even then Bernardin proved a genius at conciliation and an expert listener—skills that would prove especially valuable in Chicago, which has the nation's largest and most ethnically diverse Catholic community. An innovator as well, he designed a curriculum to teach Jewish history and culture to Catholics.

In 1972, Bernardin was appointed Archbishop of Cincinnati, where he was outspoken on political issues and became an activist fighting for jobs, racial equality, and aid for Appalachian migrants in that city. He spoke out for a halt to American bombing in North Vietnam and, to emphasize that he would not let politics interfere with the need for ecumenism, later breakfasted with the man who authorized the bombings, President Nixon. Bernardin practiced what he preached: he sold a mansion belonging to the archepiscopate of Cincinnati and lived instead in a three-room apartment above a downtown church.

After ten years in Cincinnati, Bernardin was appointed Archbishop of Chicago in August 1982. Only four months later, with the death of Cardinal Cody, Bernardin was named to his current post. In that role, he originated the rules that formed the basis for the ad hoc Committee on War and Peace for the National Committee of Catholic Bishops. At the time, he said, "There is a need for a public voice willing to take risks on the side of reversing the arms race rather than reinforcing it."

*Myra Alperson*

# *How to Protect Yourself from* Mal Ochio *(The Evil Eye)*

When I was a young boy my father took me to my grandma's house, because the family decided that the repeated headaches I was having were caused by *mal ochio*—the evil eye.

I sat in her kitchen, where the smell of tomato sauce cooking on the stove filled the room. Grandma drew the shades and the room became dark. She lit candles and placed oil and water on the table and then rubbed oil on my head and prayed. Then I felt fine, and my father and I sat with grandma and ate pasta.

While I grant that grandma may have had some special powers, the scientist part of me suggests that there may have been other reasons for my headaches to disappear. Grandma made a great tomato sauce. Right after the ritual we all ate. Who knows what curative power may have been in that sauce?

You can protect yourself from the effects of *mal ochio* by

- wearing a charm shaped like a horn *(cornicelli)*
- hanging peppers and other pointed vegetables over the door
- extending the index finger and pinky of one's hand in the sign of the horns and thrusting it toward the ground three times
- wearing a charm made of red and white plastic containing a replica of a hunchback figure *(gobbo)* with a horn-shaped body making the sign of the horns.

*Joseph Giordano*

# *Italian-American Women: Old Values, New Goals*

Anna Marie Valerio is an executive at a major telecommunications company. She is the first member of her working-class family to attend college, where she earned a Ph.D. in psychology. Valerio, thirty-three, exudes the quiet self-confidence of a woman whose intellect and skills have found a satisfying outlet. But she had to struggle hard to get there.

Although Italian-American women generally stayed away from the feminist movement of the last decade, they have been waging many of the same battles. Instead of marching in demonstrations, they have sought a quieter and, in a sense, lonelier path to self-fulfillment, trying to reconcile old values with new goals. It hasn't been easy. Until recently, young women seeking to pursue a career had few if any role models within the Italian-American community, and no real base of practical or emotional support.

"Italian women have always occupied a powerful position within the family, but traditionally they have not been encouraged to achieve in the outside world," says Valerio. "The community is uncomfortable with the idea of an independent, successful woman. It's still more acceptable to marry young and have children than to marry late and sit on a board of directors."

. . . More than other female ethnics, Italian-American women have refused to sacrifice traditional values in their search for greater options outside the home. "In a sense, we're both challenging tradition and maintaining it," explains Dr. Aileen Riotto Sirey, a New York psychotherapist and the author of a study on successful Italian-American women. "Our roles are changing, but our values have remained much the same. It's been an evolutionary process, without major eruptions."

## Different Women, Common Conflicts

There is no single portrait of today's Italian-American woman. The different social, economic, and regional backgrounds within the community make it impossible to speak of one unvarying experience. . . .

Josephine Belli is a bright, dynamic young woman. . . . At thirty, she is a dynamo of activity. In addition to studying law, she also works for the Board of Education and is chief coordinator of the annual Italian Culture Week in New York. Belli feels she's come a long way in the last few years.

"I had a lot of conflicts about having a career and going back to school, and I realized I had to reevaluate some of the traditional values of my childhood," says Belli. "It was a painful process. When I was growing up, my parents praised my intelligence and urged me to study hard, but they also warned me not to seem too smart in public, or no man would marry me. For a long time, if men discussed politics or other important issues, I didn't participate. It's only recently that I've finally rebelled and decided it's okay to be involved, to express myself. I don't worry if some people don't approve."

Married at a young age and divorced several years later, Belli wants her next attachment to be one between equals. "My marriage made it clear to me that I'm not the submissive type. Some Italian-American women know how to play the game, letting their husbands feel as if they alone make all the decisions, but I couldn't take it," she says. Belli's widowed mother, with whom she now lives, approves of her lifestyle. "My mother was a very traditional woman. She stayed at home and let my father handle everything for the family. When he died, she was devastated. She felt helpless, incapable of doing anything. She kept telling me, 'Don't let this happen to you.' She came to realize that it's good for a woman to be independent, and now she's very supportive."

Belli's decision to follow a less traditional path has not loosened her family ties. "Sometimes the family can hold you back, but I like to think of it as a source of strength," she says. "It gives me a sense of roots, of belonging, and it's a good feeling to know the family is there in times of need."

By her own definition, Gloria Peluso Drozdek had a classic Italian-American upbringing. The only daughter of a close-knit family, she attended an all-girls' Catholic school in her working-class neighborhood. Now married to a Polish house painter and the mother of two small boys, Drozdek decided two years ago that keeping house and taking care of the children just weren't enough. With her husband's support, she enrolled in a local college and is now working toward a degree.

"Although I've always been an active person who liked challenges, I was petrified to go back to school," admits Drozdek. "It was my oldest son's teacher who kept encouraging me. For a long time I insisted it was impossible, that I'd never be able to manage. Finally, I just decided it was time to try."

A robust, outgoing woman with a warm laugh and impressive energy, Drozdek carries a load which would exhaust most women. She commutes to classes in another part of town, takes care of her home and sons, manages to squeeze in study time, and still remains active in community affairs. It's not always easy. The family had to obtain a bank loan to pay for her tuition, and it's often hard to make ends meet. They can't afford childcare or a housekeeper. Sometimes Drozdek comes home so tired that she'd rather take a nap than play with the children. Occasionally her husband grumbles when she has to attend yet another meeting.

Drozdek works hard at balancing family responsibilities with her studies and outside activities—although she never doubts that her family will always come first for her. "Some people in the community can't understand why I went back to school," she says. "A lot of the Italian guys in the neighborhood keep saying to me, 'You have a husband and kids—aren't you happy?' I tell them I'm happy, but I still need something else." . . .

## Strength in Numbers

Today there is an organization that reflects this view—one that addresses the specific problems and needs of Italian-American women. Since its formation last year, the National Organization of Italian-American Women (NOIAW), headed by Dr. Aileen Riotto Sirey, has sparked an enthusiastic response. There are more than four hundred members in ten states and some fifteen hundred names on NOIAW's mailing list. Although the group includes women of various ages (from twenty to seventy-five), backgrounds, and professions, they all feel they share a common experience that is unique to Italian-Americans. There is a sense of relief and exhilaration in finally making contact with each other. NOIAW member Carol Pascocello, who heads her own public relations firm, explains: "It's wonderful to see there are other people like me out there—women with the same ethnic upbringing who've pursued a career and faced the same kind of conflicts and problems."

NOIAW is above all an action group, and it has an ambitious set of goals. Many members feel the organization's most valuable service is its "networking" system, by which women can exchange information on job opportunities that will further their careers. Italian-American women have been slow to enter the professional fields—the 1970 census showed they had the lowest percentage represented in technical or professional jobs—so they lack the connections necessary for advancement. Their occupational choices have been limited mainly to the "female ghettos" of the work force: nursing, teaching, and social work. One reason for this pattern is the traditional view among many Italian-Americans that higher education is not essential for women. When women do pursue their studies, they usually remain at home to attend local colleges, and thus have less chance of being recruited into the network channels that lead to top professional jobs.

But Italian-American women have also been held back by inner obstacles. The lack of role models and decades of negative stereotyping have fostered feelings of inferiority. "The media portray us two ways: either as fat, fertile, and preoccupied with cooking pasta, or else as the fiery, highly emotional seductress. No one ever thinks of us as being lawyers, doctors, accountants, businesswomen, or judges," says Dr. Sirey. "NOIAW is determined to fight these stereotypes, to influence not only how others see us, but how we see ourselves."

By bringing together so many accomplished and successful Italian-American women, NOIAW hopes to provide role models that will encourage the younger generation to raise the level of their aspirations. The group includes politicians, writers, artists, businesswomen, lawyers, academics, television reporters, and even an airline pilot. Says Josephine Belli: "When I see an Italian-American woman who has made it, it gives me more confidence."

Feminist writer Betty Friedan recently noted that the women's movement has reached a "second stage," in which its followers have come to realize that family and career can be given equal importance. It's ironic that this "new" discovery is something NOIAW members have known all along. While they have been slower to emerge in the professional world, it seems that Italian-American women have ended up ahead of the game.

Through its "mentor program," NOIAW has taken concrete steps to help female college students of Italian-American descent. Currently, twenty-five students are receiving career guidance from NOIAW members. "One of the reasons I helped start NOIAW was because of the special problems I encountered as an Italian-American in graduate school," says Anna Marie Valerio. "My parents couldn't totally understand my desire to achieve. They wanted me to get an education, but they didn't want me to change, to give up the old ways. I felt there was no one I could turn to who had gone through the same experience and could give me guidance—even just practical advice on what to expect in grad school. It would have been a lot easier if I had someone telling me, 'You can do it.'" . . .

## Job Insecurity

The Italian-American woman has always worked, whether it was in the immigrant factories or family-run businesses. But the concept of having a career is new and not yet fully accepted. Italian-Americans value the survival of the family more than other ethnic groups, and women play a crucial role in upholding and transmitting this message. A woman's career can be perceived as a threat to this cherished institution, and women who seek demanding professional jobs often have to cope with their own fears of appearing selfish or of losing their Italian identity and values.

Significant numbers of NOIAW's members are divorced or married to men who are not Italian-Americans. Discussion groups often touch on the need for a new dialogue between Italian-American men and women, in order to establish a more equal status. "Italian-American men, perhaps more than others, still cling to traditional roles," says Dr. Sirey.

Yet, the very solidity of the family has given Italian-American women a strong sense of themselves as being central to the life of the community. A study of successful American career women found that most of them identified with their businessmen fathers. But in a separate study by Dr. Sirey of twelve high-achieving Italian-American women, all but one said they identified with their mothers.

"We're surrounded by strong, capable women: mothers, aunts, and grandmothers who run households, making many of the really important decisions. But it's always in a family context, never in the context of a board room. We have to learn to use this strength outside the home, to apply it to our other pursuits as well," says Valerio. Adds Dr. Sirey: "We can achieve our goals while holding on to the best of our traditions. It is possible to have it all."

*Theodora Lurie*

# Women's Organizations

*American-Italian Professional and Business Women's Club (AMIT)* 31730 Acton, Warren, Michigan 48092.
AMIT furthers cultural, charitable, and social functions, emphasizing Italian culture. AMIT contributes to Italian relief and various charitable organizations and has provided scholarships to local colleges and universities.

*American-Italian Women of Achievement (AMITA)* P.O. Box 140, Whitestone, New York 11357.
Established in 1956, AMITA grants awards to women who have achieved prominence in the fields of commerce, the arts, and community.

*National Congress of Neighborhood Women* 249 Manhattan Avenue, New York, New York 11211.
The Congress provides a variety of services and training for women to improve their leadership skills in neighborhood development. It carries out its program in twenty affiliates around the country.

*National Organization of Italian-American Women* 54 Riverside Drive, Suite 5C, New York, New York 10024.
NOIAW provides a network of resources and support for professional, political, and social advancement. It publishes a quarterly newsletter and holds an annual luncheon.

*Margi Saraco*

# What Is Wrong with This Picture? Reflections on **The Godfather**

When my radical friends cottoned to the fact that I was a *Godfather I* junkie, I was quick to anticipate and disarm criticism by arguing that while it was possible for a lazy audience to understand from *The Godfather* that mafiosi went around knocking off only one another in internecine wars, making offers that couldn't be refused only to other pestilential pigs, leaving the rest of the citizenry to go about their God-fearing ways in peace, an *intelligent* audience could easily extrapolate the truth from Coppola's film—which is that the Mafia ruins small lives, destroys innocent grocers as well as rival dope-dealers. *The Godfather,* I said, bore witness to the bitter truth: evil, hydra-headed, renews itself and triumphs in the end; in America, the Corleones win.

To which my radical friends said, "Bullshit. Don Corleone and Sonny and Michael were all so damned attractive. They were killers, but one liked them just the same. Their evil was mitigated by their charm." And my brother said, "You liked it because you're Italian." And of course my friends, and my brother, were right. I had not, after all, seen *Godfather I* six times for the pleasure of witnessing the triumph of Evil over Good. I saw it because, in spite of its celebrated violence, it was perversely comforting and warm; it had a uniquely tender, cradling quality. Each time I saw Don Corleone die his rose-garden death, I was set squarely in that fabled place where families honor, respect, support, and protect one another, *touch* one another, forgive one another their sins. Viscerally I understood the Corleones better than, say, the Louds (and I liked them better, too). *The Godfather* nourished the notion that there was someone, some force, who could absolve guilt and make all the hurt go away, someone whose accepted authority could gentle and sustain us.

"Heresy," my feminist friends snorted. "You are talking about patriarchal families who have no remedy for pain, families that smother you, that protect you because you're their property. Step out of line and see what they do for you." My critical intelligence—and my own experience as a third-generation Italian—told me they were right. And yet I returned as if on a pilgrimage to an atavistic part of my nature, to the courtliness of Don Corleone, to the sanguinity and vivacity of Sonny, to the magnificent reserve of Michael—that eloquent stillness that promised everything, that promised absolution. *Godfather I* created a world analysis could not sour. I felt embraced by the film, and not just because I so rarely see the pungent gestures and rich rituals or hear the rude songs, the lyrical-vulgar dialect of my childhood, reflected in literature or art: I have a vestigial yearning to believe, damn it, that there is a safe, redemptive place, a landscape where everyone knows his or her place, where one follows, with benediction and grace, the yellow brick road to the shrine of approving family gods.

And then Coppola, in his extraordinary sequel to *The Godfather,* did more to challenge my cherished conviction that the family can be a Salvation Army than did all the harangues of my radical friends.

"Blood of our blood," we tell one another, "We will love you whatever you do, we are here for you." And then I think of the work some of those men with whom I've danced the tarantella and exchanged-blood-love do in the world (it's not pretty); and I marvel at my capacity to be seduced by the passion and authority and vigor and charm of men whose work I cannot love. And I think—looking at their wives, who have reaped the traditional rewards of traditional lives—what would have happened to those warm, smiling women if they had chosen separate identities, if their paths had violated the ethic of *la famiglia?* Would, in fact, their men have been there for them? And then I think of my brother, who is a just and generous man, whose authority I do accept, who can outcharm Sonny any day of the week, who is always there for me, who stills my restlessness and makes me feel safe, as no one else in the world can make me feel safe. And I think of my gentle father, who has learned painfully to love his maverick daughter, who defends me even when he finds my life incomprehensible. And then I think of a few bitter women, sitting outcast and alone, who are tolerated merely because they are "the blood," but who are not protected, not loved, because in some way they have violated the sacred rules of this large, lusty family composed of good men and bad men, of strong women and selfless women. I think of the strength of Italian women, of strength perverted and strength preserved. And I am painfully confused. I want all of these people to love me, to comprehend me; I want none of them to constrain or confine me. And I know that what I want is impossible.

*Barbara Grizzuti Harrison*

# *Imported from Italy*

He must be somebody's grandfather, in a navy blue button-down sweater, the same gray stubble on his head and cheeks. Why does he sit on a folding chair in a storefront window? He stares out the window, even as I walk into the store. So unaccustomed to customers as he must be, he just sits there, staring out the window, through his own reflection, into the street. Without a word he lets me walk around the store, but there is no browsing to be done. Only one part of the store brings anything to the eye. It is the emptiness that fills this man's store.

Long, shiny, white enameled meat counters, empty. Their spotless windows reflect long rows of white wooden shelves, empty. As I walk on the creaking wooden floor I wonder what this store used to be. It's so silent. I hear his raspy breathing, sounds like the leaves that are blowing along the littered sidewalks outside. I walk to the only shelf that holds any merchandise. Six gold cans of imported tuna in olive oil and four red cans of imported plum tomatoes. I pick up a can of tuna, and the legs of the gold metal folding chair scrape the floor. I stand still as he approaches. I read the ingredients, all written in Italian. He comes to me like a museum guard. I expect him to tell me not to touch things. So I return the can carefully next to the others before he arrives. I turn and for the first time I am able to see his face.

*The Godfather* (Courtesy of Culver Pictures)

You have seen his face many times. Eyes all but sewed closed. The pupils are reflections in a watery brown pool. Eyebrows so thick that they cast shadows over the lines under his eyes. The white fluorescent light shines off his bald forehead so that when I look I blink. Only if I crouch a bit can we see eye to eye. He stares straight into my chest and I wonder if he might be blind, but then he stretches his hand to take the can that I was holding and lifts it into the space between us. The top of the gold tin mirrors the ceiling and I look into that reflection as he speaks.

"This a good tuna. The best." His chapped lips continue moving after he speaks, but no sounds emerge. I nod. He nods. I want to ask him what he is doing here in this store all but ten cans short of being completely empty. I want to know if he had promised someone, a wife, a partner, himself, to remain in the store until everything has been sold. I want to know why he hasn't reordered stock, why he keeps the lights on, the door open, and the store empty. But all I ask is, "How much does it cost?"

He leans forward as though waiting for me to speak. I lean back, waiting for him to respond. Hasn't he heard me? I ask him again, but this time in Italian.

"Quanto costa questo?"

He smiles and his face ripples in wrinkles that squeeze his eyes completely closed. He places both hands on the can, as though it was a missal pressed closed in prayer. He nods his head, as though I have just said something he agrees with.

"Sei italiano?"

"Si."

Then we converse in phrases, in Italian.

"Where do you come from?" he asks.

"My grandparents come from Bari and Genova. I was born in Chicago."

"Then why do you speak Italian?"

I don't really know why I do. I just do. I can't tell him that so I say, "Because I like to." He nods as he says, "Nobody speaks Italian anymore."

"But what do you think they speak in Italy?"

"Italy is far away. I don't know. Maybe now they speak German."

We laugh. But there is a difference. His laughter causes tears to drip out of the tight corners of his eyes. Mine causes my eyes to widen. He makes no effort to remove the tears with the edge of his hand as I expected he would. Instead, the tear drops onto his now reddened cheeks, flows in between the graying stubble, and splashes onto the top of the tuna can, distorting the reflection of the latticed ceiling. When the laughter stops he speaks in broken English.

"But why to speak Italian here. We are in America. There is reason no more speak Italian."

"Why not speak Italian?" I ask.

"Because there is no more Italian here." His right hand leaves the can and waves over his head. "There is only 'mericans. 'Mericans no need Italian no more. Is no good to speak the old tongue."

I don't want to argue with him. He already seems to be tiring. So I don't respond. But he continues.

"Once ever'one want the things from Italy. Then ever'day my store she fills with the customers. My shelves they fill with the cans and ever't'ing come from Italy. It was good days. My boys they work with they father. Cut the fresh meat, put on the scale, wrap in white paper." He points to a full knife rack on the wall, a shiny white scale, and then to a roll of white butcher paper. "But is not that way no more. No. No. Nobody want the things from Italy no more." His head shook from side to side as he paused and looked around the empty store. And then, as though he had received a second wind, he resumed.

"I'm a tell you this store she use to smell like Italy. Ever' morn I open doors at six clock. Iffa close my eyes I can see Italy jus' from a smell. We have fresh basil, oh she smell so sweet. We have a rosamarie, anna all fresh spices, smell the place like they was still growin in mountains. We gotta fresh cheeses: the provolone, the Gorgonzola, ricotta, an my son he grate the Romano and Parmesan right when the customer ask for it. They cheese so fresh you think they was a cow inna back alley. Ever' day I make the fresh sausage and my wife make fresh bread an pasta. An what we no sell we eat that day. There, that shelf she was for the oil and above it we put the fresh vinegar that my brother make. They was inna green bottles. An over by the door they was barrels all fill with olives green and black that swim inna salt water. You jus' dip you hands in an they taste like they jus' off a tree. An over the counters was a hanging the pepperoni, salami, the dry peppers and cheeses and when the door open oh you should see how they swing into each other from the breeze, make a soft sound, was like a music."

As he spoke he stared at each spot until even I could see the emptiness fill with what he was describing. He walked over to the spot he was talking about and picked up an invisible box or can or bottle and described it in detail. Then he would return it to the shelf, straighten out an invisible pile, and move to another area. I followed him to the front of the store, to where the folding chair sat facing the window that reflected the empty store as it framed the autumn afternoon. He sat down, sighed, and stared out into the street, the can of tuna now in his lap. Silence. A long silence. He seemed empty of anything else to say. He just sat there, clutching that can of tuna, as though it were a handful of cards, waiting for a game of solitaire to start.

I felt like a mannequin standing in that empty window, waiting for someone to carry me away. I stared at his reflection in the window. For some reason I didn't want to turn to him to say goodbye and at the same time I didn't want to leave him. After I promised myself I would return someday I asked, *"Quanto costa quella scatola di tonno?"*

He looked down to the can in his hands. He held it up to me. "You a good boy. And for you I give this." As he held out the can, I dug into my pocket for some money. I held out a dollar.

"No, I no take a money. This for you. It's a best. You have a good lunch, no?"

I took the can. *"Grazie. Tante grazie, signore."*

"You welcome."

"I'll come back sometime. We can talk some more."

He smiled and his eyes watered. He mumbled something that sounded like, "Ever'one move away. No one comes back. But I stay. You have a good lunch, no?"

As I left the store he waved, and when I walked past the window I gave him another look and a smile. He just stared out, as he was doing when I first walked by, as though I weren't there.

*Fred Gardaphe*

# Taking Care of Mama and Papa

As every Italian-American knows, we are expected to care for our loved ones. Should we take care of Mama and Papa in our home or should we place them in a nursing home? This is our dilemma, and the solution will differ, depending on the families involved.

My family faced this dilemma when our father suddenly became very ill.

I will never forget the day I came home to my family and asked, "What are we going to do about Papa?"

The response was silence. I pointed out that taking care of Papa would be a great strain on the family and stressed the need for skilled nursing care. Papa's illness would tie everyone down. Could Mama take care of Papa? Wouldn't it affect her health?

It was my next question that broke their silence. "Perhaps," I ventured, "we should consider a nursing home?"

"Are you nuts?" my brothers replied. "Is this why we sent you to college?"

The decision was made to keep Papa at home. As time passed, he became quite frail, needing care day and night, but we all managed. Everyone helped. The priest and the family doctor came frequently, and relatives, friends, and neighbors gave support when needed.

Months later, when Papa died in his own bed, along with my grief I felt a sense of pride that my family was able to carry through old beliefs and values and give Papa this final parting gift.

Of course, my family was able to take care of our father, but what about the family with an equally strong desire and sense of obligation that lacks the means or kin to provide the necessary care?

Government programs offer little support for those who choose to take care of elderly parents themselves. Medicare, for example, will pay for an institutional facility but not for home care.

In many cases, the parents are so ill or confused that they need constant watching. Too often, however, families wait for a crisis, like a serious illness or operation, before they seek outside help. Besides feeling guilty about placing Mama or Papa in a nursing home, they worry about the neglect of the elderly reportedly widespread in the twenty-three thousand nursing homes in this country.

People in their forties and fifties are frequently pulled between the conflicting needs of their elderly parents and those of their spouses and children. They are also torn between wanting to care for aged parents themselves and turning the physical care over to professionals. Even keeping parents at home does not dispel deep reservations about hiring "outsiders" to help.

Italian-Americans in particular have inherited a tradition of taking care of their own as long as they live, an unwritten code that can be traced back to Roman times.

"If one mother can take care of ten children," an old Italian saying goes, "then why can't ten children take care of one mother?" Family obligations, loyalty, and respect for the aged are so ingrained that children who cannot treat their parents in the traditional way often suffer sharp pain and guilt.

Many families who still want to take care of their parents realize they cannot do it themselves. In the old neighborhood, the family and extended family usually lived within four square blocks. It was easier to get some help. But today, with many families living in suburbs and in smaller apartments, there is not enough space and the network is not so available. As a result, the burden falls on the shoulders of the unmarried child, or the parent is shuffled from one child to another every couple of months.

(Photo by Pamela Parlapiano)

While children are often somewhat ambivalent about the situation, there is little indecision in the minds of most elderly parents. A friend of mine tells a story about caring for his eighty-four-year-old mother at home. "Although she was bright and very much with it, she needed constant attention because of her physical condition," he recalls. "I told her, 'There's a lovely place that is more like a hotel, the staff speaks Italian, and there are lots of Italian people there.' I really painted the place up nice. She said softly, 'Tell me, Nick, do you like it?' 'Yes, Mama, very much.' 'Well,' she replied, 'you go and live in it.' "

Although tradition remains strong, there are signs that Italian-American attitudes may be changing. Dr. Donald Fandetti of the University of Maryland reports that more than 50 percent of Italian-Americans in one Baltimore neighborhood indicated they preferred independent living for the self-sufficient elderly and nursing-home care for those who require personal attention.

According to Father Emilio Donanzan, director of the Villa Scalabrini Retirement Center in Los Angeles, two thirds of the people who come to the facility prefer it to living with their children. Half of this group entered the center on their own initiative. The majority of the residents—most of whom are well into their eighties—were born in Italy.

"Most of the children want to keep their parents at home," says Father Donanzan, "but many of our elderly feel they are a burden. They feel that they can be more independent here."

In Dr. Fandetti's survey, Italian-American or ethnic-run institutions were named by 75 percent of those responding to the question, "If you had to send your mother or father to a nursing home, what type of home would you prefer?" When asked why, they said that ethnic and religious institutions provide better care and are more likely to cater to patients' language, customs, and lifestyles. Fandetti found that this attitude was also shared by the Polish-Americans questioned for his study.

There is little argument with the fact that older people are more attached to traditional values and ways of doing things, and that whatever their environment—the family, neighborhood, or nursing home—it must provide continuity with the past.

Within the family this sense of continuity is inherent in the quality of relationships among grandparents, parents, and children. In the neighborhood, it comes from the extended family, friends, the church, social clubs, and storekeepers. In the nursing home, however, the continuity has to be deliberately created. Very few nonsectarian nursing homes are sensitive to Italian-American (or any other ethnic) lifestyles despite the fact that there are good indications that the percentage of Italian-Americans among the more than 1.3 million elderly in the country's nursing homes is increasing.

Of the 22 million people in the United States over the age of sixty-five, there are approximately 1.1 million Italian-Americans. Our median age as a total population is thirty-six, ranking us only fourth behind Jews (46), Poles (40), and Irish (37). In short, we are an aging population and have little choice but to concern ourselves with the improvement of government and voluntary programs for the aging.

The increase in Italian-American elderly also means a greater need for nursing-home and extended health-care facilities. Perhaps developing specifically Italian-American settings for our aged parents is an alternative that meets the need for traditional solutions within the context of a modern American lifestyle.

## Villa Scalabrini Centers

In 1887, Bishop John Baptist Scalabrini (1839–1905) founded a group of missionary priests and brothers to specialize in the religious and social assistance of aging Italian immigrants. In 1895 he founded the missionary orders of sisters. The Order of St.

Charles, often called the Scalabrini Fathers, conducts parishes, social centers, houses for the aged, centers of migration study, newspapers, magazines, chaplaincies, and radio and television programs in the United States and in other parts of the world. The Italian-American community owes a great debt for the service the order has given these many years.

The order has nursing homes in Chicago, Los Angeles, Washington, D.C., and Rhode Island. These homes and shelters are called Villa Scalabrini.

If you have a Villa Scalabrini in your area and if you have to place Mama or Papa there you can rest assured they will be well taken care of. The relationship between the residents and the staff is excellent. It's a family. Villa Scalabrini caters to the resident's religion, language, customs, lifestyles, and view of the world. It provides continuity with the past.

For example, the Villa in Chicago has 270 beds. The staff consists of 2 priests, 12 nuns, 2 doctors, a physical therapist, a speech therapist, 4 activity directors, and 150 other staff, including nurses, nurse's aides, kitchen, laundry help, and janitors. The recreational activities are outstanding; the Villa has a bocce court and a garden for residents to work in. The holidays are celebrated in the traditional manner. The Villa has been a powerful, unifying force in the Chicago Italian-American community.

*Joseph Giordano*

# *Italian-American Homes for the Elderly*

*Villa Rosa Home* 3800 Lottsford Vista Road, Mitchellville, Maryland 20716 (301-459-4700). Rev. Anthony Dall Balcon, C.S., Director.

*St. Peters Church* 709 James St., Syracuse, New York 13203 (315-472-4451). Rev. Louis Pisano, C.S., Pastor.

*Scalabrini Villa* 860 North Quidnessett Road, N. Kingston, Rhode Island 02852 (401-884-1802). Rev. Angelo Susin, C.S., Director.

*Villa Scalabrini* P.O. Box 268, Melrose Park, Illinois 60161 (312-562-0040). Rev. Armando Pierini, C.S.

*Villa Scalabrini Retirement Center* 10631 Vinedale St., Sun Valley, California 91352 (818-768-6500). Rev. Mario Trecco, C.S., Administrator.

(Photo by Ilene Perlman)

# Preserving the Family Tradition

There is no better way of recalling past events and people who lived them than by developing an oral history project. Oral history is the tape-recording of interviews with people who were there and can remember what happened way back then.

• Select several family members and friends you'd like to interview on a special topic, e.g., immigration to the United States.
• Interview the oldest people first, for obvious reasons.
• Read about the history of Italian immigration and then prepare a series of questions *in advance.*
• Ask the interviewees to give a short autobiography of themselves.
• Avoid interrupting the speaker. Let him or her do as much talking as possible. Avoid yes and no questions. Begin with "Why" or "Tell me about" or "How." Make your questions brief. Ask only one question at a time. Save the most provocative and controversial questions until the end. Don't break into the speaker's remarks unless he or she wanders off. If that happens, gently bring the speaker back to the point.
• Pick up on important remarks. "I knew Toscanini" may be important. Don't pass it by with an irrelevant new question.
• Use a simple tape recorder and a good quality tape.
• When you have interviewed, say, a dozen or so people on the topic you may wish to ask your local public or college library or the Italian-American Historical Society whether they would like to make copies for their own collection.

If you'd like to know more about oral history, buy Willa K. Baum's excellent *Oral History for the Local History Society* (American Association for State and Local History, 708 Berry Road, Nashville, Tennessee 37204).

---

## ATTENZIONE

*Attenzione* is the only national Italian-American magazine available. Published eleven times a year, it features perceptive articles, dazzling photography, and well-written commentary about Italians here and abroad.

For more information, contact *Attenzione,* Adam Publications, 501 Fifth Avenue, New York, New York 10017.

---

# Part Two

# NEIGHBORHOOD

# Introduction:
# The Old Neighborhood

In the early part of the century, it wasn't hard to identify America's Italian neighborhoods. The Italian colony, like other immigrant groups, formed enclaves within the heart of urban America. The city streets, often crowded and unsanitary, were used as New World piazzas by the mustachioed men who delivered ice to tenement apartments and the women who carried home piecework on their heads in the traditional manner. "When the sun shines," wrote New York photographer and social reformer Jacob A. Riis at the turn of the century, "the entire population seeks the streets, carrying on its household work, its bargaining, its lovemaking on street and sidewalks, or idling there when it had nothing else to do. . . ." Pushcarts selling tomatoes and zucchini re-created outdoor markets, and the vendors' cries blended with the music of the organ-grinder. The banks, the shops, and the restaurants that catered to the Italian immigrant sprang up on the city landscape. These streets were often mapped out for the uptowner visiting the Sicilian marionette theaters or the Neapolitan caffés of Manhattan's Little Italy.

In time, the character of these neighborhoods changed. The American-born children acted less like their immigrant parents and sought integration into the national mainstream. In the prosperous 1920s, Italian-American families began moving from their original settlements to the city's outskirts. Following previous immigrants, like the Germans and the Irish, the Italians left the crowded tenements for private homes and a piece of land.

The first sign of a neighborhood is its people. Walking along the city streets, one may still hear the numerous dialects spoken by older inhabitants or by the more recent arrivals. On park benches or at outdoor cafes, residents read the newspaper *Il Progresso Italo-Americano,* America's only surviving Italian daily. Groups of women sitting in the park or in front of homes crochet table pieces for family use. Older men gathered on city-built or community-constructed courts can still be seen playing *bocce,* the Italian game similar to bowls. Nearby, others play *briscola* or *passatella.*

Hand-painted signs of small businesses and local shops are an important source of community identity. Social clubs, like *Il Circolo Culturale di Mola* or *Società Figli di Ragusa,* are formed by members from the same Italian town and display colorful signs that are banners of affiliation and pride. The predominance of Italian family names that grace the entrance of neighborhood stores indicates not only the owners but also the clientele. The windows of local lawyers read AVVOCATI, while travel agents abound with advertisements for special, inexpensive flights to Milan, Rome, and Palermo. Specialty shops, which sell imported goods from Italy, such as espresso coffee pots and ceramicware, as well as Italian newspapers, recordings, and, recently, videotapes of Italian movies, use outdoor speakers to attract and please their customers. Passing, one may hear the ever-popular "Malafemmina" sung by Luciano Pavarotti, or even one of the current Italian rock stars, such as Lucio Dalla or Pino Daniele.

Food is the tradition best maintained by Italians in America. The pushcarts are gone, but public display of fresh produce is as important for ethnic identity as it is for business. Italian families are especially fond of such items as eggplants, broccoli, artichokes, escarole, tomatoes, fresh basil, and dried red peppers sold in a bunch. Fish stores still sell seafood by its Italian names: scungilli (conch), calamari (squid), cozze (mussels), and

Italian-American newspapers

baccalà (dried salt cod). These delicacies, along with eel and octopus, make up the traditional Christmas Eve dinner. Local bakeries not only supply the daily staples of round and elongated breads and friselli, a hard biscuit with fennel seeds, but also offer artistically braided breads made in various shapes and sizes for the holidays. Pastries like cannoli, sfogliatelle, and struffoli are favorite gifts to bring when visiting friends and relatives. In the windows of small grocery shops, the caciocavallo (cheese) and the soppressata (sausage) hang delectably above the stacked boxes of pasta and the brightly colored cans of imported olive oil.

The veneration of saints is an integral part of the religious and cultural traditions of Italy, and statues are often set up on the front lawns of Italian neighborhoods.

These family "shrines" coincide with larger community celebrations for the Catholic saints sponsored by the local church or by a private organization or society. These saints are patrons of specific Italian towns from which a significant number of people from the community trace their ancestry. Thus Americans who originate from Sanza honor Our Lady of the Snows, while those from Palermo celebrate the feast of St. Rosalia. The highlight of the feasts is a procession of a life-size statue, which snakes through the neighborhood streets. The largest and best known of these events is the San Gennaro Feast of Little Italy in New York City. On a gargantuan scale, the immediate area is transformed with banners and buntings, electric lights arching over the streets, and stands offering games of chance and sausage and pepper sandwiches and zeppole, fried dough balls. Thousands of people enjoy the feast for two weeks in September.

These celebrations are instrumental in bringing together not only the local inhabitants but also the larger Italian-American community. This is feast time, a time when friends, relatives, and former residents come together to reweave their network of relations. As a participant of one feast stated, "We only see each other at a wedding or for a funeral, and then, during *the* feast." People return not only from the surrounding area but from across the country, making a flight from Los Angeles to New York an annual event. For many third- and fourth-generation Italian-Americans, the old neighborhood has become the Old World, a world of family, traditions, and roots. For those who remain, there is the pleasure in having a sense of belonging, a oneness with the past, and a place to call home.

*Joseph Sciorra*

# Italian-Americans in the United States

| State | Italian-American Population | State | Italian-American Population |
|---|---|---|---|
| Alabama | 33,837 | Montana | 16,645 |
| Alaska | 8,678 | Nebraska | 27,089 |
| Arizona | 97,523 | Nevada | 53,698 |
| Arkansas | 18,955 | New Hampshire | 45,963 |
| California | 1,144,102 | New Jersey | 1,315,632 |
| Colorado | 116,361 | New Mexico | 26,202 |
| Connecticut | 561,542 | New York | 2,811,911 |
| Delaware | 44,694 | North Carolina | 52,540 |
| District of Columbia | 8,977 | North Dakota | 3,722 |
| Florida | 461,757 | Ohio | 520,171 |
| Georgia | 52,279 | Oklahoma | 30,062 |
| Hawaii | 13,994 | Oregon | 60,769 |
| Idaho | 16,264 | Pennsylvania | 1,205,823 |
| Illinois | 640,304 | Rhode Island | 185,080 |
| Indiana | 86,040 | South Carolina | 28,474 |
| Iowa | 36,744 | South Dakota | 4,126 |
| Kansas | 28,692 | Tennessee | 41,554 |
| Kentucky | 36,001 | Texas | 189,799 |
| Lousiana | 165,015 | Utah | 31,240 |
| Maine | 31,915 | Vermont | 22,427 |
| Maryland | 185,253 | Virginia | 122,130 |
| Massachusetts | 749,583 | Washington | 106,660 |
| Michigan | 344,402 | West Virginia | 60,915 |
| Minnesota | 64,545 | Wisconsin | 119,140 |
| Mississippi | 23,098 | Wyoming | 10,916 |
| Missouri | 120,449 | | |

## What the Latest Census Tells Us

• Some 12.2 million people in the United States are of Italian parentage.

• Most Italian immigrants originally settled in New Jersey, New York, and Pennsylvania; these three states have the greatest Italian-American population.

• Most Italian-Americans live in the Northeast. The rest are about equally divided among the Middle West, South, and West.

• Cranston, Rhode Island, has the greatest proportion of Italian-Americans—38 percent. Proportions of 25 percent or more are found in Waterbury, Connecticut, Yonkers, New York, and Providence, Rhode Island.

• Few contemporary Italian-Americans were born in Italy—about 7 percent, or approximately 800,000 people. Some 3 million are second generation, born in the United States but with mother or father born in Italy.

• Most Italian-Americans live in urban or suburban areas.

• The Italian-American family remains intact. Far more remain married than their non-Italian counterparts in the general population.

Bread store, 259 Bleecker Street, February 3, 1937 (Photo by Berenice Abbott, Courtesy of Museum of the City of New York)

# New York City

## Little Italy

Mulberry, Chrystie, Forsyth, Mott, Elizabeth, Delancey, Hester, Canal Streets, the Bowery, the Lower East Side, Greenwich Village—these and others are the teeming lower Manhattan streets and neighborhoods that were the first homes for millions of European immigrants who arrived in the United States in the late nineteenth and early twentieth centuries.

They were not, like their Anglo-Saxon predecessors two hundred years before, dreaming of creating a new world of political freedom or hoping to open an unexplored continent. Nor were they refugees from Europe's nineteenth-century revolutions. They were, rather, Irish fleeing oppression and starvation, Jews escaping anti-Semitism, Italians running from grinding poverty, the hopeless *miseria* in the *mezzogiorno* (the south) and Sicily.

The Southern Italians, the *meridionali,* moved into what is called today Little Italy, into the very walk-up tenements occupied by those who had come earlier, the *settentrionali* (northerners). Soon they poured into slum neighborhoods left by upwardly mobile Irish and Germans. They and their large families crowded—1,100 per acre in some sections at the turn of the century—into cold-water railroad flats, usually with outside toilets. Still, they rarely complained, for even in New York's cruel winters and sizzling summers, their shelter in this Little Italy was vastly superior to their miserable homes in Italy.

They could not speak English, so these impoverished immigrants rarely, if ever, mingled with non-Italians. They clung to their large families and friends, their Italian Catholic (so different from Irish Catholic) churches, their own concepts of honor. Compounding their isolation, they huddled together according to regional, even village, origin—western Sicilians on one street, eastern Sicilians on another, Calabresi on another, Abruzzesi on another. (Mulberry Street is still Neapolitan territory.)

All the same, their lives were vastly better than in Europe. Even in the slums, there were physicians and dentists, storefront baby clinics, and, above all, the public schools. The literate children of illiterate peasants began to prosper in business, enter the universities, distinguish themselves in the professions and public service.

However, many *meridionali* chose to stay in a contracted Little Italy, surrounded by proliferating skyscrapers and gentrified housing. Few Americans understood their traditions and festivals, but were attracted—and still are—to the neighborhood's sights, sounds, and smells, delicious food, and charming exuberance and spontaneity. As a hit song cried out: "Oh tell me what street/compares with Mott Street/in July." Today, excellent restaurants are to be found everywhere in Little Italy, pizza parlors are ubiquitous, and pasta of all kinds, polenta, osso buco, zabaglione, caffè espresso, zuppa inglese, and wines are commonplace.

Today's residents of Little Italy are mostly American-born, quintessential savvy New Yorkers. But they cannot and will not—nor would anyone want them to—give up their special ethnic personality. The people of Little Italy—*questa razza indomabile* ("this indomitable race") have slowly and gently helped make New York the unique and exciting metropolis it is today.

Notwithstanding the intrusion into the area of a host of expensive, trendy shops, non-Italian restaurants and food stores, the spread of Chinatown, and the influx of yuppies (young upwardly mobile professionals) into the new high rises and converted lofts, Little

Italy perseveres. The Italian-Americans from other New York neighborhoods and the suburbs feel compelled from time to time to return—for spiritual refreshment and for a reminder of the rich inheritance they carry with them from generation to generation.

*Lorraine Mottola*

### Recommended Restaurants

*Angelo's of Mulberry Street*  146 Mulberry St. (between Hester and Grand streets) (212) 266-8527.
Italian cuisine at its finest in this delightfully charming world-famous restaurant.

*Benito's I*  174½ Mulberry St. (212) 226-9171.
The best cannoli cream and strawberries in the world.

Bread peddlers on Mulberry Street, New York, ca. 1910

*Il Cortile* 125 Mulberry St. (between Canal and Hester streets) (212) 226-6060.
This stylish and attractive restaurant in the midst of Little Italy breaks from the strong Neapolitan tradition of the area by specializing in Northern Italian fare of high order, well served, and moderately priced. Reservations suggested.

*Ferrara's Pastries* 195–201 Grand St. (between Mulberry and Mott streets) (212) 226-6150.
The most famous pastry shop in the world. Just completely redecorated and more beautiful than ever. Plenty of seating, second-floor café, and of course seating outdoors.

*Puglia* 189 Hester St. (between Mulberry and Mott streets) (212) 966-6006.
Singing, piano playing, violins, and a festive party atmosphere every day and night.

*Vincent's Clam Bar* 119 Mott St. (corner of Hester St.) (212) 226-8133.
At the same location since 1904; famous for their seafood and secret sauce.

Clam seller, Mulberry Street, New York, ca. 1910

# Three Little Italies

***Brooklyn—Carroll Gardens.*** Originally settled by the Dutch in 1636 (who called the area Breuckelen), Carroll Gardens today is predominantly an Italian-American community. The area is distinguished by its brownstones—the beautiful row houses which were originally built for wealthy merchants in the late 1860s.

Recently, through community efforts, a section of Carroll Gardens (bounded by Smith, Hoyt, President, and Carroll streets) was declared a Historic Landmark District.

The Carroll Gardens Association, a grass-roots movement started about twenty years ago and headed by community leader Salvatore "Buddy" Scotto, decided to act to save the community they called home.

Says Scotto, "My parents told me to look for a home out on Long Island, where I could raise my family in a safer, more congenial environment. I dragged my feet over the prospect of moving, until I finally realized that I just did not want to leave. I loved this neighborhood—I wanted to stay here!"

Scotto and his group began their community consciousness-raising activities with a $60,000 government-funded tree-planting program and moved on to bolder, federally funded projects, including the Carroll Gardens Senior Citizens Center and the Court Street Day Care Center.

There was an unoccupied old factory on Court Street, known as the Doehler Dye Building. The Carroll Gardens Association sought to convert the building into moderately priced cooperative apartments and received the support of Father George Voiland, pastor of St. Mary Star of the Sea Church on Court Street and a highly respected member of the community. Because of his affirmation of the project, community support followed. The city loaned $1.6 million (at 1 percent interest) toward the conversion. Result: 125 affordable apartments known as the Carroll Gardens Cooperative.

The neighborhood renewal has been a boon to the family-run shops and restaurants on Court Street. Some of the fine area restaurants include Helen's (complete with open kitchen) at 396 Court Street and Casa Rosa at 384 Court Street. Some of the most interesting specialty shops in the area are Esposito's at 357 Court Street, a third-generation family store featuring quality homemade sausages and fine cheeses; Balsamo's, 434 Court, featuring the freshest selection of fish, and Frank Monteleone Pastry at 355 Court.

Of course, no Italian-American neighborhood is complete without its traditional religious feast, and in Carroll Gardens the feast celebrated originated in Mola di Bari, a small town on the Adriatic coast. The Van Westerhout Mola Social Sport Club and the Circolo Cittadini Mola, both at 447 Court Street, sponsor the four-day feast in honor of the Madonna Maria SS. Addolorata, the patroness of Mola di Bari. The feast is held every year on the last weekend in August. Money raised sustains the club and their many charitable activities—one of which is the support of orphans in Mola.

***Staten Island—Rosebank.*** Staten Island was discovered by the Italian explorer Giovanni da Verrazano in 1524, and today, appropriately, the Italian-American area rests at the foot of the bridge that bears his name. The Italians first settled in the Rosebank area in 1880, when Staten Island was considered a playground for the rich.

The immigrants lived in Rosebank for twenty-five years before they could finally persuade the bishop of the diocese to give them their own church. In 1905, the first Italian Catholic parish was founded on Staten Island—St. Joseph's Church (rebuilt in 1957) at 171 St. Mary's Avenue.

Rosebank's traditional Italian-American religious feast occurs in mid-July and is sponsored by Our Lady of Mount Carmel Society at 16 Amity Place.

(Courtesy of *Il Progresso*)

The celebration lasts for several days, beginning on a Sunday with an 11 A.M. High Mass in Italian at St. Joseph's Church, followed by a procession through Rosebank, complete with two marching bands and attendants bearing flags of the Pope, Mount Carmel, the United States, and Italy.

The society maintains a shrine at its site on 16 Amity Place. It was built by an Italian immigrant, the late Vito Russo, father of the society's current president. The meticulously detailed mosaic shrine is now open to visitors seven days a week.

Also located in Rosebank is an impressive memorial to the contributions of two prominent Italians in America: Giuseppe Garibaldi and Antonio Meucci. The Garibaldi-Meucci Museum at 420 Tompkins Avenue is a New York City Landmark Site and is in the National Register of Historic Places. The museum memorializes Garibaldi, who lived there for eighteen months while in exile from Italy during his fight for Italian national unity. The museum is also dedicated to the memory of Antonio Meucci, a struggling scientist who was recognized by the United States Supreme Court in 1886 as the true inventor of the telephone in 1857.

The building itself was constructed around 1845, and is a fine example of Gothic Revival architecture. When Italy's president, Sandro Pertini, came to the United States in March 1982, he visited the museum as the guest of its chairman, Vincent R. Polimeni, and the Order of the Sons of Italy.

(Photo by Pamela Parlapiano)

(Photo by Pamela Parlapiano)

(Photo by Patricia Beemer)

For those who wish to shop in the area, Bay Street, in the heart of Rosebank, has several outstanding stores. Montalbano's at 1134 Bay Street is the oldest store in the area, and it brims with many fine fresh and imported Italian specialties. The DeLuca General Store at 1253 Bay Street is a browsers' delight, offering a potpourri of various items for dozens of different uses.

*Queens—Corona.* The swamplands of Corona began to attract Italian immigrants around 1893. Here they built one- and two-family homes made of wood and brick and surrounded them by the most remarkable gardens. To them, Corona swampland seemed to offer all the possibilities of country living.

St. Leo's Church, founded in 1904, has always served many ethnic groups, though the parish today is mainly comprised of Italian-Americans and offers Masses in Italian.

Not far from St. Leo's is a modest, charming chapel dedicated to Our Lady of Mount Carmel. According to Monsignor A. J. Baretta, pastor of St. Leo's, "The chapel was built by immigrants in 1925. Today, the chapel still enjoys the regular attendance of the sons and daughters of the original builders. It is a mission of St. Leo's, and our priests celebrate regular weekday and Sunday Masses in Italian there."

Though many sons and daughters of immigrants have left Corona, for many others, an attachment to the old neighborhood outweighs any desire to move. Together, these

(Photo by Patricia Beemer)

residents and businessmen, without the help of large-scale federal aid, have pooled their efforts to build up trade, attract new businesses, and beautify the area.

The focal point of the Corona Heights district, and a source of pride to all, is the triangular park at 108th Street and Corona Avenue known as Lisa Square. A few years back, the park fell into disrepair and was derisively called "Spaghetti Park." Joseph Lisa, Sr., then the Democratic District Leader, decided to act; with the cooperation of the New York City Parks Department, he turned "Spaghetti Park" into a beautiful, immaculate square.

A visitor to the small park will see the American and Italian flags flying side by side, an active bocce court, and well-tended greenery.

Like other areas, Corona enjoys its social clubs, where the men gather to play cards and drink coffee. Most prominent of these is the Calabrese Club at Fifty-first and Corona avenues, opposite the park.

The most popular and interesting area restaurant is the Parkside at 107–01 Corona Avenue. Celebrities and locals alike enjoy the hearty menu offerings. But the Parkside is more than food. At the time of the Italian earthquake, more than $5,000 was raised by the restaurant to aid the earthquake victims. Civic citations from all over—including the Papal Office in Vatican City and the Oval Office in Washington, D.C.—are proudly displayed on the walls.

On hot summer days, people travel for miles and wait in line for a taste of one of the more than twenty-five flavors of delicious Italian ices from the shop of Peter Benfaremo at 52–02 Corona Avenue. Two tempting Italian delis highlight the area: the Maselli Family Deli at 53–14 108th Street is open seven days a week and offers fine Italian imports and brick-oven breads; the Corona Park Salumeria at 107–22 Corona Avenue, run by Giacomino Nuccio, offers, among other items, a selection of fine Italian cheeses.

*Anne Marie Riccitelli*

## ITALIANS IN NEW YORK

• The largest number of Italian-Americans lives in Brooklyn.

• Italians are the largest single European national group in all of New York City and New York State.

• Of the seven million people living in New York City, 11.35 percent are Italian. In New York State, Italians represent 11.03 percent.

• The next highest European national group, the Irish, represented only 4.4 percent of New York City and 5.75 percent of New York State.

• Although Brooklyn has the highest number of Italians, Staten Island has the largest proportion of Italians—28.11 percent. Manhattan has the smallest—3.55 percent.

# New Jersey

The more than 1,315,000 Italian-Americans living in the state of New Jersey today make up about 18 percent of the state's total population. They are overwhelmingly the descendants of poor immigrants who came to this country in large numbers in the second decade of this century. In the 1980s, their children and grandchildren are an important force in the state's professional, commercial, intellectual, and political life. But their progress has not been easy or without impediment.

The first authenticated visit to what is now called New Jersey was by the Florentine navigator Giovanni da Verrazano, who sailed into Sandy Hook in 1524 and dropped anchor in Upper New York Bay. It is believed that the first Italian settlers arrived in the Dutch colony of New Amsterdam, now New York, around 1635, and some probably found their way across the Hudson River to the town of Bergen, now Jersey City.

Early records contain references to one Michaele Mellinot of Savoy, a prominent landowner who apparently was the first Italian to live among the Dutch and the British. In 1800, Giovanni Battista Sartori founded a spaghetti factory in Trenton, the first in the United States. We know that in 1805, Lorenzo da Ponte, who had written the brilliant libretti for Mozart's *Don Giovanni, Le Nozze di Figaro,* and *Cosi fan Tutte* several years before, owned a grocery store in Elizabeth.

Aside from these fragments, documentation of Italian immigration before the U.S. Civil War is hard to come by, because until the separate sovereignties in Italy were unified in 1861 after years of war, Italy was not recognized as a nation and therefore did not appear as such in the immigration records. It is almost certain, however, that about 4,500 Italians arrived in New York between 1820 and 1850, mostly from the north of Italy.

These pre–Civil War newcomers were not so much immigrants as refugees—political exiles, scholars, and tradesmen—who sought a place to live permanently and safely. They became skilled craftsmen—barbers, silk workers, stonecutters, sculptors, and bottle makers—as well as importers of cheeses, cooking oils, and wines. Some became bankers; for example, beginning some time in the 1870s, a Newark clothing merchant named Manzano deposited the savings of customers who planned to send it to relatives in Italy and by 1880 had transformed his entire business into the Bank of Commerce, today's Bank of Manzano.

Beginning in the late 1870s, immigrants from the *mezzogiorno* found work in factories. Many were artisans—shoemakers, tailors, leather workers; others became manual laborers. Some invested in neighborhood stores and taverns. And an important group became farmers. In 1878, Seccho di Casale, who had established the first Italian newspaper in New York, *L'Eco d'Italia,* brought over, in a body, the first group of *contadini* (peasants). In the pine barrens of southern New Jersey, he established in Vineland a farm community that developed into one of the most famous in the United States.

Of the more than 157,000 Italians living in New Jersey in 1920, many were printers, mechanics, and electricians, as well as workers in the earlier immigrants' occupations. In 1910, the stonecutters in Newark became the first to form a union.

Before World War II, immigrants from the same areas in Italy tended to concentrate in the same cities—northerners in one, southerners in another, Sicilians in another. Following this *campanilismo* pattern, they formed *mutuo soccorso* (mutual aid) societies and associations devoted to patron saints that helped maintain the viability of the various Little Italies by providing social and recreation facilities in poverty areas. Their poverty notwithstanding, some Italians managed to get university educations and were then able to organize professional societies—the Dante Alighieri Society, formed in 1909, for example—to help provide the social services needed to foster closer harmony among people who came from different areas in Italy.

Nevertheless, progress came all too slowly. A 1939 study in Newark revealed that half of the city's first-generation Italian-Americans felt that their national origin prejudiced their opportunities for jobs and professional careers. They were right. Only after World War II did the second generation move rapidly into the professions and university faculties.

Discriminated against in private industry and excluded from the professions for many years, Italians could and did advance rapidly in politics. Today, mayors of important cities, government officials, and other powerful political figures whose names end in a vowel are anything but rare.

Nevertheless, Italian-Americans, although Roman Catholic, had to contend from the beginning with Catholic immigrants who had preceded them. Many Italians were anti-clerical, and most were far less rigid in their observance than the largely Jansenist Irish Catholics who controlled the church in the United States during the nineteenth century. Indeed, they viewed the Italians as enemies of the Pope, and during the wars for the unification of Italy, Irish volunteers, including the father of "Boss" Hague of Jersey City, had fought against Italians in defense of the Holy See and the papal states. Faced with Irish Catholic animosity, the Italians established their own parishes from the 1880s onward. To this day, there is only one Italian-American bishop in New Jersey, Celestino J. Damiano of Camden.

Today it can be said that, as a group, the descendants of the first-generation stonecut-ters, political refugees, farmers, and laborers are being granted the status they have earned. Peter Sammartino is Chancellor of Fairleigh Dickinson University; Rocco Morano is a former president of New Jersey Bell Telephone; Marie Garibaldi, recently appointed to the New Jersey Supreme Court, is the first Italian-American to hold that position. In sum, notwithstanding remaining subtle forms of discrimination, Italian-Americans are enjoying a chance to enrich American life with the legacy brought by their ancestors to the New World.

*Jennifer Figurelli*


## Recommended Restaurants

*Bel 'vedere* 247 Piaget Ave., Clifton (201) 772-5060.
Specialties: ostriche champagne, gamberi e sogliola alla ghiotona.

*The Homestead* 800 Kuser Rd., Trenton (609) 890-9851.
Specialty: chicken cacciatore.

*Ferraro's Italian Restaurant* 8 Elm St., Westfield (201) 232-1105.
Specialties: handmade fusilli alla Ferraro, filled cannelloni.

*Valentino's* 1441 Rt. 23, South Butler (201) 492-0200.
Specialties: sweetbreads, red snapper Livornese.

*Il Tulipano* 1131 Pompton Ave., Rt. 23, Cedar Grove (201) 256-9300.
Specialties: clams oreganata, cavatelli, penne, bass and sole.

# Hartford

## History and Neighborhoods

Hartford, Connecticut's largest city (population 300,000), and its capital since 1873, also is the home of many of the state's more than 500,000 Italian-Americans. Until the large-scale immigration from the old country began around 1870, however, the city had only a few hundred inhabitants of Italian birth or ancestry. While Hartford was established in 1633 as a fort by Dutch settlers from New Amsterdam (New York) and was first settled permanently by the English two years later, the first Italian names did not appear in the town records or main newspaper, the *Connecticut Courant,* until the 1790s.

The huge influx of Italians to Connecticut after 1880 (five thousand per year) consisted overwhelmingly of individuals from the *mezzogiorno.* They congregated in the Little Italy area around Front Street and Windsor Avenue. Here the community had its general grocery, cheese, and other stores specializing in Italian food; here mutual-aid societies and such ethnic churches as Saint Patrick–Saint Anthony were located; here *Santa Pasqua* (Holy Easter, the Feast of the Lamb) and *Carnevale* were celebrated.

Most of those who settled in Hartford's Little Italy from 1880 to 1924 (when the United States imposed immigration quotas) were laborers or small merchants. But there were also entrepreneurs who helped establish Hartford's prominence as a national insurance and regional banking center. Among them were Pietro Antonio Loraia (Leroy) and his sons, who helped found the Antonio Andretta and Palloti Bank, the largest Italian commercial bank in New England.

Hartford's Italian-Americans also established no less than forty-seven mutual-aid fraternal, political, athletic, and cultural organizations between 1892 and 1974. In the first decade of the twentieth century, some of the smaller self-help organizations, which were composed of individuals from the same town, were subsumed under the Hartford Lodge No. 333 Order Sons of Italy. The most recent organization is the Italian-American Historical Society of Greater Hartford, founded in 1974.

Religiously, the community has long been overwhelmingly, and for the most part, traditionally, Catholic. Italian evangelical Protestant churches made some inroads in the Italian-American community, particularly during the 1920s and 1930s among its poor, to whom they offered practical assistance (soup kitchens, food packages, loans). But Roman Catholicism kept the allegiance of the majority of Hartford's Italian-Americans.

In the first quarter-century of the postwar era, the city's downtown Catholic churches were weakened both by the drift to the suburbs and the liturgical liberalization initiated by Vatican II. But during the 1970s and early 1980s, the pendulum swung the other way, as church after church saw a return of many third- and fourth-generation Italian-Americans who revived traditional religious and ethnic rituals, processions, and festivals. (An excellent overview is *The Italians in Their Homeland, in America, in Connecticut,* Storrs, Conn.: University of Connecticut, 1976.)

## A New Little Italy

In the late 1950s and early 1960s, the city's long-standing Italian neighborhood along the old east side was torn down to build Constitution Plaza. Gradually, Italian-Americans came to congregate in Hartford's south end, which, along with a two-mile strip of the Franklin Avenue business section, has become a new Little Italy. It is replete with the smell of dried meats and the sound of old women haggling in their distinct dialects with the area merchants. The area is served by such import stores as Mangiafico, where a variety of Italian cheeses and meats can be found. Customers can be seen stopping in the midst of shopping to throw out their arms to *paesani* they haven't seen for a week. Children press their noses to the glass counters.

Hartford's Italian-Americans have contributed a great deal to Connecticut's political life. In 1909, Salvator d'Espoto became one of the first two Italian-Americans elected to the state legislature. Francis Pallotti, a graduate of Yale Law School, served as Connecticut's secretary of state for seven years (1923–1929); he was the first Italian-American to serve a statewide position and later became a superior court judge. More recently, Ann Uccello was elected the city's first woman mayor. She later accepted a major position in the Department of Transportation during the Nixon Administration.

A local radio personality may be better known than all the politicians combined. She is Zia Giuliana, whose Thursday program of advice on family matters on radio station WRYM has caused her to be called the "Dear Abby of Italian radio."

## Reaching Beyond Hartford

As Connecticut's largest Italian-American community, Hartford houses a number of institutions whose influence reaches well beyond the city's boundaries. One is the *Connecticut Italian Bulletin,* which was founded in 1950 by Venn S. Sequentia and is the state's most widely read and respected Italian newspaper.

In 1970, the government of Italy established a consulate in the city and made Riccardo Di Loreto, a travel agent, vice-counsel (Di Loreto had been lobbying to have Italy open a consulate in the city since 1968, when that government's consulate in New Haven closed). It is Hartford's only foreign diplomatic mission of any kind.

*David Szonyi*

## Recommended Restaurants

*Hartford*
**Gionfriddo's** 283 Asylum St. (213) 247-0032.

*West Hartford*
**Dino's Italian Kitchen** 29 Crossroads Plaza (213) 236-4531.

*Norwalk*
**Perillo's Ristorante** 274 Connecticut Ave. (213) 852-1024: 838-7737.

*Bridgeport*
**La Scogliera Restaurant** 697 Madison Ave. (213) 333-0673.

*Fairfield*
**Three Brothers Pizzeria & Restaurant** 601 Kings Highway E. (213) 367-5359.

# Boston

Take one of America's oldest cities. Choose a neighborhood that once housed redcoats and patriots and people it with grandmothers draped in black, children playing bocce in the streets, and cafés where loud conversation and very little English can be heard. Pepper it with some of the best Italian restaurants in the country and you have Boston's North End.

The contrast of Southern Italian life against a backdrop of American Puritan architecture and history makes the North End fascinating. Generations of Italian families inhabit brick buildings of three and four stories built from foundations that once housed this country's first settlers. Women yell to one another from upper-story windows. Old men gather on the Prato to play checkers and tell tales of how things used to be. Young men in tight jeans and designer sunglasses make staccato conversation by the jukebox playing the latest hits from Italy in the local coffee bar. Squat shopkeepers display citrus fruits in sidewalk stands. Nearby, mothers sit and chat on chairs outside their apartments, keeping a protective eye on the activity down the block.

Isolated by the Fitzgerald Expressway, which keeps traffic flowing in and out of Boston, the North End stays aloof from the mainstream of the city, keeping its own tempo and traditions. On Saturdays, a street by the waterfront becomes an affair of massive crowds vying for good buys in fresh produce, breads, meats, pastries, and fish sold in outdoor carts year-round.

Boston bluebloods and brahmins pour out of their Beacon Hill and Back Bay abodes to rub elbows on Blackstone Street, where bargaining is a tradition older than the Revolution. Young boys and old men call out their wares from behind well-stacked carts in accent and manner that are definitely Italian. If you don't like the price, wait. Before you can turn your head you've made a deal.

A skip across Blackstone Street along the stretch of Boston's Freedom Trail, the smell of fresh fish and fruits changes to garlic and tomatoes. Proceed down Salem Street into the heart of the North End and the challenge becomes how to walk a block without eating.

The brick and cobblestone corners of the North End are over three hundred years old. From the mid-1600s, the North End housed colonists and Puritans. Cotton Mather, famous for his outspoken support of witch-hunts, lived in this neighborhood. If a man kissed his wife in public, he was given due punishment in the stocks that stood in North Square. The American Revolution was plotted in neighborhood pubs that seemed to have kept "the English-speaking world of the 17th and 18th centuries excessively alcoholic," according to historian G. B. Warden.

Throughout the eighteenth century, the North End remained one of the most heavily populated areas in Boston. A fashionable section of town with brick cottages opening onto streets cobbled with shells from the sea, it was the home of wealthy merchants and shipbuilders who enjoyed living near their warehouses and shipyards. But the prestige of the neighborhood declined steadily after the Revolution and hit bottom during the early 1800s when masses of Irish immigrants flowed into Boston to escape the potato famine. Around this time, Boston's population erupted from a peaceful 25,000 to 560,000. The wealthy had long escaped the loss of property values by moving out of the North End into Dorchester and Beacon Hill, renting their homes to indigent Irish families. Within a few years, the North End became known as a neighborhood of poverty and debauchery. Families lived without sanitation facilities, eighteen to twenty in a room. People contin-

(Photos by Pamela Parlapiano)

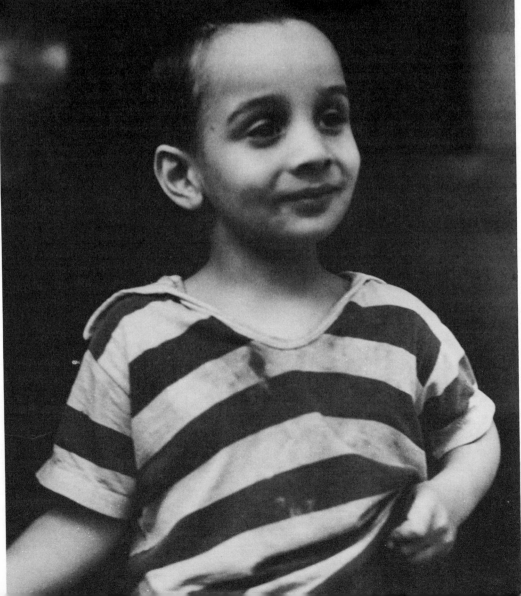

ued to pour in until the North End rivaled Calcutta in population density per square foot.

Boston opened settlement houses to help the immigrants and formed the North End Union in 1890. Here, the immigrants could take classes in various trades and skills. The neighborhood became increasingly Jewish and Italian as immigration continued.

By the 1920s the North End triangle bordered by Salem, Prince, and Endicott streets became almost entirely Italian as the Jews moved to other neighborhoods. Not a trace of the once flourishing Jewish culture can be found in the North End today.

Amidst the poverty and isolation of the immigrant ghetto, the people pursued their age-old Italian customs, adapting them to the ways of Boston life to give them strength against the exploitative conditions of their work.

The Italian traditions can be felt in the many festivals and feasts celebrated through these streets in the summer. The Sicilians have their holidays of St. Joseph, St. Agrippina, Madonna de Sorcorso, and the fishermen's feast. Neapolitans have their feast of St. Lucia, St. Rocco, and the feast of Madonna della Cava. But the feast of St. Anthony is by far the North End's biggest fete. This summer finale, usually held in late August, brings

(Photo by Pamela Parlapiano)

(Photo by Pamela Parlapiano)

out the confetti, which falls like snow from roofs and upper balconies. Schoolgirls draped like angels tape dollar bills to the robe of St. Anthony of Padua Montefalcione, a sidewalk chapel statue paraded through the town. Donations on the robe may total twenty thousand dollars by the end of the day.

On the upper edge of the North End, overlooking the ocean, many neighborhood residents of generations past and present find peace at Copps Hill, Boston's second oldest cemetery, founded in 1659. Evidence of musket practice mars tombstones set crooked and cracked in the overgrown grass. Three hundred years of life and culture can be sensed in this cemetery. Sit on a sepulcher that once covered a secret tunnel to the sea where plotting revolutionaries stored their munitions and watch children playing stickball by the wharf where people once watched the battle of Bunker Hill.

But the nature of the North End is changing. Because of its proximity to downtown Boston, property values have exploded in the past few years. Young professionals are purchasing property and condominiums, helping to target the North End as Boston's latest up-and-coming section. The rift between the Italian-born and the American-born generations widens as gentrification breaks bonds that seemed forever fortressed in these colonial brick edifices.

*Lark Ellen Gould*

### Recommended Restaurants

*Felicia* 145A Richmond St. (617) 523-9885.
Considered the cook of the celebrities, Felicia cooks for Luciano Pavarotti and Wayne Newton when they come to town, and Bob Hope flies her to Palm Springs once a year to cater the Desert Classic. Felicia's special creation is Chicken Verdicchio. This is a breast of chicken cooked with lemon, mushrooms, and artichoke hearts, sautéed in Verdicchio (imported white wine)—served in a garish setting of statues and red tablecloths with opera accompanying the inexpensive meal.

*Lucia Ristorante* 415 Hanover St. (617) 367-2353.
This is a gallery of mirrors, marble, and murals where elegant meals of tortellini and fresh seafood are served at moderate prices. Linguine alla Marco Polo, Lucia's best, has calamari, octopus, clams, mussels, shrimps, and sole sautéed in garlic and olive oil and then simmered with Italian tomatoes and fresh parsley.

---

# HOW TO PLAY BOCCE

Bocce is played in a measured, somewhat concave area, about sixty feet long and eight feet wide. A "regulator peg" sits in the center and there are foul areas at each end of the alley. The goal of the game is for a player to get the balls as near to the target ball as possible. Here are some specifics:

• As few as two people can play, each receiving two throws per chance. Otherwise, three to six people can be on each squad. They have four shots each and take alternate turns.

• There are three fundamental shots: the straightforward bowl; the called shot, in which the ball *must* hit a target; and the aerial shot, when the target is designated beforehand.

• All balls, including the target ball, or *pallino,* are bowled from behind the foul line at the end of the alley. The target ball has to come to a halt at least five feet from the regulator peg.

• If a straightforward bowl displaces the other balls, it is disallowed and other balls are substituted. Also, when an aerial bowl or a called shot misses the target and disturbs other balls there is a disqualification.

• The first player to tally 15 points (18 in team play) wins.

*J. A. Cuddon*

---

# Providence

Rather than being a melting pot, Rhode Island—home to a number of ancestry groups—is composed of fiercely loyal ethnic communities. The result: a colorful patchwork of heritage and culture in the smallest of the fifty states.

The Italian-American population of Providence, the state's capital, is nearly 20 percent, while North Providence, Johnston, Cranston, and Warwick have higher percentages.

*L'Eco del Rhode Island* (243 Atwells Ave.) was established in 1897, the only Italian-American publication in the state. Originally published in Italian, it is now written in English. Every Thursday, *Echo*'s readers are treated to a hefty variety of news stories, features, profiles, and arts and entertainment specials. The newspaper continues to expand as second- and third-generation Italian-Americans become increasingly more aware of their heritage and culture.

The flavor of Italian heritage and culture remains strong in the state's Little Italy—officially marked by Atwells Avenue and called Federal Hill, just outside downtown Providence.

Atwells Avenue plays host to a number of festas during the course of the year. They include Columbus Day celebrations, Easter and Holy Week observances, city-pride fairs, and, most notably, the Festa di San Giuseppe, which runs from the last week of April through May 1. The festa transforms the business center, closing its streets, painting traffic lines of red, white, and green, and creating a pedestrian walkway of carnival sights, outdoor musical entertainment, and processions. Up to 175,000 people visit the festa each year, cramming into a space less than one mile long.

March 19, the calendar's St. Joseph's Day, presents a preview of the festa to come, with massive celebrations held at area city halls and parks and long lines of zeppole lovers waiting outside of Federal Hill bakeries.

Aside from being a festival ground, Federal Hill is home to a number of families that immigrated to Rhode Island and stayed in the Atwells Avenue area. Those families are now meeting an increasing number of new neighbors, many of whom are young Italian-American professionals who have moved back to the place of their childhood.

The city's ethnic neighborhoods do not stop at Atwells Avenue's gates, however. Large concentrations of first- and second-generation Italian-Americans still inhabit the city's North End, Silver Lake, Mount Pleasant, and other corners. These, like Federal Hill, have been or will be thoroughly rejuvenated with the help of Providence's first Italian-American mayor, Vincent A. Cianci, Jr. Cianci took full advantage of federal grants the city never before tapped and rebuilt the ethnic neighborhoods and downtown Providence to display grandly both the historical and ethnic traditions once nearly lost.

Among those traditions are the Italian architectural ones, which have led to the erection of ornamental street lamps, bricked walkways, and Roman piazzas.

At the opening of Atwells Avenue, the city erected an archway to welcome visitors with the Italian symbol of hospitality, *la pigna,* which hangs from the center of the stone arch. Religious and cultural monuments have been refurbished and newer ones, including downtown Providence's modern stone sculpture of Giovanni da Verrazano, were put into place. The renovations marked the rebirth of Italian heritage and pride and have attracted the attention of national and international media.

*Doreen Dimitri*

## Community Organizations

**Federal Hill House** 9 Courtland St. (401) 421-4722.

Federal Hill House provides day care programs, a senior citizens' program and meal site, and an afternoon youth program. Italian classes are also offered.

**Italo-American Hotline and Information and Referral Service** 1746 Cranston St., Cranston (401) 942-8151.

The hotline, offered by the Filippo Mazzei Lodge Order Sons of Italy in Cranston, was instituted in April 1984 to serve the Italian-American community throughout the state by providing up-to-date information on programs and services available to them. The service is free and open to everyone.

**The Providence Heritage Commission** Providence City Hall (401) 421-7740.

The Commission was founded in 1979 to commemorate important events and developments in the city's history and diverse ethnic heritage.

**International House of Rhode Island** 8 Stimson St., Providence (401) 421-7181.

International House was established in Providence in 1963 to fill the needs of foreign visitors associated with the state's colleges, hospitals, industrial plants, and research institutions. A variety of ethnic fairs are offered each year at the house, where programs include an international women's club, foreign language classes, ethnic dinners, culinary arts, and tours to acquaint people with the Rhode Island community.

**United Italian-Americans, Inc.,** 2322 Cranston St., Cranston (401) 943-7221.

Unitam promotes better understanding of the Italian-American culture. The group, which boasts a prestigious board of directors of state leaders and professionals, awards scholarships to students of Italian and to Italian-American students as well. Every year, Unitam holds a gala dinner honoring unsung heroes in the Italian-American community.


## Food Shops

Providence is bursting with gourmet specialty items easily found on Federal Hill.

**Providence Cheese** 407 Atwells Ave. (401) 421-5653.

Francis Basso operates and owns this nationally recognized shop that offers pasta made of unusual ingredients. Basso's spinach pasta is the popular favorite, while the carrot and beet recipes run a close second. Providence Cheese also offers a *tavola calda*— a hot table—for hungry Federal Hill visitors. There you'll find Basso's own cheeses made with goat's milk, stuffed peppers, and other hot specialties.

**Gourmet Gallery** 405 Atwells Ave. (401) 273-9240.

Here you will discover the special hard-to-find utensils that make Italian cooking so pleasurable. Pasta machines, espresso makers, and the like are all at shoppers' fingertips.

**Merola's Omelettes** 318 Broadway.

One block away is a small, unassuming luncheonette on Broadway. Merola's Omelettes offers the best in hot frittata sandwiches, including eggs and potatoes, eggs and tomatoes, and the famous zucchini frittata. But there's more for the soup lover. Escarole and beans, minestrone, and pasta fagiuolo allow Merola's patrons to feel right at home.

"These are the dishes my mother cooked for us," said owner Ralph Merola. "My father liked them so much he decided to open a restaurant."

*Doreen Dimitri*

*Recommended Restaurants*

*Joe Marzilli's Old Canteen* 120 Atwells Ave. (401) 751-5544.

*The Chalet* 1021 Mineral Spring Ave., North Providence (401) 723-6084.

*Boccaccio's* 1500 Oaklawn Ave., Cranston, R.I. (401) 423-6882.

## BRICK OVEN

This brick oven was built in 1946 at the original Palmieri's Bakery on Ridge Street in Providence.

Now run by Anthony Palmieri, the third generation in a family of bakers, the bakery produces the most popular Italian bread loaves in the state. Palmieri's crunchy crust and special texture keep the business growing.

"The brick oven is the secret," Palmieri said. "There's really no special recipe."

Original Palmieri's Bakery (Photo by Kathy Lamorte)

# Philadelphia

In 1853, the first Italian Roman Catholic parish was founded in this country—St. Mary Magdalen de Pazzi, established at Seventh and Montrose streets in South Philadelphia. At the time of its founding there were fewer than two hundred Italians in all of Philadelphia, most of whom were from Northern Italy. But when Southern Italians began to emigrate in huge numbers by the 1880s, many came to Philadelphia to settle near St. Mary's.

Once established in Philadelphia, immigrants spread throughout the area according to occupation. A large number of Italians moved to the northwest section of the city, which attracted laborers who wanted to work on the railroad then being built. Northwest Philadelphia also served as a stopping point for Italians who would soon move on to work in the northern and western Pennsylvania coal mines. A number of Italians moved to the Main Line suburbs of Wayne and Stratford to work in stone quarries and take landscaping jobs on the estates of the rich.

But South Philadelphia drew the largest number of Italians for several reasons: a small Italian community had already been established there at St. Mary's parish, and it was close to construction and textile companies, which were the largest employers of Italians in the late nineteenth and early twentieth centuries. Italians living in South Philadelphia lived in boardinghouses with their *paesani* (those who came from the same section of Italy) or would rent one bedroom of a row house.

Today, more than a quarter of a million Italians reside in the South Philadelphia area. South Philadelphia's Italian Market, which runs up Ninth Street from Federal to Christian streets, is a noisy and bustling row of shops and stalls. Butchers hang hogs' heads and sides of beef in their windows; live crabs desperately attempt to claw their way out of open bushels; fruit is piled high on stands set up at curbside.

The Ninth Street open-air market was originally established by Jewish clothing merchants in the 1880s. By 1905, the Italians, moving into the area, set up fruit and produce carts.

Anyone armed with a little money and a large shopping bag can pick up almost anything. Irv's, near Washington Avenue, specializes in women's dresses and jeans. Various Asian merchants up and down the street sell T-shirts and accessories. DiBruno's and Claudio, King of Cheese sell all kinds of domestic and imported cheeses, including low-fat and low-salt cheeses. Sarcone's Bakery, at the top of the market near Christian, features, among various kinds of bread, homemade pizza shells and pepperoni loaf. If looking at slabs of beef or fish makes you hungry, you can buy a roast pork or tripe sandwich at Willie's, on Christian just off Ninth.

If you're buying fruits or vegetables from the stalls, comparison shop. It doesn't take much effort, because the vendors usually call out their prices continuously. The vendors also usually describe their inventory: "I got watermelons! Peaches! Grapefruit! I got tomatoes! Oranges! Apples!" or "Peaches! Sweet as sugar!"

The crowded conditions give the market a charm no suburban mall could hope to match. Worried about the pileup of trash, the Ninth Street Businessman's Association President, Harry Crimi, recently proposed that air-pressurized trash receptacles be built into manholes, which would suck trash away. But, for now, the trash, along with the noise and bustle, will remain.

*Joseph DiGiuseppi*

## Cheesesteaks and Hoagies

Cheesesteaks and hoagies are South Philly's major contribution to the gastronomic world. A cheesesteak is a thinly sliced minute steak fried with oil on a griddle, topped with American cheese, provolone cheese, or Cheese Whiz and put in a soft Italian roll, to which are added fried onions, hot peppers, mushrooms (rarely), and sometimes tomato sauce.

Hoagies (known elsewhere as subs or heroes) are made with provolone cheese and a variety of Italian cold cuts, such as capocollo, boiled ham, salami, and Italian ham, in a soft Italian roll. Add thick tomato and onion slices, olive oil, lettuce, and hot peppers to taste.

South Philly food is best eaten at an outdoor stand. You don't sit down, you lean on the counter to make sure you don't get oil all over yourself. You can get a cheesesteak or hoagie (or both) at Pat's King of Steaks, Ninth Street and Passyunk (Pa-shunk) Avenue, where you can see pictures of celebrities ranging from Sylvester Stallone to Rocky Graziano; Geno's, across the street from Pat's, which also features a twenty-five-cent cup of coffee, and Oregon Steaks, Oregon Avenue and Juniper Street.

You can eat indoors, sitting, at Ragozzino's, 737 South Tenth Street, a block away from the Italian Market, or Emil's, Broad and Moore streets. Either way, have fun and don't use too much hot pepper.

## Radio

Dalmazio DiCristofaro hosts the Italian-language program "Italy of Today" on WFLN, 95.7 FM. Broadcast on Sundays nine-thirty to noon, "Italy of Today" features Neapolitan, operatic, and popular music. (Call to request your favorite.) In between, hear commentary as well as soccer scores and standings. News is beamed via satellite from RAI, the Italian radio-television network.

Frank Sinatra fans have a variety of all-Sinatra programming. Frank sings solo weekdays from eleven to noon on WPEN, 950 AM. Catch Ol' Blue Eyes on the weekends on "Friday with Frank," 6 to 10 P.M. Fridays, and "Sunday with Sinatra." Both shows are broadcast in stereo on WWDB, 96.5 FM.

## Recommended Restaurants

**Dante and Luigi Corona di Ferro** 762 South Tenth St. (215) 922-9501.

Known sometimes as Dante and Luigi's, sometimes as Corona di Ferro, this warm and comfortable restaurant originated as a boardinghouse for immigrants from Abruzzi. Dante's atmosphere reflects its strong Italian tradition: tables with red-checked tablecloths fill up two rooms with high ceilings and portraits on the walls. The staff keeps the Italian tradition of hospitality, as well: the service is prompt and friendly. The large menu changes daily, but the homemade macaroni dishes and large antipasto are always available. (Smaller portions are available for children.) Dante's doesn't accept credit cards, but the prices are extremely reasonable. In an area known for Italian restaurants, Dante and Luigi's is outstanding.

**Cent'Anni** 770 South Seventh St. (215) 925-5558.

Taking its name from the toast that wishes you a hundred years of life, this restaurant's decor is reminiscent of an old-fashioned Mulberry Street dining room. Cent'Anni is a small place with a bar in the back and little Christmas lights twinkling around plants. Specialties include chicken Giacomo, which is chicken cooked with artichokes, peppers,

Typical row house block in South Philadelphia (Photo by Steven Marinelli)

(Photo by Joseph DiGiuseppe)

Statue of Christopher Columbus, Marconi Plaza, South Philadelphia (Photo by Joseph DiGiuseppe)

and mushrooms, as well as fettuccine Alfredo. Cent'Anni serves special dishes on certain nights, such as frutti di mare, a shellfish combination cooked and served over linguini.

**Marra's** 1734 Passyunk Ave. (215) 389-9042.

This noisy and informal restaurant in the middle of a shopping area has been a South Philly favorite for a long time. You can play Frank Sinatra and Tony Bennett favorites on the jukebox, and large tables in the back room can accommodate groups of diners. Marra's bakes its pizzas in a brick oven, and all sizes and combinations are available. Broiled or fried seafood combinations and a variety of pasta dishes are served as well.

**Palumbo's** Eighth and Catherine streets (215) 627-7272.

Palumbo's began as an immigrant boardinghouse, but is better known as a Philadelphia entertainment landmark. It is one of Philadelphia's few nightclubs; entertainers such as Jimmy Durante and Frank Sinatra have appeared there. Comedians David Brenner and Joey Bishop got their start at Palumbo's and usually come back to play the place. During the season, young entertainers show their stuff alongside more established stars.

Palumbo's Nostalgia Room Restaurant is open year-round. Its red velvet walls display pictures of the entertainers who've appeared at the nightclub. Dishes include scungilli, calamari (squid), and rigatoni with sausage.

**Ralph's** 760 South Ninth St. (215) 627-6011.

A block away from the Italian Market on Ninth Street, Ralph's is a bustling, old-fashioned restaurant. Seating consists of two rows of small tables on either side of a wide middle aisle that leads directly from the front door to the kitchen. Ralph's specializes in lasagne and in old-time favorites such as escarole, tripe, squid, and red peppers in oil and garlic. Children's portions are available. A banquet room on the second floor is available for private parties.

**Strolli's** 1528 Dickinson St. (215) 336-3390.

Strolli's was a small restaurant in the back room of a tavern that attracted neighborhood people until the Philadelphia newspapers got hold of it. Now reservations are practically a necessity, and the little room is constantly crowded. But the food that first attracted the locals remains the same, and prices remain inexpensive compared with other Italian restaurants. Specialties include veal piccante, which is slices of veal sautéed in lemon, butter, and herbs; stuffed eggplant, and pasta and beans. Viewing the walls, you can see glowing newspaper reviews, a life preserver, and a memento of John and Carmella Strolli's trip to the Vatican.

**Victor's Café** 1303 Dickinson St. (215) 468-3040.

The Victor in the name stands for RCA Victor: this restaurant was a record store before the Depression. Restaurateur John di Stefano kept the opera records from his father's inventory while collecting others, and now Victor's back room holds thousands of operatic selections. Diners can request their favorite aria and listen to Caruso, Gigli, Lanza, or Pavarotti as they eat. Victor's features lasagne, veal dishes, and pasta.

## Organizations

**America-Italy Society of Philadelphia** 1420 Walnut St., Suite 1206, Philadelphia, Pa. 19102.

This nonprofit organization promotes ties between Italy and America. The society sponsors lectures and conferences on Italian culture and politics, screens Italian films, maintains a collection of Italian books and magazines, and conducts Italian classes at all levels.

*Columbus Civic Association of Pennsylvania, Inc.* 1312 South Tenth St., Philadelphia, Pa. 19147.

*Columbus Day Committee of Philadelphia* 912 South Eighth St., Philadelphia, Pa. 19148.
   Philadelphia's Columbus Parade is held the Sunday before Columbus Day, when bands, clubs, and fraternal organizations march down South Broad Street. The parade begins at Federal Street and ends at Columbus's statue at Marconi Plaza, Broad Street and Oregon Avenue. Many Italian restaurants and bakeries sell food at Marconi Plaza after the parade.

*Order Sons of Italy in America (O.S.I.A.)* Grand Lodge of Pennsylvania, 1520 Locust St., Philadelphia, Pa. 19102 (215) 732-7501.
   The Sons of Italy sponsors civic and social activities, sponsors scholarships, and publishes the monthly *Sons of Italy Times,* the back page of which is written in Italian.

*Philadelphia Chapter UNICO National c/o Unico Village, Inc.* Seventy-second and Brant Place, Philadelphia, Pa. 19153 (215) 365-1828.
   UNICO stands for Unity, Neighbors, Integrity, and Charity. This Southwest Philadelphia organization runs Unico Village, a retirement home, and raises funds for senior citizens and the mentally retarded.

*Joseph DiGiuseppi*

# *Pittsburgh*

The Italian-Americans are not only one of the largest nationality groups in Pittsburgh, their climb upward from immigrant days has been one of the most spectacularly successful, especially in politics.

   The Pittsburgh Italian community boasts a mayor, Richard Caliguiri; the first Italian-American chief judge of a U.S. circuit court of appeals, Ruggiero Aldisert; a state supreme court justice, Stephen Zappala; and Allegheny County controller, Frank Lucchino. In addition, both the bishop of the Catholic Diocese of Pittsburgh, Anthony Bevilacqua, and the auxiliary bishop, Anthony Bosco, are of Italian heritage.

   There are an estimated 50,000 Italian-Americans in Pittsburgh's 400,000 population, and 180,000 in Allegheny County's 1.6 million. Most Pittsburgh Italians originally hailed from the Southern Italian regions of Abruzzi, Calabria, and Sicily.

   Sometimes they came literally as a community. For example, many of the Italians in the Oakland section of Pittsburgh originated in Gambarale, a small Abruzzi town. It is said that anyone born in Gambarale has a 50-50 chance of emigrating to the Panther Hollow section of Oakland.

   Another virtual community immigration was from Ataleta, also in the Abruzzi mountains, to settle in the Bloomfield section of Pittsburgh. Atalesi say there are more of them in Pittsburgh now than lived in their native city during its 155 years as a town.

   Sicilians settled in the Lower Hill and Manchester sections of Pittsburgh and in Duquesne, a town upriver on the Monongahela. Immigrants from Calabria made their homes in the Lower Hill and those from Naples in the East Liberty section.

There was one major exception to the rule that Pittsburgh's Italians came from the south. The town of Sant'Alessio outside Lucca is the ancestral home of two large Pittsburgh families well known in the restaurant and bakery business—the Tambellinis and the Barsottis.

When the Italians came to the United States in the 1890s and early 1900s, many came as laborers (the *padrone* system). A large number who came to western Pennsylvania went into the coal mines, but that was usually temporary. Italian immigrants quickly moved into construction work of all kinds—residential, commercial, industrial—and into small businesses, with an emphasis on groceries, produce, and restaurants, and into tailoring and barbering.

Italian-Americans are prominent in the construction business, and many a Pittsburgh householder has found that when he or she needs a roof fixed, a lawn landscaped, a chimney repaired, a floor installed or tiled, or an addition constructed, an Italian-owned business is recommended by knowledgeable neighbors.

National churches were established here, but often the Italians found themselves served by non-Italian priests. The diocese frequently felt it had fulfilled its obligation by assigning one Italian-speaking priest to a parish. Some Pittsburghers assert that this is why the church in Pittsburgh never had the hold, particularly on Italian men, that it did with other immigrant groups.

But the story has had a triumphant ending. The first non-Irish priest to break into the bishopric here was of Italian descent. When Anthony Bosco, who had grown up in Pittsburgh's Northside neighborhood, was elevated to be auxiliary bishop in 1970, the event was approved by more than Italians. Bishop Bosco recalls with amusement how a Polish parishioner pumped his hand with the congratulatory, "You're not a Slav, but at least you're not Irish!"

Then in 1983 came the appointment of Anthony Bevilacqua from Brooklyn as bishop of the Pittsburgh diocese. The breakthrough was complete.

In Pittsburgh today there is only one remaining predominantly Italian neighborhood —Bloomfield, flanking Liberty Avenue two miles from downtown. Immaculate Conception Church is the anchor for a community with small shops and restaurants and other Italian-oriented businesses.

Only a few shops remain on Larimer Avenue in East Liberty, once an Italian-American hub community.

The Italian Nationality Room, one of nineteen nationality rooms at the University of Pittsburgh, recreates the atmosphere of a fifteenth-century Tuscan monastery. Each student bench is carved with the name and founding date of an Italian university, while the painting on the rear wall features Elena Cornaro, the world's first woman university graduate.

The night on which the Pittsburgh Italians perform is always a highlight of the three-night Pittsburgh Folk Festival, in which twenty to twenty-four of Pittsburgh's nationality groups participate. The Italians, along with the other groups, operate a food booth and an exhibit booth each night throughout the festival, which usually is held on the weekend before Memorial Day. For detailed information, including the night of the Italian stage performance of music and dancing, call (412) 227-6812.

The Italian Day Triad is a three-day festival in mid-July, including a mass, brunch, community visits to the elderly and entertainment for handicapped children, and Italian Day at Kennywood Amusement Park near Pittsburgh. For information, call the Pittsburgh office of the Italian Sons and Daughters of America, (412) 261-3550.

At the Church of Madonna di Castello in Swissvale (just east of Pittsburgh), the Feast of St. Anthony is celebrated June 13 and also the first Sunday in September; the Feast of

St. Simeon, the second Sunday of October; and the Feast of Our Lady of Mt. Carmel, the third Sunday of October. For information call (412) 271-5666.

## Recommended Restaurants

Included in this list are specific recommendations by Mike Kalina, restaurant critic for the Pittsburgh *Post-Gazette:*

*Caffé degli Amici* 4627 Liberty Ave. (Bloomfield neighborhood) (412) 687-1070.

*Emilia Romagna Ristorante* 942 Penn Ave. (downtown) (412) 765-3598.

*Piccolo Piccolo* 1 Wood St. (downtown) (412) 261-7234.

*un Poco di Roma* 2930 South Park Rd., Bethel Park (South Hills) (412) 833-9009.

*Poli's* 2607 Murray Ave. (Squirrel Hill neighborhood) (412) 521-6400.

*Rico's* 2330 Evergreen Rd., Ross Township (North Hills) (412) 931-1989.

*F. Tambellini* 139 Seventh St. (downtown) (412) 391-1091.

*Louis Tambellini* 860 Saw Mill Run Blvd. (Overbrook neighborhood) (412) 481-1118.

*Tambellini-Woods* 213 Wood St. (downtown) (412) 281-9956.

*Clarke M. Thomas*

# Chicago

The first Italians to reach Chicago—four men, in 1850—emigrated from Northern Italy and settled in the downtown area, then the city's red-light district. As Italian immigration to Chicago increased at the turn of the century, areas of Chicago began to be inhabited by people who had once lived in the same regions in Southern Italy.

The Near North Side became known as Little Sicily; a South Clark Street community was predominantly settled by Calabresi; the Grand Avenue community was made up of mostly Terminesi; a large Tuscan community settled near Twenty-fourth and Oakley; the Roseland/Pullman area was settled by large groups of Piemontesi, Calabresi, and Venetians; and the suburban community of Chicago Heights was largely Amasenesi and Marchegiani.

From a total of four Italians in 1850 to more than sixteen thousand in 1900, Chicago's Italian population has grown to more than five hundred thousand today. And so, where are the Little Italies?

As early as 1937, Chicago's Little Italies had begun disappearing. The Chicago *Tribune* ran an article entitled "Wrecker's Ax Sounds Requiem of Little Italy," October 10, 1937:

"The neighborhood surrounding Grand Avenue and Halsted Street, which for three generations has been a copy of a Southern Italian village, is tumbling down. . . .

Gradually throughout the years the factories of an industrialized Chicago have crept up on the cottages and flats that at one time housed a population of 70,000 to a square mile."

This area was but one of many peculiar Italian settlements, of which only fragments remain today. Chicago's Italian population settled in areas that later proved to be prime real estate. The Near West Side neighborhood, known as Taylor Street, once housed the largest concentration of Italians. This area was first drawn by the Eisenhower Expressway, then quartered by the Dan Ryan Expressway, and finally gutted by the University of Illinois at Chicago.

Those Little Italies that did not fall prey to urban renewal eventually disintegrated as second and third generations of Italian-Americans climbed the economic ladder and left the inner-city areas.

Though the city centers of Italian-Americans have disappeared, there is a strong show of Chicago's Italian-American community at the various religious and social festivals. The largest of these is the Feast of Our Lady of Mt. Carmel, held every year (since 1894) in mid-July in Melrose Park, a suburb just west of the city. Every August, there is a large Festa Italiana held on Chicago's Navy Pier, which has grown in popularity each year.

A new show of Italian-American life has cropped up on Harlem Avenue, the street that forms the western border of the city. Running north from North Avenue to Foster Avenue, new Italian delicatessens, cafés, bakeries, restaurants, grocery stores, import stores, and specialty shops have created a renaissance of Italian-American culture.

The Italian-American community of Chicago and its suburbs are united socially and served by *Fra Noi*, the largest Italian-American monthly newspaper in the United States, published by the Scalabrini Fathers of Villa Scalabrini.

There has also been a resurgence of interest in preserving Italian-American history in Chicago. Professor Dominic Candeloro guided the Italians in Chicago project. The collection of this project is housed in the Italian Cultural Center in Stone Park, Illinois.

The Italians of Chicago, though not as obvious a population as before, continue to influence the style of life and culture of Chicago. Italians are still alive and strong and scattered throughout the city and its suburbs, thriving as little pieces of Italy.

*Fred L. Gardaphe*

## Recommended Restaurants

### DOWNTOWN–NEAR NORTH

**Como Inn**  546 N. Milwaukee (312) 421-5222.

Practically a Chicago landmark, the Como Inn serves classic Italian food in a setting that brings to mind Renaissance Florence. Any dish prepared alla Yolanda (named after the owners' mother) is certain to be robust.

**Danilo's Restaurant**  1235 W. Grand (312) 421-0218.

Danilo's is located in a refurbished old neighborhood house. The stracciatella here does justice to its Roman origins, pasta dishes are knowingly prepared, and the veal melts in your mouth.

**Enzio's Ristorante**  21 W. Goethe (312) 280-1010.

Tucked into Chicago's Gold Coast, Enzio's offers fine food with an attention to detail that shows up in fresh chopped herbs and nuances of flavor.

*La Strada* 155 N. Michigan (312) 565-2200.

If you want to impress someone, the glittery location and the food here will do it. Try a half-order of pasta and a piatto secondo of zuppa di pesce, cotoletta valdostana, or chicken scarpariello, and forego dessert. If you care to order a pasta not on the menu, the chef will probably be able to accommodate you.

*Mangia Italiano* 1560 N. Wells (312) 951-8707.

Anyone who is homesick for Italy should perk up at the sight of Mangia Italiano's dining room. The white linen tablecloths, heavy silverware, and bottles of mineral water give one the illusion of dining in Trastevere instead of Chicago's Old Town. Italophiles will also appreciate the food, particularly zingy dishes like spaghetti alla puttanesca.

*Salvatore's Restaurant* 525 W. Arlington Place (312) 528-1200.

Veal chop Salvatore is memorable here, and seafood dishes are attentively prepared. Ordering a half-dish of pasta is recommended, because you may want to save room for the tempting desserts. Salvatore's is located in what seems like a large, old-fashioned palazzo.

## NEAR SOUTH

*Al's Bar-b-que* 1079 W. Taylor (312) 226-4017.

In a city famous for its Italian beef sandwiches, Al's are rated tops by everyone from *Chicago* magazine to the Taylor Street crowd. Be prepared to wait and to inhale your beef at the counter or in your car. Don't miss the wonderful greasy fries. A fresh Italian ice from Mario's across the street will cool you down after this heady experience.

*Bruna's Ristorante* 2424 S. Oakley (312) 254-5550.

Located in a Tuscan neighborhood, Bruna's offers some well-made examples of that cuisine. The mixed greens salad is a prelude to savor, and the bolognese, primavera, carbonara, and anchovy pasta sauces are flavorful. Veal dishes are tender, and shrimp diavolo will please those who like their food spicy.

*Febo's* 2501 S. Western (312) 523-0839.

Febo's slogan, "Famous for Nothing," belies the home-cooked quality of the food and friendly atmosphere here—every other table seems to be populated with neighborhood locals. Febo's is strong in traditional pastas and meat dishes, with several Northern Italian offerings.

*Florence Restaurant* 1030 W. Taylor St. (312) 829-1857.

Florence Scala, a community organizer who fought to defend this neighborhood, Chicago's most famous Little Italy, runs this jewel of a restaurant in her family's build-ing. The pasta with Gorgonzola sauce is creamy and flavorful, and the pasta with walnuts is a delightful innovation. Fresh meat and fish specials are offered daily.

*La Fontanella* 2414 S. Oakley (312) 927-5249.

Chicago Alderman Vito Marzullo, who hails from this neighborhood, often recom-mends La Fontanella. Arancini and caponata are notable appetizers; green noodles in cream sauce and fettucine Alfredo stand out, and veal saltimbocca is mouthwatering. Veal dishes parmigiana and francese and chicken Sylvia are also delectable.

*Vernon Park Restaurant* 1073 W. Vernon Park (312) 226-9878.

There's no sign above the door to this neighborhood hideaway, but the Bridgeport politicians and University of Illinois students and faculty who eat here don't need one. The fresh clams, hearty pastas, robust red wine, and lack of anything resembling decor will delude you into thinking you're at Nonna's in the old neighborhood—and the prices aren't that much higher.

*Giannotti's* 7711 Roosevelt, Forest Park (312) 366-1199.

Long a stalwart of the western suburbs, Giannotti's offers generous portions of traditional Italian-American cuisine. Try a seafood salad, mussels, clams, or scampi as an appetizer. Pasta alla montanara, with ham, basil, olives, and onion in a tomato base, is delicious. Red snapper alla livornese and veal dishes are recommended. The atmosphere is a little heavy on wrought iron and elaborate chandeliers.

*La Capannina* 7353 W. Grand Ave. (312) 452-0900.

Fresh, high-quality ingredients and talented preparation make La Capannina a star on Chicago's restaurant scene. The diverse menu yields such delights as linguine with mussels, paglia e fiena, steak alla pizzaiola, and saltimbocca. La Capannina is run by a Barese family, who began it in a side-street storefront.

*Ristorante Italia* 2631 N. Harlem (312) 889-5008.

Don't let the storefront Italian bar dissuade you from entering—there's a pleasant dining room in back. This family-run restaurant specializes in homemade pastas, and there's a wonderful zuppa di pesce with pasta. The locals who frequent the bar, sipping espresso and cappuccino and bantering in Italian, add a homey feeling.

*Sicily Restaurant* 2743 N. Harlem (312) 889-1040.

Arancini start a meal off here nicely, and there is a wide selection of pasta dishes, including one named for Al Capone. A noisy band and jovial clientele provide local color and give this place a fun atmosphere.

*Slicker Sam's* 1911 Rice (1 block north of Lake St.), Melrose Park (312) 345-5368.

The emphasis is on seafood in this casual spot, with its checked tablecloths and thatched-grapevine ceiling. Clams can be had fresh, steamed, or baked, and mussels and calamari are good alternatives. The pastas are served in generous portions, and the linguine with red calamari sauce is rewarding. Even after granita di limone the bill should pleasantly surprise you.

*Pamela De Figlio*

# St. Louis

George D. Wendel is a nationally recognized authority on the problems of American cities. As director of St. Louis University's Center for Urban Programs, he has to be a dispassionate observer of cities and their peoples.

But Professor Wendel, a tall, moustached, nicely disheveled man, admits to a flaw in his academic objectivity. The flaw is a weak spot for the Hill, the fifty-two-square-block neighborhood on the south side of St. Louis that, for more than seventy-five years, has

(Photo by Steven Marinelli)

been home to the city's Italian-American community. "I'm an aficionado of the Hill," he says. "Hell, they made me an honorary son."

Every Saturday morning, Wendel and other Hill devotees drive to the area to do their shopping. They park their cars on narrow residential streets lined with small, immaculately kept houses, then stroll from store to store with shopping bags on their arms. They buy their bread from the Missouri Bakery or Amighetti's, prosciutto from Volpi Italian Foods, and meat from John Colombo's market.

If food alone were enough to make a neighborhood work, it could well explain why the Hill continues to amaze urbanologists and sociologists. But we do not live by bread alone, even when the bread comes from Amighetti's. You have to put down your knife and fork long enough to look at the history and the people that have created, atop the gently sloping ground of the highest point in St. Louis, one of America's most thriving neighborhoods.

"The Hill is a rare mix," says Wendel. "A magic combination you won't find very often these days. It may be because it's so out of whack with time that it's as strong as it is."

Meaning? "Well, for instance, it violates every law known to city planners. Planners hate the kind of mixed usages you find on the Hill. They go crazy over things like having a saloon on one corner, a grocery store on another, an auto repair shop in the third, and a residence on the fourth."

For the most part, the Hill's fourteen hundred families live in one-story brick houses built on narrow lots. The yards are small, but usually adorned with flowers or trellises, often setting off a statue of a madonna. Streets are uniformly narrow and normally clogged with parked cars, making driving an adventure. There is no commercial district, shopping mall, or retail strip; the stores are scattered in ones and twos on corners and on side streets. Given the history of similar neighborhoods in other cities, it is easy to understand why Norton Long, professor of urban affairs at the University of Missouri–St. Louis, says that "an architect would take one look and predict that the whole thing will become a slum."

If the Hill has proven anything over the years it is that it is not fated to the same ending as Little Italies in other parts of the country. Its distinction lies not in the red, white, and green fire hydrants dotting the streets, but in the civic-mindedness of the residents, who are determined not to see their neighborhood reduced to ashes. And nobody has displayed more of that determination than the Reverend Salvatore E. Polizzi, the acknowledged leader of the Hill.

Polizzi is dedicated to bringing young people—especially young married couples—into the Hill, sometimes at the expense of older residents. While many view the success of this crusade as the major reason for the growth and stability of the area, others have accused Polizzi of an insensitivity occasionally bordering on crassness. But Polizzi is only too aware of the checkered history of the Hill in the twentieth century, and particularly of how its alternating developmental and regressive phases were at the whim of external events, economic speculators, and carpetbaggers of various kinds.

In the first two decades of this century, the area thrived because of its location near some of Missouri's richest Cheltenham clay mines, the principal source for building-bricks in the Midwest. Among the mining population, the Hill established its identity as a Milanese Italian stronghold.

The Hill people survived the Depression largely because of the Democratic ward political organization that had grown up in the twenties. Louis "Gene" Gualdoni, and, later, Louis "Midge" Berra, delivered huge majorities to Democratic Party candidates, who in turn provided jobs when work was hard to come by. This political paternalism and sense of security prevailed until the end of World War II, when the young people of the Hill began to grow restless. Drawn by the same ambitions as other war veterans, they began drifting off to the relatively wider spaces of the suburbs.

By the mid-fifties, the exodus of young Italian-Americans had not only led to a consolidation of the older generation, but had also encouraged an influx of non-Italians into the area who rented rather than bought. This trend continued until the mid-sixties, when the neighborhood arose and banded together to prevent a drive-in theater from being built on a vacant lot on a corner of the Hill.

Polizzi formed a neighborhood organization called the Hill 2000, a name expressing the hope that the neighborhood would still be thriving at the turn of the century. The nonprofit corporation is funded from the proceeds of the annual "Hill Day" festival in mid-August, a celebration that draws huge, enthusiastic crowds to the neighborhood.

Among other activities, the Hill 2000 has opened youth and day-care centers, built a park, started an employment and housing office, and spawned more than two dozen similar organizations in other St. Louis neighborhoods. Its most celebrated achievement took place in 1971, when residents forced the state of Missouri to build an overpass—financed with Hill Day contributions—across a new highway so the Hill wouldn't be split up.

Unlike many other neighborhoods enjoying a revitalization, the Hill has not attracted an urban gentry. Young doctors, lawyers, and other professionals settle elsewhere. The

Hill's new residents are pretty much like the old ones—working class, Catholic, and Italian.

According to urbanologist Wendel, this is an important difference for would-be emulators to keep in mind. "The Hill is not a suddenly fashionable old neighborhood," Wendel observes. "It is what it has always been. If other neighborhoods in St. Louis or other cities in America want to learn from it, they should look at it and choose from it, cafeteria-style."

*Kevin Hortigan and*
*Richard Feminella*

## Recommended Restaurants

*Candicci's* 7010 Bonhomme (west of Central) (314) 725-3350.
Moderately priced pasta, chicken, beef.

*Charlie Gitto's Pasta House* 207 N. Sixth St. (314) 436-2828.
Not far from Busch Stadium, Pasta House Downtown features salads, pastas, sandwiches. Charlie Gitto's on the Hill, 5226 Shaw Ave. (314) 772-8898, offers seafood, pasta, chicken.

*Godfather's Ristorante* 12280 Dorsett Rd. (near I-270) (314) 434-8234.
Known for its fettuccine padrino.

*Gooma's* 12280 Dorsett Rd. (near I-270) (314) 434-8324.
A disco in an Italian garden atmosphere.

# New Orleans

They may have been wise churchmen, but when the Council of Nicea met back in A.D. 325, its members just didn't have the wisdom to predict the problems they would cause 1,615 years later in A.D. 1940 at a spot in the New World to be known as New Orleans.

In drawing up the Christian calendar, the council members declared that Easter would henceforth be celebrated on the first Sunday following the fourteenth day of the Paschal full moon. No problem, except that in 1940 the ole Paschal moon came early, thus pushing Easter up to March 24.

Obviously, the man in the moon isn't Italian, because the early Easter meant that March 19, the feast day of St. Joseph, would fall right in the beginning of Holy Week.

Four decades ago Lent and especially Holy Week were more strictly regarded as periods of fasting and abstinence. So, the city's archbishop, Joseph Francis Rummel, was perplexed. The custom among local Italians of making altars out of food and feasting in honor of St. Joseph seemed inappropriate for such a sacred time of the year.

Thus, the bishop asked that the altars and celebrating be postponed for two weeks until April 2, nine days after Easter.

This created a schism among local Italians. Some reasoned that St. Joseph might not take kindly to having his day tampered with. Besides, the saint had friends in high places who wouldn't mind a bit of Lenten levity. Others reasoned that the bishop was the boss and agreed to go along with his request.

What emerged was a classic New Orleans solution to a problem. Instead of a celebration delayed, there was a celebration doubled. Some Italians feasted on March 29, others waited until April 2. Both factions got to double dip in honoring St. Joe. . . .

Italians celebrate differently in New Orleans because New Orleans' Italians are different. Whereas immigrants from continental Italy, particularly the southern part, settled throughout the United States, and primarily the East Coast, the immigrants who came to New Orleans were insular. They were from the island—Sicily.

Anthony Margavio, a professor of sociology at the University of New Orleans who has done extensive research on the local Italian culture, estimates that the ancestry of at least 90 percent of the local Italians traces back to Sicilians. . . .

Among the local Sicilians is a subgroup of sorts whose ancient ancestors split from Albania to escape the conquests of the Ottoman Turks. They turned left at the Adriatic Sea and sailed for nearby Sicily. These latter-day Sicilians, sometimes referred to as *Arbreshe,* were also part of the migration to Louisiana. Their family names (such as Amato, Chetta, Chisesi, Ciaccio, Clesi, Cuccia, Foto, Grisaffi, Lala, Lamana, Schiro, Sciambra, Tortorich, and Manale) are quite common in New Orleans and although frequently thought to be Italian in origin, are technically Albanian.

Although the original Albanian settlers were also Catholic, their services were conducted in the Greek, as opposed to the Latin, rite. Most of the Arbreshe came to the states from the Sicilian town of Contessa Entellina. That town's name flutters on the banner of the New Orleans–based Contessa Entellina Society.

Each September the society's members hold a procession and mass. In doing so, its members walk a well-worn path. Founded in 1886, the society is one of the very oldest continuing Italian organizations in the United States.

It doesn't march alone. September is also the time for processions in honor of St. Rosalia. The saint was a daughter of a Sicilian noble family who chose to live her life in penance and labor. She lived in a cave on Mount Pelegrino three miles from Palermo. Rosalia seemed especially adept at dealing with pestilences, not only in ancient Sicily but locally as well.

When Italian farmers in Kenner were losing their cattle and mules during a plague, they prayed to Rosalia for intercession. The plague ceased and in 1899 the town's St. Rosalia procession began.

Across the river in Harvey, Italian farmers began a similar celebration. The saint is still honored in both towns.

As a peace-making concession, each town holds its procession on a different Sunday. Traditionally, the privilege of having the first procession is alternated annually. Yet another tradition has it that those in the procession walk barefoot, but traditions are sometimes altered by affluence and the temperature of the sidewalk.

Whichever procession local Italians may happen to be marching in, their ancestry likely traces back to the migration to Louisiana predating the early twentieth-century flow of other Italians throughout the rest of the United States.

They came to Louisiana propelled by the force of history: theirs and ours.

In Sicily, the continuing conquests and raping of the land had left the peasant farmers poor. They worked on the turf of absentee landlords who divided the harvest with midlevel managers. The farmers continually were left with little. Inevitably there were peasant uprisings.

Rosary beads, flowers, and individual candles placed at statue of St. Anthony (Photo by Joseph DiGiuseppe)

(Photo by Pamela Parlapiano)

Meanwhile there was an agricultural revolution going on in the United States. In the days following the Civil War, the local demand for Mediterranean citrus had declined, thus leaving extra cargo space in British frigates. Simultaneously, the Louisiana sugar industry no longer had the service of slaves to work its cane fields.

With the help of the state, the sugar plantation owners looked for a new crop of farmers. They tried importing workers from the American Midwest as well as Scandinavians, Germans, and even disgruntled Chinese coolies. Eventually, the Sicilian farmers, who needed a place to go, and the Louisiana sugar bosses, who needed the farmers' services, found each other.

A study on Louisiana immigration by Dr. Jean Scarpaci reveals that "the Italians gained a reputation as being industrious and ambitious." Apparently so—there arose such a demand for Italians that the state formed an Immigration League to attract them to the state. A New Orleans Italian, Vincent Lanata, was hired as an agent and promised two dollars for each of his countrymen that he delivered to the state.

Many immigrants signed contracts in which the cost of passage would gradually be deducted from their pay. For that commitment, they often got a bumpy ride.

As testimony to life on the ships were the passenger lists recording the names, occupations, destinations, nationalities, and possessions of the travelers. One column was reserved to check off shipboard deaths. All too often that column was filled with the names of infants. . . .

Those who survived endured the hardships so that they could get away from Sicily. In spite of that, Margavio suggests, many of them planned to return to their mother country someday. "They didn't want to stay," the professor argues, "they only wanted to sojourn. Their goal was simply to make enough money to put aside so that one day they could buy that little piece of land they loved so much in Sicily and live a nice life."

Instead, many of them eventually gave up farming and joined the turn-of-the-century movement to the cities. In New Orleans, they relocated in what was then the city's poorer areas: the French Quarter, Algiers, and Carrollton. Of those Italian settlements the largest was in the Quarter, where the Sicilian population swelled to the extent that the section bordered by Dumaine Street, Esplanade Avenue, Dauphine Street, and the river became known as Little Palermo. Amidst Spanish architecture in a neighborhood called the French Quarter, the Italians were predominant.

As sudden urbanites, the Sicilians became merchants—quite often in businesses, small and large, related to food. The smoothness of the transition from the cane field is a phenomenon that has amazed Margavio and a colleague on the UNO sociology faculty, Jerome Salomone.

"What we've found to be particularly interesting, actually you may even use the word 'astonishing,'" Margavio reveals, "is the rapidity with which the Sicilians, predominantly illiterate peasants, moved into the merchant ranks in New Orleans. I don't know of any parallel, but in 1900 a majority, a little more than 50 percent of all the Sicilian immigrants in New Orleans, were some form of merchant—it's incredible. In Chicago or New York, their counterparts would have been in the construction trade. But in New Orleans, they were merchants."

Why?

A paper prepared by the two professors suggested two reasons, as explained by Margavio:

"Because Sicilians dominated in New Orleans, things were different. In other places Sicilians didn't dominate. And among Sicilians there was a strong sense of economic independence, 'whatever you do, be your own man.' They combined their strong family commitment with that economic individualism, 'be your own man, work for yourself, don't work for anybody else. Be your own boss.'

"To run a business back at that time, a person didn't necessarily have to read and write but did have to know numbers. Nobody can run a business without knowing numbers. They knew their numbers because they always enjoyed gambling. They worked with numbers all the time with card games and games of chance. In order to do that, they had to fool with numbers in some way or another."

From that setting, the Italians began the gradual business of assimilation, blending themselves into the cultural stew. Some became prosperous. The Maestri family made a fortune in the furniture business and then in real estate. Many remained poor. As with all ethnic groups, politics is generally the first step toward respectability. In the urban America of that period, political machines provided the inroad for the caravan of immigrants. One of the sons of the Maestri family followed that road to City Hall to eventually become mayor.

For most, however, the road passed through hostile territory. The process of acceptance for the Sicilians shouldn't have been any more difficult than that of any of the other European ethnic groups that came before. Unfortunately, the Italians were burdened by stereotypes which, like all stereotypes, were overstated.

During the peak years of Italian immigration, the mayor of New Orleans was Joseph Shakspeare. His Honor didn't like Italians and that sentiment was reflected by City Hall. In answering an inquiry addressed to the Mayor from an Ohioan who was curious about the nature of Italians, Shakspeare's secretary had written in part that "epidemics nearly always break out of their quarter."

New Orleans, a city wrung out of cypress swamps, had always been particularly susceptible to disease. During much of its history, the town's main nemesis was the feared yellow fever. For poor, uneducated, foreign-speaking immigrants (of any nationality) clustered together in crowded conditions, the chances of contracting and eventually spreading disease was particularly high.

Such was the fate of the Italians during their period of immigration. They were, of all ethnic groups, generally the most prone to disease. But that was simply because they were the latest to arrive. They were the least assimilated; thus, the prevention and cure of local disease was most foreign to them.

A study of the Italians during the 1905 yellow fever epidemic by Jean Trapido emphasized the cultural clash. Most cases of the outbreak centered in and around the Italian section of the Quarter. Stunting the disease was difficult because many Italians were suspicious of health authorities, especially those who wore uniforms. There was also a distrust of doctors.

What was perceived by some outsiders, including the mayor, as a carelessness toward disease was really the unhappy plight of foreigners lumped together in a strange world. It was hard for native-born New Orleanians to understand that there was a reason for the immigrants' mistrust of uniformed health authorities—the Sicilians had fled from a land where a uniform often meant suppression.

Of all the images hung on the Italians, however, the cruelest has been the gangster stigma. In fact, in New Orleans the Mafia has probably been the cause of more dastardly rumors than crimes. It's an old New Orleans custom, whispering about different places around town that are allegedly owned by THE MAFIA.

Part of the folklore of the city has been the suggestion that the Mafia in the United States began in New Orleans. There are stories about early racketeering, primarily along the riverfront, to which the terms "Mafia" and "Black Hand" were applied. But there is no evidence of any international Sicilian-controlled criminal cabal.

A more accurate statement about the relationship of the city to the Mafia is that the national hysteria about the organization was triggered by a nasty incident in New Orleans.

It was a misty night in October of 1890 when David Hennessy, the city's police chief, was fatally shot as he approached his Girod Street home. As he lay dying, Hennessy reportedly whispered to Bill O'Connor, a police captain, that his assailants were "Dagoes." During the hours before his death, Hennessy had talked to doctors, clerks, and his mother. Never once had the charge been repeated. Yet, based on the testimony of one man, a dragnet of suspicious Italians was ordered.

From there the story takes many ugly turns leading to the mob slaughter of Italians as they stood trapped in the parish prison. In the trial of those accused of the Hennessy murder, six Italians had been found not guilty. No decision was made on the other three.

Outraged, a citizens' protest rally grew into a mob. The mob overran the prison in search of Italians, any Italians. Eleven Sicilians, consisting of three that had been acquitted the day before, the three that had had a mistrial declared, and five that had not been on trial at all, were either lynched or shot. Eight other imprisoned Italians hid themselves well enough to escape death.

Mob action became an international incident. The government of Italy protested to Washington. Eventually, the federal government agreed to pay damages to the families of the victims. But the greatest damage was to reputation.

Rousing the rabble during all this was Mayor Shakspeare. The incident had become a darling of the national press, which was at the peak of its "yellow journalism" phase. As part of the after-the-crime hysteria, the mayor released to the press a list of "ninety-four Mafia murders" in New Orleans. The press screamed the news in headlines across the country and the word "Mafia" became part of the American lexicon.

Author Richard Gambino's study of the Hennessy incident pointed out that Shakspeare glossed over the fact that the ninety-four murders on the list took place over a twenty-five-year period. Neither did the mayor mention that the roll was put together by simply listing every homicide victim in the city with an Italian-sounding name. That included some listed as "identity unknown" and also several Spanish names.

Also unmentioned was the fact that ninety-one of the murders were unsolved. The three that were, were all love triangle passion crimes. For none of the ninety-four murders was there any hard evidence of a Mafia connection.

Yet, the papers loved the story and without questioning spread the word across the country. The Mafia mystique had been planted. . . .

Joseph Maselli bristles at the Italian stereotypes. Maselli is the founder and president of the American-Italian Federation, an umbrella group that coordinates the efforts of more than twenty Louisiana and Gulf Coast Italian-American organizations ranging geographically from the St. Joseph's Italian Society of Houma to the Shreveport Progressive Men's Club. . . . The federation operates from the offices of his wholesale business on South Salcedo Street serving as the nerve center for Italian-American pride.

"There are two words that are important to Sicilians that the movie *The Godfather* made light of," Maselli complains. "One is the word 'godfather.' A godfather is a person selected to be the guardian of your child. To the Sicilian it's an honor to be selected as a godfather. The other is the word 'family.' The family unit has always been important to Sicilians—a part of their way of life." . . .

But the truth is there is not much about local Italians that needs to be defended. They are clearly among the leaders of the community. Italians have provided mayors, . . . councilmen, and police chiefs. . . .

Somehow, the Italians have thoroughly assimilated but have maintained their identity better than most other ethnic groups. Weaving *paesani* still puff down the street for the St. Joseph's Day parade and the classified section of the newspaper still runs a special column in March listing the location of the altars.

Most of all, the Italians have a monument to their success. Rising on Poydras Street, within blocks from the site where Hennessy was shot, the Italian Piazza may one day be the focal point of Italian-Americanism.

If the plans come to fruition, there will be restaurants and shops surrounding the piazza. An American-Italian Activities Center will house a study center. . . .

Already the piazza's complex fountain system has won notoriety. It has been pictured and written about in architectural magazines and in both *Time* and *Newsweek.* It is huge with columns made from water sprays and a pool running down an incline shaped like the map of Italy.

One day the famous St. Joseph's altar in front of the church by the same name of Tulane Avenue may be located in the piazza. The place's very existence has already added an event to the city's crowded festival calendar. Columbus Day is now celebrated there, with a festival. For Italians the famine of recognition is over, the piazza is a bountiful harvest. St. Joseph has been good.

It was the weekend of St. Joseph Day in 1978. The platform at the piazza was packed as assorted dignitaries did their part to dedicate the new piazza. The speech making was muted by noise. Over at the fountain, bare feet caused tidal waves throughout the map of Italy.

A teen-aged daughter of Italian-Americans began at the northern border and raced down the incline toward the south. Reaching the Sicilian end, she stepped up on the edge. Perhaps without realizing it she had just splashed through her heritage. The road through Sicily ended in New Orleans.

*Errol Laborde*

### Recommended Restaurants

*Impastato's* 3400 16th St., Metairie (504) 455-1545.
The specialty here is homemade pasta.

*Sclafani* 1315 N. Causeway Blvd., Metairie (504) 835-1718.
Sclafani offers local specialties and an Italian salad bowl.

*Tortorici's* 441 Royal St., New Orleans (504) 522-4295.
A Festivo Dinner is the specialty of the house.

678 Green Street, San Francisco, CA 94133

**ITALIAN-AMERICAN
ARTISTS
IN CALIFORNIA
1850 to 1925**

# San Francisco

Columbus Day is celebrated like New Orleans' Mardi Gras. Italian art is so popular that the exhibit of the Vatican Collection drew 616,000 visitors. Four Ruffatti pipe organs voice song into the city, opening night at the opera is the year's biggest cultural event, and the local sports hero is named Joe Montana. Rome? Naples? Try San Francisco, California.

This city with the Mediterranean climate, like Rome built on seven hills, has seen a resurgence in interest in all things Italian. It manifests itself in the grand, like the Bufano statues that brighten the city, or the Galleria in the financial district's Crocker Center, a glass-domed arcade styled after Milan's Galleria Vittorio Emmanuelle. It can also be seen in the minutiae of life, like the proliferation of shops selling gelato, which has replaced American ice cream as the favored frozen dessert.

The neighborhood that was, and still is, the most distinctly Italian in San Francisco is North Beach, an area that runs north between Russian and Telegraph hills. At its center is Washington Square, dominated by the beautifully sculptured twin spires of the Church of Sts. Peter and Paul. Although Italians are no longer the largest ethnic culture in the area in terms of numbers, the atmosphere is certainly Mediterranean. Italian bakeries and delicatessens lure their customers with the bait of freshly baked breads, pastries, *focacce*, and sliced meats, and most of the streets' doorways seem to lead into restaurants featuring Italian cuisine.

The history of Italians in the City by the Bay goes back more than 130 years, when the Gold Rush was in full swing. Like almost all who came to seek their fortunes, they soon discovered that reality was a harsh teacher. The fortunes they longed for were phantoms, and the dream they held of returning to Northern Italy as *signori* was replaced by the stark necessity of finding food, shelter, and occupation in a country whose customs and language were a mystery.

Those who did not return to Italy settled in and around San Francisco. Many found lands in the fertile San Joaquin and Sacramento valleys and returned to the farming they had left behind. Others became the nucleus of a thriving fishing community, which burgeoned not just near San Francisco but extended all along the coast of California. The Italians of Fisherman's Wharf were so successful in the San Francisco area that they soon drove all other immigrant groups out of the fishing business.

As the years passed the new *Americani* became an integral part of the city's life, and Italian businessmen played an important role in the growing city's thriving economy. Probably the most important entrepreneur of San Francisco's Italian-American community was Amadeo Peter Giannini. Atypical of his contemporaries in the banking industry, he saw how the other lending institutions ignored the needs of the less affluent and made it difficult for the immigrants to secure loans—"foreigners" who often couldn't speak English. On August 10, 1904, Giannini opened the doors of his Banco D'Italia, which later became known as the Bank of America. After the earthquake of 1906, when fires destroyed much of San Francisco, Giannini saved the bank's assets by moving them out of town until the danger was over. Within a week Giannini's fledgling operation was taking deposits, and while the other banks were waiting for their vaults to cool off, Giannini was lending money to rebuild the ruins. North Beach, which was left with twenty thousand homeless Italian families, was the first section of the city to be rebuilt.

North Beach stood alone as the center of Italian culture for many years, but like the Germans and Irish, whom the Italians displaced in their search for stability and cohesive-ness, so too were the Italians displaced. The street that marked the southern boundary of North Beach—Broadway—has become the city's flesh district, a boulevard bathed in a perpetual neon daylight lined with topless nightclubs and massage parlors. Chinatown, once restricted to the south of Broadway, quickly spilled over into the once predominantly Italian neighborhood. The sons and daughters of the original Italian community left the old neighborhood for the suburbs, and for a while North Beach was home of the Beats of the fifties and early sixties. A reminder of that era still remains on Columbus Avenue: Lawrence Ferlinghetti's City Lights Bookstore. Only recently has interest in revitalizing North Beach shown results, and today the emigration has slowed, even reversed slightly as younger Italian-Americans try to find the sense of community that their parents enjoyed.

## Places to Visit in San Francisco

The Musèo Italo-Americano, at 678 Green Street, is the first museum of its kind in the United States. It is housed in Casa Fugazi, a building donated to the Italian community for cultural programs. It was founded atop a North Beach café by Paola Bagnatori and Giuliana Haight Nardelli, and is dedicated to preserving, researching, and displaying the works of Italian and Italian-American artists and providing educational programs for the appreciation of Italian and Italian-American art, culture, and history.

Photographs, sculpture, and craftwork are on display, and admission is free. The museum tries to exhibit eight different displays each year and presents a good overview of what contemporary Italian and Italian-American artists are doing.

The North Beach Museum is located above the Eureka Federal Savings and Loan Building at 1435 Stockton Street. Its displays are changed regularly and present to the public a photographic record, as well as artifacts, of life in the North Beach area throughout its history.

## Recommended Restaurants

The greatest sin that can mar your soul in San Francisco is a sin of omission . . . not eating at one of the city's many fine restaurants. The international flavor of the city extends to its cuisine, and Italy's contribution to the art of cooking has done much to enhance San Francisco's reputation as one of the finest dining cities in the nation. For a great pizza, try Tommaso's on Kearny near Broadway, but prepare for an hour's wait for a seat. For ice cream, there are many Gelato's locations around the city. For breads and pastries the best place is always just around the corner, whether in North Beach or not, because Italian bakeries are everywhere, like Il Fornaio's two San Francisco shops. And of course there are the restaurants.

*Fior d'Italia* 601 Union St., sits on North Beach's Union Square (415) 986-1886.

Established in 1886 Fior d'Italia is San Francisco's oldest Italian restaurant, and although no longer at its original location, the new restaurant still maintains its antique look.

"We offer the most authentic Northern Italian cuisine in San Francisco," says manager Joseph Musso. Less emphasis is placed on pastas as a side dish; risotto (rice in broth with different seasonings) and the cornmeal-based polenta are offered instead.

*La Pantera* 1234 Grant Ave. (415) 392-0170.

Walking through the door, you might get the impression that you've entered a faded photograph from a family album. The restaurant looks exactly as it did when it opened in 1907 and is typical of the style of family restaurants of that era. At La Pantera, family style means family style: you get what they serve. There are no menus, and waiters bring out the courses in quantities appropriate to the size of your party.

*Modesto Lanzone's* Opera Plaza (601 Van Nest Ave.) (415) 928-0400.

If you'd like to combine a little culture with the cuisine, try the incomparable Modesto Lanzone's. Whereas in other Italian restaurants the walls are decorated with photos or posters of Italy, Lanzone's Opera Plaza room could double for one of the finest art galleries. Paintings from his private collection hang there, and like the food are there for the enjoyment of his patrons.

*Veneto's* Mason and Bay (415) 986-4553.

*Bruno's* 20th and Mission (415) 824-2258.

*La Trattoria* 1507 Polk (415) 771-6363.

*Via Veneto* 5356 College Ave. Oakland (415) 652-8540.

*Giovanni's* 2420 Shattuck Ave. Berkeley (415) 843-6678.

*Salerno* 2468 Shattuck Ave. Berkeley (415) 549-2662.

*Paul Giles*


# Selected Guide to Italian Festivals in the United States

**CALIFORNIA**
San Jose   ITALIAN-AMERICAN CULTURAL FESTIVAL. Early October, annual, two days. Contact: (408) 293-7122.

**CONNECTICUT**
Hartford   FESTA ITALIANA. Early September (weekend following Labor Day), annual, two days, Franklin Avenue. Contact: Mr. Ruggier, radio station WRYM, (203) 666-5646.

**DELAWARE**
Wilmington   ITALIAN FESTIVAL. Early–mid-June, annual, eight days. Contact: St. Anthony's Church, Ninth and Dupont streets, Wilmington, Del. 19805 or telephone (302) 421-3747.

**INDIANA**
Clinton   LITTLE ITALY FESTIVAL. Early September, annual, four days. Contact: Rita Muciarelli, 849 North St., Clinton, Ind. 47842 or telephone (317) 832-6606.

**LOUISIANA**
Independence   LITTLE ITALY FESTIVAL. Late April, annual, one day. Contact: Dr. Harry Becnel, chairman, (504) 878-6324.

## MARYLAND
Mitchellville   ITALIAN SPRING FESTIVAL. Mid-May, annual, one day, Villa Rosa Home. Contact: Rev. Anthony Dal Balcon, 3800 Lottsford Vista Road, Mitchellville, Md. 20716 or telephone (301) 459-4700.

## NEBRASKA
Omaha   SANTA LUCIA FESTIVAL. Late July–early August, annual, four days. Contact: Omaha Visitors Bureau, Omaha-Douglas Civic Center, Suite 1200, 1819 Farnam St., Omaha, Neb. 68183 or telephone (402) 444-4666.

## NEVADA
Reno   ITALIAN FESTIVAL. Early October, annual, eight days, Eldorado Hotel. Contact: Rhonda Carano, (702) 786-5700.

## NEW JERSEY
Holmdel   HERITAGE FESTIVALS AT HOLMDEL. June and September, weekends, annual, Garden State Arts Center. Contact: Garden State Arts Center, Telegraph Hill Park, Holmdel, N.J. 97733 or telephone (201) 442-8800.

## NEW YORK
New York City   FEAST OF SAN GENNARO. Mid-September, annual, eleven days, Mulberry St., Little Italy. Contact: (212) 226-9546.

New York City   FESTA ITALIANA. Mid–late July, annual, ten days, Carmine St. between Sixth and Seventh avenues. Contact: Our Lady of Pompeii Church, Carmine St., New York, N.Y. 10014 or telephone (212) 755-4100.

## OHIO
Columbus   ST. JOHN'S ITALIAN FESTIVAL. Early October, annual, two days, Ohio State Fairgrounds, Multipurpose Building. Contact: Benny Andreoni, 5306 Poplarwood St., Columbus, Ohio 43229 or telephone (614) 294-5319 or (614) 885-1036.

## OKLAHOMA
McAlester   ITALIAN FESTIVAL. Late May, annual, three days, Schiller Field. Contact: Chamber of Commerce, Box 759, McAlester, Okla. 74501 or telephone (918) 423-2550.

## RHODE ISLAND
Providence   COLUMBUS DAY FESTIVAL. October (around Columbus Day), annual, one day, Federal Hill. Contact: Rhode Island Department of Economic Development, 7 Jackson Walkway, Providence, R.I. 02903 or telephone (401) 277-2601.

## WEST VIRGINIA
Clarksburg   WEST VIRGINIA ITALIAN HERITAGE FESTIVAL. September (Labor Day weekend), annual. Contact: 104 East Maine St., Clarksburg, W.Va. 26301 or telephone (304) 622-1986.

## WISCONSIN
Milwaukee   FESTA ITALIANA. Mid–late July, annual, four days, Lakeshore. Contact: Italian Community Center, 2648 North Hackett St., Milwaukee, Wis. 53211 or telephone (414) 963-9613.

*Paul Wasserman and Edmond L. Applebaum*

*Part Three*

# FOOD AND DRINK

# Introduction:
# The Family Dinner

For me there is no greater pleasure than to eat together with family and friends. The larger the group, the better I like it. At the meal, amid the platters of pasta, family members reaffirm their bonds to one another. While I have a greater awareness of all this at holiday celebrations, when the Giordanos gather at Grandma's on Christmas Day, these familial feelings actually have their roots in the daily ritual of deciding what to eat, shopping, preparing food, and the discussion around the table. The way we carry out these activities is not randomly arrived at, but follows a pattern that can be traced to the eating habits of past generations. It is far more important in sustaining family relationships than we think.

When I recently visited Italy, I decided to explore the subject a little further. To any visitor, it is obvious that eating in Italy is a joyful, time-consuming, even somewhat ceremonial event. The food is wonderful; lunch takes three hours; restaurants with tables stretch into the streets; waiters serve your meals with great dignity. Most small restaurants are still family run and so the attention given to the preparation of the food, the service, and the ambience produce a nurturing feeling close to what I feel when I sit in my own home.

One afternoon, after a remarkable lunch, I found myself talking about the nature of Italian eating habits with Ermgelo Muzzellini, chief chef of the Cavalieri Hilton in Rome. Besides being one of Italy's great master chefs, Muzzellini is also a scholar of cuisine— and an expansive talker. As a third-generation Italian-American, I was curious about what a great chef and gourmet thought about American eating styles. "Italian-Americans are in many ways more Italian than most modern-day Italians are," explained Muzzellini. "They live and eat like Italians in the 1880s did. When I come to New York, it always reminds me of what my grandmother said life used to be like here—the food, the way it is eaten and served. It amazes me the way Italian-Americans have maintained this."

What did the chef think of the kinds of foods Italian-Americans ate? Were they authentic? "Oh," he said with a laugh, "some of it is very authentic. You can get anything in New York that you can get in Rome. But the thing that amazes me is that Americans eat pasta from *cans.* This, to me, is not good." (I assured him that most Italian-Americans would agree with him.) He continued, "But I like the holidays you have—Christmas, Thanksgiving. The feasts have a wonderful feeling of plenty. The Italian-Americans seem to take many of the dishes from Italy and mix them with American roasts and meats. It is very nice—the food, the family atmosphere, the way traditions are kept."

After meeting with Muzzellini, I wondered how successful my family has been in maintaining traditional Italian foods and eating habits. I was raised in a family where we ate together every night. When your work schedule interfered, your place was set anyway and dinner was waiting when you arrived home. There was a definite pattern to each week. Tuesday was spaghetti, and it was particularly special because the family would also watch Milton Berle on television. Of course Friday was fish night. Saturday's lunch was always some variety of a hero sandwich—peppers and sausages or salami and provolone. On Sunday, dinner always followed the last Mass and would be a big baked pasta or a roast.

When I returned from Italy, I found a section on Italian-American families buried in a study of cultural patterns in American eating habits. Dr. Judith Goode, an anthropologist and director of urban studies at Temple University, and two of her colleagues observed the eating habits of third-generation Italian families in two Philadelphia neighborhoods. They found a definite pattern of behavior that was carried over from the Old World to the New World.

• There is strong male dominance (father) in deciding what foods are to be served. If the men do not like certain foods they are not made part of the menu.

• Men are very much involved in having access to wholesalers and in getting fresh produce—meats, fruits, and vegetables. The men are also involved in large-scale shopping during the week.

• There is a cycle of certain meals from week to week. Tuesday and Thursday are spaghetti and macaroni nights; Sunday is also a sauce meal. The other meals vary and are given less importance. For holidays and special occasions, there is also a repetition of certain traditional dishes.

• There is a great deal of emotional involvement and discussion about food, particularly for sauce meals, but there is no agreement about what is a "good" sauce—how much spice, how thick, or what the color intensity should be. Still, each household has a particular way of preparing its sauce; when the family cook does not meet these standards, there are complaints from the other family members.

• The mother has a great deal of control over the kitchen. However, in third-generation families where mothers work, the grandmother is active in preparing meals and teaches the granddaughter how to cook. Mothers-in-law are also very much involved in teaching their daughters-in-law how to cook in the style of their husband's family.

How well these family patterns have held up under the pressures in this country to homogenize the customs of Italian-Americans and other ethnic groups is a test of our ethnic strengths. Early in this century, our immigrant grandparents resisted the message that they must abandon their traditions, change their dress, language, and food habits, if they were to make it in America. For example, oil, garlic, peppers, and the exotic flavors of Italian and other ethnic cuisines were seen by puritanical Anglo-Saxons as too passionate, foods that would only excite the individual and stir the blood. Therefore, the blandness of the Anglo-Saxon diet was seen as preferable to the sensuality of Italian and other ethnic foods. The pressure to conform and the unavailability of raw ethnic foods in some parts of the country forced other immigrants to abandon their native cuisine. There were limits: tapioca pudding never supplanted cannoli cream.

There are strong pressures on Italian-Americans to change their food and eating habits. The frantic pace of our lives and the increasing number of working mothers make it almost impossible for families to get to come for dinner during the week. A recent study indicated that families eat dinner together seldom as to only three times a week or less.

All the same, while these forces have affected Italian-Americans, we have resisted giving up our distinctive foods and family meals with unusual tenacity. Aside from the fact that we have a tradition of fine eating which dates back to Roman times, our concern with food, eating, and the pleasures of a good dinner are interwoven with our strong concept of family.

*Joseph Giordano*

(Photo by Pamela Parlapiano)

# Traditional Recipes

## Pasta Fatta in Casa (Homemade Egg Pasta)

Every fine Italian cook has his or her secret for making good pasta. Some use water, some water and salt, some only flour and eggs, some oil. It all boils down to fresh eggs and good flour and, most of all, strong arms. The size of eggs varies greatly and therefore the quantity of flour; the weather has something to do with the pasta too, since the flour absorbs less egg when it is damp. Italian girls used to receive pastry boards when they married, and it was considered heretical to make pasta on anything else—but marble works just as well. It will stick a little to the marble but is easily removed with a spatula. Even Formica can be used, although it does make your life a little more difficult.

In making flat pasta we calculate 3/4 egg a person to about 75 grams (scant 2/3 cup) of flour. But all this depends on the quality of the flour and the flour absorption of the egg. If necessary add flour, and do not be afraid of going beyond the quantities suggested. We use an electric pasta machine to roll out our pasta; a hand-operated machine works just as well. We never seem to have the time to roll the pasta out by hand, but pasta that has been entirely rolled by hand is thought to be more porous, so that the sauce clings better to the pasta.

Here is our recipe for fettuccine for four. Of course again this depends on appetites, and whether the pasta is to be served as a first course or a main course. We think this quantity is sufficient for four as a main dish.

**2 1/2 cups all-purpose flour**
**3 large eggs**
**1 tablespoon extra virgin olive oil**

Pour the flour onto a wooden or marble surface and make a well in the center. Break the eggs into the well and add the olive oil.

With a fork begin to beat the eggs and oil in the center and begin to incorporate the flour, holding the wall of flour so it doesn't collapse and let the eggs through. When the eggs have absorbed enough flour to be less liquid, begin to knead the dough, pushing it with the heel of the hand until all the flour has been absorbed. (If using a pasta machine it is not necessary to work the pasta too much, as it will be kneaded in the machine.) Knead the dough with the heel of the hand, folding over and giving a quarter turn each time until the dough is smooth. This should take about 10 minutes. Add flour as necessary. Put the dough under an overturned bowl to rest for 30 minutes.

Clean off the work surface, then prepare a little mound of flour to the side for dusting the pasta or flouring the rolling pin as necessary. Divide the dough into two pieces. Replace one half under the bowl. Flatten the dough on the board with the knuckles into a round flat ball; dust lightly with flour. With the rolling pin, begin to roll from the center outwards, turning the dough a quarter turn each time. Rub the rolling pin with flour occasionally to keep the dough from sticking. Roll until the sheet of pasta is thin enough to wrap around the rolling pin. At this point roll it around the pin and, putting very light pressure on the pasta, roll the pasta toward you. Starting with the hands in the center, quickly slide the hands toward the outside of the rolling pin, exerting a light, even pressure on the dough. Roll up the sheet, turning the pasta sideways each time (90 degrees) until the sheet is as thin as desired, dusting with flour as needed so that the pasta does not become sticky. The sheet should be round and beautifully thin, but this comes with practice; don't be discouraged if it seems a bit thick. Place the sheet of pasta on a tea towel or wooden surface to dry. (Do not leave it on marble.) Repeat this with the reserved ball of dough.

The pasta should dry in 15 to 25 minutes, depending on the season. It will have a parchment look and feel dry when you touch it. It must not be too dry or it will break when cutting—and if underdried it will stick together.

Roll up the sheet of pasta loosely and, using a sharp knife, cut to the desired width. As the pasta is cut, lay it on clean tea towels. The pasta is now ready to cook. Be careful with the cooking time, as it will only take a minute or so. If there should be pasta left over, it can be stored in the refrigerator in a plastic bag for up to 3 days.

To make pasta by machine: Follow the preceding recipe up to putting the dough under the bowl.

After 30 minutes, divide the dough into 6 pieces. Prepare the pasta machine and dust the large rollers lightly with flour.

Using the large rollers, run one piece of pasta through 10 times, using the largest opening. Fold the pasta in thirds each time and lightly dust with flour when sticky. After 10 times the pasta should be smooth. Now put the rollers on the second largest opening and run the pasta through one time. Move to each successive notch, stopping when you get to the desired thickness (we usually cut fettuccine on the next to last opening). Repeat with the other pieces of dough.

Let the pasta dry about 10 minutes before cutting. Remove the large roller and attach the fettuccine cutter. Run the pasta through and place the fettuccine on clean tea towels. Repeat with all the pasta pieces.

To make pasta dough with a food processor: Put all ingredients in the bowl fitted with the steel blade and process until a ball is formed or is well mixed. If it does not form a ball, turn out and knead a few times until the dough sticks together. Dust with flour and set aside to rest. This pasta needs more flour.

*Pasquale Bruno, Jr.*

# Parmigiana di Melanzane (Eggplant Parmesan)

SERVES 6, AS A FIRST COURSE

This dish is supposed to have originated in Campania, but it is prepared all over Southern Italy and in Sicily. Slices of hard-boiled eggs are often placed on the layer of mozzarella, and in certain small villages in Campania they put melted chocolate between the layers. The dish can be prepared well in advance and then reheated until bubbling, but it may also be served at room temperature. Our recipe—the best one we've come across for this dish—was given to us by a Neapolitan friend.

3½ pounds eggplant

Coarse salt

1 medium onion, chopped

2 tablespoons extra virgin olive oil

2 cans (each 1 pound) Italian plum tomatoes, undrained and coarsely chopped, or 3
    pounds very fresh ripe tomatoes, peeled, seeded, and coarsely chopped

1 cup fresh basil leaves, tightly packed, or 1 tablespoon dried basil

Peanut oil

All-purpose flour for dredging

3 ounces freshly grated Parmesan cheese

Freshly ground black pepper

12 ounces grated mozzarella cheese

Peel the eggplant and slice ½ inch thick. Arrange in a large colander and sprinkle with coarse salt. Put a plate with a weight on it on top of the eggplant, and set aside for 1 hour.

Meanwhile, make the tomato sauce. In a heavy saucepan, sauté the onions in the 2 tablespoons of olive oil on low heat until transparent. Add 1 teaspoon coarse salt and the tomatoes to the onion, mashing them together with a wooden spoon. Add half the basil and cook for 15 minutes. Set aside.

Rinse the eggplant and pat dry with paper towels.

Pour 1 inch of peanut oil into a large skillet and heat until hot. Put about 1 cup flour into a large bowl. Flour the eggplant slices lightly; toss in a sieve to eliminate excess flour. Flour only enough eggplant to fry at one time, adding more flour to the bowl if needed. Fry the eggplant until lightly colored; drain on paper towels.

Preheat the oven to 350° F. Oil a 14 × 9½-inch baking dish.

Put a layer of a third of the eggplant into the baking dish; sprinkle with a third of the Parmesan and some freshly ground pepper and cover with a layer of half the mozzarella. Add a layer of half the tomato sauce and top with half the remaining basil leaves. Repeat the layers, ending with eggplant slices sprinkled with the remaining Parmesan.

Bake, uncovered, for 30 minutes. Serve hot or tepid.

NOTE: This dish freezes well; in fact it's a good idea to double the recipe and freeze one. If frozen, remove from the freezer and leave at room temperature 30 minutes. Bake for 30 minutes at 200° F, 30 minutes at 300° F, and 20 minutes at 350° F, or until bubbly.

# Spaghetti all'Aglio, Olio, e Peperoncini
(Spaghetti with Oil, Garlic, and Hot Red Pepper Flakes)

SERVES 8

We like to eat this very simple spaghetti late at night or when there's nothing in the house and we're all hungry. It is very fast and delicious. Use a large frying pan because the whole dish will be assembled and mixed together in it. The sauce is prepared at the last minute, as the water heats and the pasta cooks.

**1 cup extra virgin olive oil**
**2 tablespoons garlic, sliced**
**Coarse salt**
**1/2 teaspoon hot red pepper flakes, or more to taste**
**11/2 pounds packaged spaghetti or spaghettini**
**5 tablespoons fresh parsley, chopped**

Heat the oil, add the garlic and salt to taste in a skillet. Sauté the garlic gently while stirring with a wooden spoon.

When the garlic has browned, remove the skillet from the heat. Add the pepper flakes and stir constantly to keep them from burning (if burned, they become very bitter). Return the skillet to low heat.

Meanwhile, bring 7 quarts water and 2½ tablespoons coarse salt to a boil in a large pasta pot. Cook the pasta until *very* al dente, just barely cooked; it will cook a little more in the frying pan. Add 2 cups cold water to the pasta pot to stop the cooking process.

Drain the pasta, add to the sauce, and mix thoroughly on the fire for at least a minute. Add the parsley and mix.

# Fettuccine di Casa (Our Fettuccine)

SERVES 6

This is a fairly standard pasta all over Italy, but it is so good that we have it often in our houses. It's also very simple to prepare.

**10 ounces mushrooms, cleaned and thinly sliced**
**7 tablespoons unsalted butter**
**2 cups fresh or frozen peas**
**4 ounces prosciutto, in julienne strips**
**3/4 teaspoon coarse salt**
**1/4 teaspoon freshly ground black pepper**
**1 pound fresh fettuccine**
**6 tablespoons Parmesan cheese, freshly grated**
**3 tablespoons heavy cream, or as needed**

Bring 5 quarts water and 1½ tablespoons coarse salt to a boil in a large pasta pot.

Sauté the mushrooms in 5 tablespoons of the butter until they exude liquid. Turn up the heat and cook for 5 or 6 minutes.

Cook the peas in the boiling water. As soon as they surface, cook for 3 minutes, then remove with a sieve and add to the mushrooms. Add the prosciutto. Cook for 5 minutes on medium flame, then season with the salt and pepper.

Put the remaining 2 tablespoons butter in the bowl in which you will mix the pasta and put the bowl on top of the pot of boiling water. As soon as the butter has melted, remove the bowl. Boil the fettuccine until al dente. Add 1 cup of cold water to stop the cooking process, then drain the pasta and mix in the heated bowl with butter and the Parmesan. Add the mushroom mixture and the cream. (This pasta must not be dry. If necessary, add another teaspoon of cream.) Serve immediately.

# Peperoni della Nonna (Granny's Stuffed Peppers)

SERVES 8

A cheerful dish that is particularly attractive with the contrasting red, yellow, and green colors of the peppers, this can be served as an antipasto or for a light lunch or supper dish. The recipe is very old and was given to us by Signora Morpurgo.

**Coarse salt**
**1 large eggplant, peeled and cut into 1/2-inch dice**
**8 large red, yellow, and green peppers**
**2 tablespoons minced onion**
**4 tablespoons extra virgin olive oil, or more as needed**
**3 to 4 ripe tomatoes, peeled, seeded, and cut into 1/2-inch dice**
**5 ounces oil-packed tuna, drained**
**1/3 cup capers, rinsed**
**5 ounces pitted black olives, Gaeta or oil-cured**
**4 tablespoons fine dry bread crumbs**

Preheat the oven to 400° F. Oil one or two ovenproof serving dishes.

Sprinkle salt over the eggplant and set aside for 30 minutes in a colander, with a plate and weight on top of the eggplant. Wash, pat dry, and set aside.

Cut the peppers in half lengthwise and seed, then cut one of the peppers into 1/2-inch dice. Arrange the pepper halves in the ovenproof serving dishes, cut side up; reserve. Reserve the diced pepper separately.

In a skillet, sauté the onions over low heat in 3 tablespoons of the oil until transparent. Add the eggplant, reserved diced pepper, and tomatoes and sauté for about 10 minutes. Add the tuna, capers, olives, and bread crumbs, and cook for 2 to 3 minutes, stirring, adding the remaining 1 tablespoon oil.

Fill the reserved pepper halves with this mixture. Pour a thin trickle of olive oil over each pepper and bake for 15 minutes. Lower the oven to 375° F and continue baking for 50 to 60 minutes longer. Serve hot or cold.

NOTE: These peppers can be frozen after cooking. Thaw and heat before serving.

# Spaghetti alle Vongole (Spaghetti with Clam Sauce)

SERVES 8

The clams around Naples are small shellfish that resemble snails, and have a pronounced flavor that this recipe brings out. Spaghetti alle Vongole is a traditional Christmas Eve dish in many parts of Italy. The clams are sprinkled with cornmeal and soaked before being cooked because it encourages them to open and allows the sand to come out of the shell.

**4 pounds baby clams**
**Coarse salt**
**1 handful of cornmeal (about 1/3 cup)**
**1 cup plus 2 tablespoons extra virgin olive oil**
**2 garlic cloves, crushed**
**1/2 teaspoon hot red pepper flakes**
**2 tablespoons chopped parsley, plus additional parsley for garnish**
**Freshly ground black pepper to taste**
**12/3 pounds spaghetti or vermicelli**

Scrub the clams well to remove surface dirt and rinse them two or three times in cold water. Fill the kitchen sink with cold water and add 2 fistfuls of salt. Place the clams in a colander and immerse in the water. Sprinkle a handful of cornmeal over the clams, cover the colander with a lid, and leave for at least 5 hours, overnight if possible. Rinse the clams three times and drain.

Add 3 tablespoons salt to 8 quarts water in a large pot. Bring to a boil.

Meanwhile, heat 2 tablespoons oil in a 12-inch skillet and add the clams. Cover and cook over a high flame for 3 to 4 minutes, shaking the pan continuously so that all the clams are exposed to the heat. Cool slightly and discard clams with closed shells. Set aside 3 cups of clams in their shells to be served on top of the pasta.

Strain the pan juices through a strainer lined with one thickness of paper towel and set aside 2/3 cup of the liquid. Shell the remaining clams and add to the reserved pan juice liquid.

Heat the 1 cup oil in a 12-inch skillet and add the garlic. Fry until lightly browned, then add the hot pepper flakes, the shelled clams with their broth, and the chopped parsley. Simmer for 1 minute and season to taste with salt and pepper. Remove from the heat, reserve.

Cook the pasta in the 8 quarts boiling water. The pasta must be very al dente, so taste often to make sure it does not become overcooked. When ready, stop the cooking process by pouring in 2 cups cold water. Drain and add the pasta to the skillet with the clams. Mix rapidly and thoroughly over moderate heat and serve hot, placing the reserved clams in their shells over the pasta. Garnish with more parsley.

*Jo Bettoja and Anna Maria Cornetto*

# Polenta al Pomodoro con Salsiccia (Polenta in Gravy)

SERVES 6–8

**POLENTA**
1 cup finely ground yellow cornmeal
1 teaspoon salt
1 cup cold water

Boil 3 cups water. Mix cornmeal, salt, and cold water in a bowl. Gradually add the mixture to the boiling water, stirring continually. Reduce heat and cover. Continue cooking over low heat about 5 to 10 minutes, stirring frequently.

**GRAVY**
2 pounds sweet Italian sausage, cut in small pieces
2 cloves garlic, minced
1 can (28 ounces) Italian plum tomatoes
2 cans (12 ounces) tomato paste
1 teaspoon basil leaves
1 teaspoon oregano
Salt and freshly ground black pepper
2 cups water

Brown the sausage over medium heat. Remove the sausage from the pan and drain the fat. Add the 2 cloves garlic; brown slightly. Add the tomatoes and tomato paste. Add the water and stir. Sprinkle in the herbs and season to taste. Return the sausage to the pan. Let the combination cook at a slow simmer for 2 hours in an uncovered pot. Stir occasionally.

Serve on a large platter with gravy on top, or you may prefer to serve sauce separately.

Another way to enjoy this cold-weather dish without gravy is to refrigerate the cornmeal after cooking. Leave in refrigerator overnight, cut the meal in blocks, and fry the individual squares in butter or margarine. Serve with honey or maple syrup.

# Cavatelli alla Conserva di Pomodoro
(Cavatelli with Tomato Sauce)

SERVES 4 AS A FIRST COURSE OR SIDE DISH

In some locales this pasta is also known as gnocchi or seashells. The rolling and forming of the pasta is not done for aesthetic reasons; the ridges and the small pockets in the cavatelli help to pick up and hold the sauce.

**SAUCE**
1 clove garlic, peeled and put through a garlic press
2 tablespoons olive oil
1 can (28 ounces) Italian plum tomatoes, undrained
2 tablespoons tomato paste
2 tablespoons finely chopped fresh parsley
2 teaspoons oregano
Salt to taste

**PASTA**
2 cups sifted unbleached flour
3/4 tablespoon vegetable oil or melted vegetable shortening
1/2 cup or more hot water
1 teaspoon baking powder

To make the sauce: Use a nonaluminum 2- to 3-quart sauté pan or saucepan. Over medium heat sauté the garlic in the oil for about 2 minutes. Put the tomatoes through a food mill and add to the garlic. Add the tomato paste and mix thoroughly. Add the parsley and oregano. Bring the sauce to a slow boil. Turn down the heat. Keep the sauce at a slow simmer (small bubbles) uncovered for 30 to 40 minutes. Taste and add salt if necessary.

To make the pasta: Use a fairly large mixing bowl. Put the flour into the bowl. Add the shortening. Add the 1/2 cup hot water and mix with your hands for about 2 minutes. Add the baking powder.

Mix thoroughly with your hands until the dough comes together in a ball. At this point, if the dough feels stiff, add a little more hot water. The dough should be quite soft and a bit spongy. Take the dough out of the bowl and knead for 4 to 5 minutes.

Cut a piece of the dough about the size of a plum off the ball and keep the rest covered with a towel. Stretch and roll this piece between your hands to form a sausagelike shape.

Place the dough on the counter and, with the lightest amount of pressure, roll your hands over the dough to stretch and thin it out. Cut in one-inch slices. Continue until you have used all the dough.

Fill a large pot with 8 quarts of water. Add 3 tablespoons of salt and 2 tablespoons of oil. Cover and bring water to a boil. Place in cavatelli and cook for 15 minutes or until tender. Do not overcook.

Place cavatelli on a large platter, pour sauce over it, and sprinkle with Parmesan cheese.

# Fennel: Cure-all and Culinary Treat

I have found few ingredients more regrettably understated in our present food culture than fennel—*finocchio* to Italians. Yet this sweet licorice-flavored ingredient is steeped in herbal lore and tradition. Besides its long-standing appeal to Mediterranean cooks, fennel's various components have been considered antidotes for numerous ailments. Throughout the ages fennel was brought forth to treat everything from coughs, colic, and abdominal cramps to evil and obesity. The ancient Greeks attributed bravery and longevity to the imbibing of fennel infusions.

The venerable herbalist Culpeper proclaimed fennel's purgative qualities in his writing. Fennel, he noted, "expels wind, provokes urine, and eases the pains of the stone and helps it to break." Herbal prescriptions of yore include "gripe water," a fennel-based brew for flatulence in infants; a soothing eyewash made by leaching the essence of fennel seeds into boiling water; a cough expectorant made by mixing fennel oil (expressed from the seeds) with honey; and an insect repellent also made from the oil. Even Longfellow proclaimed the medicinal attributes of the prolific herb. Fennel, he intoned,

> Was gifted with the wondrous powers
> Lost vision to restore.

Fennel, in its various herb and vegetable forms, is wending its way into prominence once again through a renewed interest in the health-giving qualities of herbal concoctions and the still-developing American cuisine. Although it is still those of Mediterranean heritage who capitalize on fennel's versatility in the kitchen, fennel can often be found in large produce markets in most cosmopolitan areas. It is easiest to find in fall or winter, when it is harvested.

There are three types of edible fennel, all imparting the characteristic scent and flavor of anise to varying degrees. Common or wild fennel is grown for its seeds and leaves. The seeds, a popular seasoning for Italian sausage, may also flavor cookies, breads, and other baked goods. The feathery leaves can be brewed into a calming tea. Used either fresh or dried, they mate famously with fish dishes—especially soups, stews, and sauces. Fennel leaves help lessen the oiliness of fish such as salmon or mackerel.

A French waiter in a street cafe in Marseilles enlightened me about the inventive French use of dried fennel twigs. He ignited the stalky pile, deftly flambéing my grilled *daurade* until the fish was perfectly redolent of fennel smoke.

*Carosella* or Sicilian fennel has tender young stems that can be eaten like asparagus or broccoli rabe. While visiting me in San Francisco, my grandmother discovered a field of these fragrant stalks growing wild. We were at a roadside rest on our way up to Sonoma wine country when she scurried off into a weed patch. Using her dress as an apron, she began to fill it with the wispy vegetation.

"Mama!" bellowed her daughter, my Aunt Jenny, *"che fai?"*

*"Finocch', c'è il finocch',"* came the excited cry of discovery, as she tugged furiously at the wild weeds she'd not seen so rampant since her girlhood in Sicily.

I pulled a net sack from my car and together we picked, ignoring Aunt Jenny's bewildered gaze. My grandmother showed me which of the top stalks would be the most tender.

That evening Grandmother regaled ten of my friends with a sumptuous meal of spaghetti with marinara sauce, laced with mounds of fennel sautéed in olive oil, and topped with toasted bread crumbs and Parmesan cheese. Months later I attempted to duplicate the meal but was thwarted by my hand-picked batch of ropelike fennel. My octogenarian grandmother, I'm afraid, took her instinct for tender weeds to her grave.

For this reason I use the third type of fennel, Florence fennel or sweet fennel. Florence fennel, the one resembling squat celery with thick overlapping basal stalks, most arouses my sense memories in the way Proust's madeleine did for him. I associate this fennel with many past lavish holiday feasts that brought my large Italian family together. Fennel appeared on the antipasto tray to *enhance* appetites before the meal, at various intervals of the day-long meal to *quell* appetites, and always before the meal's culmination.

The humble appearance of Florence fennel belies its full culinary worth. Its sweet licorice flavor adds a new and refreshing dimension to raw vegetable salads (cut away the darker green top woody stalks), but there are many ways to enjoy cooked fennel.

Braising in stock or a seasoned liquid brings out fennel's unique flavor. Sautéing it in butter with a simple herb also highlights its pleasant taste. Sage, sweet basil, marjoram, or tarragon all mingle nicely with fennel. Its sweetness is a wonderful foil for Italian cheeses—pair it with a Gorgonzola and ricotta mixture or the Danish havarti. Or bake stalks of fennel stuffed with Parmesan and bread crumbs (see recipe for Finocchio Parmigiano).

Steamed or parboiled fennel goes well with a light cream sauce. Or it can be puréed as a soup or sauce base itself. Fennel and tomatoes yield a hearty, peasant pasta sauce.

In other cuisines fennel appears with lentils, rice, potatoes, and even apple pie. In fact, the torta di finocchio e nocciole, a dessert fit to crown any grand repast, is a furtive way to introduce this "cultured" vegetable to an unschooled palate.

## Growing Florence Fennel

The fennel plant *(Foeniculum dulce)* is hardy and free of pest and disease problems. It is a cool-season vegetable—an annual in most parts of the United States, a perennial in mild regions. Botanically it belongs to the Umbelliferae family with celery, carrots, chervil, and parsley.

If you live in a very mild region, you can start finocchio in autumn or winter and harvest it in spring. If you live in the north, plant it in May and harvest it in midsummer. Fennel requires about 100 days of frost-free weather from the time of planting. It will withstand the cold, but a frost will kill it, and a very hot temperature will cause it to bolt (run to seed).

Sow seeds at a depth of 1/2 inch, about 4 inches apart. When the plants are 3 inches tall, thin them to stand at 8-inch intervals in rows. To guard against bolting, water the plants adequately throughout growth. Periodic applications of rich manure will help produce succulent, thick-fleshed bulbs. Mulching will also encourage tender stems.

Harvesting can usually take place 90 to 120 days from the time of planting, when the basal stalks are fully developed, measuring 2 1/2 to 3 inches in diameter. Much wider than that will yield a stringy woody plant. Dig up the entire plant, remove the roots, and cut back the upper branches.

*Camille Cusumano*

## Fennel Recipes*

---

* The following recipes use Florence fennel and only the basal stalks. The weight or measurements refer to the fennel after the top stalks have been cut away.

# Finocchio Stufato con Burro Salvia
(Braised Fennel with Sage Butter)

SERVES 6

1 stick (1/4 pound) butter, at room temperature
2 tablespoons minced fresh sage
1 tablespoon fresh lemon juice
2 large bulbs (about 2 1/2 pounds) fennel, cut into 2 × 3-inch strips
2 cups poultry stock
1/4 cup dry sherry
2 tablespoons olive oil

Preheat oven to 375° F. Combine the butter, sage, and lemon juice, creaming with an electric beater or a wooden spoon. Roll the butter mixture into an oblong, wrap in plastic wrap, and refrigerate.

Spread the fennel strips in bottom of a greased 2-quart baking dish with a cover. Pour the stock, sherry, and oil over the top of the fennel and cover.

Bake for 30 minutes. With a slotted spoon, remove the fennel to a serving dish. Dot with the sage butter and serve immediately.


# Crema di Finocchio (Cream of Fennel Soup)

SERVES 4

5 tablespoons unsalted butter
1/2 cup chopped onion
2 1/2 cups chopped fennel
1 cup heavy cream
1 cup chicken or veal stock
Watercress leaves, for garnish
Freshly ground black pepper

Heat the butter in a 2-quart soup pot. Add the onion and fennel and cover. Cook until the fennel is soft, about 12 minutes. Purée the mixture, along with the cream.

Return the soup to the pot and stir in the stock. Cook just until heated (do not boil) and serve immediately. Garnish each serving with a few watercress leaves and pepper.

# Finocchio Parmigiano (Baked Fennel Parmesan)

SERVES 4

2 cloves garlic, minced
1/2 cup Italian seasoned bread crumbs
1/3 cup grated Parmesan cheese
2 medium bulbs fennel (about 11/2 pounds), sliced lengthwise
1/2 cup olive oil
2 tablespoons chopped fresh parsley

Preheat oven to 375° F. Combine the garlic, bread crumbs, and Parmesan. Spread the fennel strips, inner stalk up, in a 9-inch-square baking dish.

Fill the fennel stalks with the bread crumb mixture. Pour the olive oil over all. Bake for 25 to 30 minutes, until the fennel is tender. Garnish with the parsley and serve as a side dish.

# Insalata di Finocchio e Crostacei (Fennel and Shellfish Salad)

SERVES 4 TO 6

4 cups water
1 stalk celery, quartered
1 carrot, halved
1 onion, quartered
8 peppercorns
1 teaspoon salt
1 medium bulb fennel (about 3/4 pound), cut into 1/4 × 11/2-inch strips
1/2 pound bay scallops
1/2 pound medium shrimp, shelled
3 tablespoons minced Italian sweet peppers
1 stalk celery, minced
1 clove garlic, crushed
2 tablespoons chopped pimientos
1 teaspoon whole-grain-style mustard
1 teaspoon dried chervil
1/4 teaspoon crushed red pepper
1/4 cup white wine vinegar
3/4 cup virgin olive oil
1/2 cup Italian olives

In a 2-quart pot, combine the water, celery, carrot, onion, peppercorns, and salt. Bring to a boil and cook 30 minutes. With a slotted spoon, remove and discard the vegetables and peppercorns.

Add the fennel, scallops, and shrimp to the stock. Cover the pot and remove from heat. Allow to sit 10 minutes, then drain and set aside.

In a large salad bowl, combine all the remaining ingredients except the olives. Mix well. Add the shellfish and fennel and toss to coat well. Add the olives and toss. Serve chilled or at room temperature.

# Pesce Spada con Finocchio Salsa (Swordfish with Fennel Sauce)

SERVES 4

1 large bulb fennel (about 1¼ pounds), chopped
4 tablespoons unsalted butter
4 tablespoons olive oil
3 cloves garlic, minced
2 tablespoons chopped fresh basil
2 tablespoons fresh lemon juice
1 teaspoon fennel seeds, crushed
4 slices (½ pound each) swordfish steak
¼ cup melted butter and lemon juice (half and half) for basting

Boil enough water to cover the fennel. Add the fennel to the boiling water, simmer 5 minutes, and drain. Purée and set aside.

Heat the butter and oil in a saucepan. Add the garlic and sauté 3 minutes. Slowly stir in the fennel purée, basil, lemon juice, and fennel seeds. Cook just until heated through. Keep warm until the fish is cooked.

Preheat the broiler. Brush both sides of the swordfish with the melted butter and lemon juice. Place the steaks on broiler pan and broil 2 inches from the heat about 7 minutes on each side (depending on thickness of fish), until flesh is no longer translucent. Baste several times during cooking. Serve immediately with the fennel sauce.

# Specialties of the House*

## Spiedini alla Romana
(Skewered, Deep-fried Mozzarella Sandwiches)

SERVES 8–12

**SANDWICHES**
14 slices ordinary supermarket white bread
12 slices mozzarella cheese, each slice about 1/4 inch thick (see instructions below)
Flour for dredging
5 eggs, well beaten
Oil for deep frying

**ANCHOVY SAUCE**
8 tablespoons butter
10 anchovies, chopped
1 tablespoon finely chopped fresh parsley
1/4 cup drained capers, optional
1/2 cup brown beef gravy, available in cans

Trim the crusts from the bread to make neat squares (see note). If you can purchase mozzarella cheese in a loaf shape (the loaf size is approximately that of a loaf of bread) cut off 12 slices, matching the shape and size of the bread slices as closely as possible. Make 2 stacks of sandwiches with bread slices top and bottom.

If a regular package of mozzarella is used, proceed differently. Cut the bread squares in half to make 28 rectangles. Cut the mozzarella into 24 slices, matching the shape and size of the rectangles of bread as closely as possible. Make 4 stacks of sandwiches with slices of bread top and bottom.

Secure each stack with 2 skewers, to hold the sandwiches together as they cook. Dredge the skewered sandwiches in flour. Coat thoroughly with the egg and place the sandwiches on a rack until ready to fry. This may be done a 1/2 hour or so in advance.

Preheat oven to 400° F.

Heat the oil for deep frying and when it is very hot and almost smoking add the sandwiches. Cook about 3 minutes, turning once, or until golden brown all over. It may be necessary to fry the sandwiches in 2 batches. Drain on paper toweling.

Combine the sauce ingredients in a saucepan and simmer briefly, stirring until the anchovies are "melted" and the sauce smooth.

Place the skewered sandwiches on a buttered dish and bake about 5 minutes, or until sandwiches are piping hot throughout. Remove the skewers and cut each sandwich crosswise into 2 or 3 portions. Serve with the anchovy sauce spooned on top.

*Mario's Restaurant*
*2342 Arthur Avenue*
*Bronx, N.Y. 10458*

---

* Selected by each restaurant.

# Fettuccine Verdi alla Gargiulo

SERVES 4–6

1 small onion, julienned
1/4 cup olive oil
2 ounces raw mushrooms, sliced
2 ounces butter
3 ounces Italian prosciutto, julienned
2 ounces peeled tomatoes, chopped
3 ounces boneless breast of chicken, part-roasted and julienned
2 ounces heavy cream
Pinch of nutmeg
Salt and freshly ground black pepper to taste
1 pound green fettuccine
Grated Parmesan cheese (optional)

In a 12-inch skillet, sauté the onion in the oil until golden, then add the mushrooms and sauté for 2 more minutes. Add the butter, prosciutto, tomatoes, and chicken. Simmer 6 minutes.

Blend into this mixture the cream, nutmeg, salt, and pepper.

Separately boil the fettuccine in 2 quarts salted water. Drain.

Place the fettuccine in a warm serving dish. Pour the chicken mixture over it, add the Parmesan, and serve.

*Gargiulo's Restaurant*
*2911 West 15th Street*
*Brooklyn, N.Y.*
*(718) 266-0906; ES2-9456*

# Spaghettini alla Puttanesca, Versione Bianca

SERVES 1

3 peeled garlic cloves, chopped
2 tablespoons olive oil
1/2 cup chicken broth
2 leaves fresh basil
1/8 teaspoon chopped fresh parsley
12 pitted Gaeta olives with their own juice
1 pinch Accent (optional)
1 chopped anchovy
Salt and freshly ground black pepper to taste
4 ounces spaghettini

In a small pan, sauté the garlic in the oil. When the garlic is browned, add the rest of ingredients except the spaghettini. Let the sauce simmer uncovered about 10 minutes, until somewhat thick.

In a separate pot, cook the spaghettini al dente, drain, and add to the sauce. Let the whole thing simmer for about 1 minute and serve hot *without* cheese.

*Ennio & Michael Ristorante*
*504 LaGuardia Place*
*New York, N.Y. 10012*
*(212) 677-8577*

# Fusilli con Broccoli di Rapa

SERVES 2

1/2 pound fusilli
Pure olive oil
3 or 4 whole cloves garlic, peeled and cracked
11/4 cups water
1 teaspoon salt
1/8 teaspoon pepper
1/8 teaspoon crushed red pepper or to taste
2 cups fresh broccoli rape, washed and stems trimmed short

Cook fusilli until al dente in salted, boiling water. Drain and rinse pasta in a colander. Set aside.

Cover the bottom of a 3-quart saucepan with about 1/4 inch olive oil. Sauté the cloves of garlic until lightly browned.

Remove pan from stove and add 11/4 cups water, and salt, pepper, and crushed red pepper to taste. Return pan to stove and add broccoli rape, turning it until it begins to shrink. Cover and let simmer for 5 minutes.

Remove cover and add fusilli. Toss and turn pasta and vegetable until fusilli is hot and the two are evenly mixed. Serve with a slotted spoon, then pour some of the liquid on top.

*Sal Anthony's*
*55 Irving Place*
*New York, N.Y. 10003*
*(212) 982-9030*

# Pasta al Pesce

SERVES 6

MARINARA SAUCE

2 large cloves garlic, minced
3 pounds onions, sliced or chopped
1/2 cup olive oil
1 teaspoon salt
1 teaspoon freshly ground white pepper
1 can (28 ounces) tomatoes (crushed or peeled)
3 teaspoons chopped fresh parsley
3 fresh basil leaves (chopped or crushed)
1 teaspoon dry white wine

3 cloves garlic, minced
1/2 cup olive oil
2 tablespoons chopped fresh parsley
1/2 teaspoon oregano
1 teaspoon freshly ground white pepper
Salt to taste
12 mussels
12 littleneck clams
6 jumbo scallops, cut in half
6 jumbo shrimps
1/2 pound fillet of sole
1/2 cup dry white wine
1 cup clam juice
1 pound linguini
1 cup marinara sauce

To prepare marinara sauce: Brown the garlic and onions in the oil until the onions are a golden color. Add the remaining ingredients and simmer for about 20 minutes.

To prepare pasta al pesce: Brown the garlic in the oil, add the herbs and seasonings, and cook over medium heat for a few minutes. Add all the fish and shellfish. Simmer uncovered for 10 minutes. Add the wine and clam juice. Slowly bring almost to a boil.

Meantime, add a teaspoon salt and a few drops oil to 4 quarts boiling water. Return to a boil and add the linguini, stirring gently. Bring to a boil and cook for 10 minutes.

Drain the linguini and mix in the sauce and the pesce, toss, divide, and serve.

*Restaurant Italia*
*1909 Wilshire Boulevard*
*Santa Monica, Cal. 90403*
*(213) 453-3333*

# DESSERTS

## Pignoli Cookies

1 package (6 ounces) almond paste (do not use canned paste)
2 egg whites
1 cup confectioners' sugar
1/4 cup unsifted flour
1/2 teaspoon baking powder
1 jar (6 ounces) pignoli (pine nuts)

Break up almond paste. Add egg whites. Cream until smooth with electric beater.

Combine dry ingredients and add to almond paste. Wrap in plastic wrap and refrigerate until cold and stiff.

Preheat oven to 300° F.

Dip teaspoonfuls out with spoon. Make round ball and roll in the nuts. Place on greased cookie sheet 1 inch apart.

Bake for 15 to 20 minutes, or until brown. Remove from oven, cool on tray for 5 minutes, then remove cookies with spatula and cool further. Store in plastic bag or tin for 1 week, then serve.

## GELATO

One product making a big hit in America is gelato—Italian ice cream. Gelato is smoother and richer than American ice cream—the chocolate is dark and rich and the *fragola* tastes like fresh strawberries. Apparently, gelato machines (designed in Italy) pump less air into the mixture, making the flavors stronger and the texture denser than those of ordinary ice cream. Other Italian gelato flavors are *gianduia* (chocolate with bits of hazelnut), *amaretto* (almond), *torrone* (nougat), and *zabaglione* (vanilla with marsala wine).

## Strufoli

Vegetable oil (fill a deep saucepan 2/3 full)
2 cups sifted all-purpose flour
1/4 teaspoon salt
3 eggs
1 teaspoon vanilla extract
Milk (if needed)
1 cup honey
1 tablespoon sugar
1 cup chopped walnuts
1 tablespoon candy sprinkles

Place the vegetable oil in a deep pot (fill two-thirds only) and heat at low temperature until very hot.

In a large bowl, mix the flour and salt.

Make a well in center of the flour and drop each egg in (one at a time), mixing slightly after each addition. Add vanilla to egg mixture.

Mix together to make a soft dough. Turn dough onto a lightly floured surface and knead 100 to 125 counts. If the dough becomes hard to knead, wet hands with milk, then knead again. (Milk will make dough moist and at the same time add flavor.) When the dough is spongy, it is ready to cut.

Divide dough in half (cover the other half with damp cloth so it won't dry out). Cut in strips and roll to length of pinky. Then cut each rolled strip in pieces, about 1/4 inch wide.

Drop one or two into hot oil to test. When strufoli bubbles, oil is hot enough. Then drop a few at a time into the hot oil. Do not overcrowd the pot. Fry until golden brown, turning occasionally with a slotted spoon. Remove with slotted spoon and place on brown paper to absorb the oil.

Place the honey and sugar in a skillet and cook over low heat until the honey starts to bubble. Remove skillet from heat. Place the chopped nuts in the heated honey and stir well. Place the strufoli in the honey and coat well. Remove from skillet. Add the sprinkles to decorate.

## BUYING FOOD BY MAIL

**Dean & De Luca's** 121 Prince St., New York, N.Y. 10012 (212) 254-7774. De Luca's catalog lists its cheeses, herbs, baked foods, and specialties.

**Balducci's** 424 Avenue of the Americas, New York, N.Y. 10011 (212) 673-2600. Balducci's is a food store that seems like a department store. Almost everything appears to be available, including baked goods and homemade foods. Catalog available.

**Alba Italian Pastry Shoppe** 7001 Eighteenth Ave., Brooklyn, N.Y. 11204 (718) 232-2122. A marvelous family bakery that specializes in retail and mail orders.

# Italian Cheeses

**Albini**   Made of a mixture of goats' and cows' milk, it comes from Northern Italy. This cheese has a mellow, pleasant flavor. It is becoming increasingly rare.

**Al Pepe**   A hard peppery cheese.

**Ancona**   A cheese of the pecorino group.

**Arovature**   Made of the milk of the water buffalo. Like other cheeses of this type, it is rare and becoming rarer.

**Asiago**   Made from partly skimmed cows' milk, cured for one year or more. Available soft or aged, it can be used as a table cheese or for grating.

**Asin**   A sour-milk cheese with a washed crust and a whitish, buttery, soft paste. There are sometimes a few eyes.

**Bel Paise**   Creamy texture, with a touch of tartness. Fine cheese with many uses.

**Benrade**   Made from cows' milk with 10 percent goats' milk. It is colored yellow with saffron and cured about two months.

**Bertolli**   A ewes'-milk cheese that is firm, yellow, and piquant.

**Bocconi Giganti**   A name given to a number of Italian cheeses that resemble smoked, well-aged provolone.

**Caciocavallo**   Cows' milk cheese, smooth, firm-bodied, gourd-shaped. It has a light tan crust that is not edible. Delicate, mildly smoky flavor. It is used as a table cheese; when cured for six months or longer, it can be used for grating.

**Caciotta**   A soft, buttery, saffron-colored cheese that is cured about ten days. Its flavor ranges from sweet and mild to slightly piquant.

**Canestrato**   A strong Sicilian yellow-white ewes'-milk cheese aged about six months. It is pressed in a wicker mold, whose imprint remains on the cheese, giving it its name. In the United States, an incanestrato is made from cows' milk by a process ordinarily used for Romano.

**Casigliolo**   A cheese much like caciocavallo, made in Sicily. It is also called panedda and pera di vacca.

**Castelmagne**   Blue-veined cows' milk cheese.

**Chiavari**   Sour milk whole cows'-milk cheese, made in Genoa.

**Ciclo**   A small soft cream cheese.

**Cotronese**   A ewes'-milk cheese from Calabria seasoned with whole peppercorns.

**Cremini**   A mild cheese spread.

**Cremino**   A soft cream cheese, sold in Northern Italy wrapped in foil.

**Emiliano**   Similar to Parmesan, with a dark oiled surface, a light yellow interior, a granular texture, and a mild to sharp flavor, depending on the length of the cure. Winter cheese is ripened twenty months; spring cheese at least two years.

**Erbo**   Similar to gorgonzola; seen as a round, rindless sausage, often in a tin, in countries other than Italy.

**Fontal**   A table cheese made from whole cows' milk. The name is restricted by law to a cheese made in the Val d' Aosta. The cheese is a thin compact disk, with a few holes scattered through a straw-colored or white paste.

**Fontina**   Made from cows' milk, somewhat yellowish and soft. For table use. Very good cheese for cooking as it ages and hardens.

**Fontinelli**   A semidry, flaky, sharp cheese.

**Fresa**   A caciotta, soft, mild, sweet cows'-milk or goats'-milk cheese from Sardinia.

**Gorgonzola**   Italy's principal blue-veined cheese.

**Grana**   Generic name that describes finely grained hard cheeses made from partly skimmed milk and matured in distinctive drums for at least a year.

**Lodigiano**   A grana cheese from Lodi, it is presented as a cylinder of convex faces, colored dark with oil. The interior is yellow, and the cheese is sharp, fragrant, and a little bitter. It has less fat and larger eyes and is slower ripening than Parmesan, and is cured for as long as five years.

**Mel Fino**   One of the newer cheeses, it is a blue Bel Paese.

**Milano**   A soft, fast-ripening Italian cheese. Similar to Bel Paese, it is also called fresco quardo. It is cured about twenty days, is yellow, has a thin rind and may be enclosed in muslin bags.

**Mozzarella**   A soft white cheese that can be shaped in a variety of ways. Originally it was made from buffaloes' milk, now from cows' milk. It is most famous in America as a topping used on pizza. However, many claim it is best when fresh, only a few days old. Try it sliced with olive oil and salt or sample it with a variety of vegetables such as tomatoes, roasted sweet peppers, hot peppers, and of course good bread!

**Parmigiano Reggiano**   The hardest of all cheeses, usually used for grating, especially for pasta dishes. Parmesan is a golden-yellowish cheese and is aged very carefully.

**Pecorino Romano**   Is a hard grating cheese made from sheep's milk and is sharper and tangier than Parmesan. They are interchangeable in many dishes. This, too, is aged carefully, and the taste of the cheese is strengthened with age.

**Provolone**   Comes in many forms, since it is often shaped by hand. Good for table use and cooking.

**Ragusano**   A spun-curd hard white cheese that is steeped in brine and sometimes smoked. The rind is thin, smooth, golden yellow for table use; dark brown, rubbed with olive oil for grating. The cheese is sweet when young, strong when aged.

**Ricotta**   A fresh, uncured cheese that is bought in containers. It is made from the whey of cows' milk. You can slice dry ricotta like a cream cheese, but ricotta is most often used in such dishes as lasagna, manicotti, and baked ziti and in desserts such as cannoli and cheesecake.

**Roma**   A soft cream cheese.

**Romanello**   A very hard cheese, made from partly skimmed milk. Sharp, well cured, it bears a basket imprint. The interior is white with small openings.

**Salame**   A small soft cream cheese. This name also refers to a large sausage-shaped provolone.

**Sardo**   A Romano type made in Sardinia from a mixture of cows' and ewes' milk. It is also made in the United States and Argentina.

**Scanno**   A ewes'-milk cheese, cured by treatment in a solution of iron oxide in sulphuric acid. The exterior is black, the interior a deep yellow. It has a buttery consistency and tastes burned.

**Sposi**   A small creamy cows'-milk cheese.

**Stracchino**   Generic term for a type of creamy Lombardy cheese.

**Toscanello**   A very hard, ewes'-milk cheese from Tuscany that is used for grating.

**Toscano**   A ewes'-milk cheese much like Romano.

**Trecce**   A spun-curd cheese that is braided and eaten fresh.

**Tuscano**   A semihard cream-colored Parmesan cheese from Tuscany.

# Italian Wines

| | |
|---|---|
| Aglianico del Vulture | Basilicata—dry deep red wine |
| Albana di Romagna | Emilia-Romagna—dry-medium white table wine |
| Aleatico di Portoferraio | Tuscany—sweet red dessert wine |
| Amarone della Valpolicella | Veneto—dry red table wine |
| Asti Spumante | Piemonte—sweet sparkling white wine |
| Barbaresco | Piemonte—dry red table wine |
| Barbera | Piemonte—dry red table wine |
| Bardolino | Veneto—dry red table wine |
| Barolo | Piemonte—dry red table wine |
| Brachetto | Piemonte—dry red table wine |
| Brunello di Montalcino | Tuscany—dry red table wine |
| Capri | Campania—dry white table wine |
| Carema | Valle d'Aosta—dry red table wine |
| Castelli Romani | Lazio—dry or semisweet white or red table wine |
| Chianti | Tuscany—dry red table wine |
| Chiaretto del Garda | Veneto—medium-dry pink table wine |
| Cinqueterre | Liguria—semisweet white table wine |
| Ciro | Calabria—sweet red table wine |
| Corvo Bianco | Sicily—dry white table wine |
| Corvo Rosso | Sicily—dry red table wine |
| Cortese di Cavi | Piemonte—dry white table wine |
| Dolcetto | Piemonte—dry or sweet sparkling table wine |
| Est! Est! Est! | Lazio—dry white table wine |
| Frascati | Lazio—medium-sweet white table wine |
| Freisa | Piemonte—dry red table wine |
| Frescciarossa | Lombardy—dry red or white table wine |
| Galestro | Tuscany—dry white table wine |
| Gattinara | Piemonte—dry red table wine |
| Gavi | Piemonte—dry white table wine |
| Giro | Sardinia—sweet red dessert wine |
| Gragnano | Campania—dry red table wine |
| Greco di Tufo | Campania—medium-dry white table wine |
| Grignolino | Piemonte—dry red table wine |
| Grumello | Lombardy—dry red table wine |
| Inferno | Lombardy—dry red table wine |
| Ischia | Campania—dry white table wine |
| Lacrima Christi | Campania—medium-dry white table wine |
| Lambrusco | Emilia-Romagna—medium-sweet red sparkling wine |
| Lugana | Veneto—dry white table wine |
| Marsala | Sicily—sweet brown dessert wine |
| Malvasia | Lazio—sweet gold fortified wine |
| Moscato Fior d'Arancio | Sicily—sweet gold fortified wine |
| Moscato del Salento | Puglia—sweet gold fortified wine |
| Nebbiolo | Piemonte—dry red table wine |
| Nobile di Montelpulciano | Tuscany—dry red table wine |

| | |
|---|---|
| Orvieto | Umbria—dry or semisweet white table wine |
| Passito | Sweet amber fortified wine |
| Piccolit | Friuli—sweet white table wine |
| Pinot Blanc, Pinot Grigio | Dry white table wine |
| Recioto | Veneto—sweet red table wine |
| Riesling | Dry or sweet white wine |
| Rubesco | Umbria—dry red table wine |
| Santa Maddalena | Alto Aldige—dry red table wine |
| Sassella | Lombardy—dry red table wine |
| Soave | Veneto—dry white table wine |
| Spanna | Piemonte—dry red table wine |
| Taurasi | Campania—dry red table wine |
| Tocai | Friuli—dry white table wine |
| Valgella | Lombardy—dry red table wine |
| Valpantena | Veneto—dry red table wine |
| Valpolicella | Veneto—dry red table wine |
| Valtellina | Lombardy—dry red table wine |
| Verdicchio | Marche—dry white table wine (try with shellfish) |
| Vernaccia San Giminiano | Tuscany—dry white table wine |
| Vin Santo | Tuscany—sweet white table wine |

# MARCELLA HAZAN'S COOKING CLASSES

She wrote *The Classic Italian Cookbook* (Knopf) and *More Classic Italian Cooking* (Knopf). Her husband, James Hazan, wrote *Italian Wine* (Knopf). Their classes are often held in Italy from April to October, where they teach marketing principles, hold comparative wine tastings, conduct restaurant banquets, and prepare farmhouse dinners and fish feasts on the Adriatic. For information, write: Hazan Classics, P.O. Box 285, Circleville, N.Y. 10919.

# Some of The Best Italian Cookbooks

Bettoja, Jo, and Anna Maria Cornetto. *Italian Cooking in the Grand Tradition.* Garden City, N.Y.: Dial Press/Doubleday & Co., 1982.

Bruno, Pasquale, Jr. *The Great Chicago Style Pizza Cookbook.* Chicago: Contemporary Books, 1983.

Deep-dish Chicago pizza. A how-to plus an extraordinary array of recipes. Well-illustrated and authoritative.

Bugialli, Giuliano. *Giulano Bugialli's Foods of Italy.* New York: Stewart, Tabori & Chang, 1984.

A stunning yet practical book of Italian food and cooking with 250 photographs by *Time-Life* picture editor John Dominis. 125 recipes from the entire peninsula.

Candler, Teresa Gilardi. *The Northern Italian Cookbook.* New York: McGraw-Hill, 1977.

A large variety of recipes—lower in calories than Southern Italian cooking—using fruits, vegetables, and wines.

Casale, Anne. *Italian Family Cooking.* New York: Fawcett/Columbine, 1984.

"Reading the recipes [in this book] is the next best thing to sitting in a kitchen in Rome, watching dinner being prepared," said one critic. More than 250 recipes, lucid and easy-to-follow.

Hazan, Marcella. *The Classic Italian Cookbook.* New York: Harper & Row, 1973.

Regional cuisines for every taste.

————. *More Classic Italian Cooking.* New York: Knopf, 1978.

Two hundred and twenty new recipes that convey the vast variety of scent and taste of Italian cooking.

Loren, Sophia. *In the Kitchen with Love.* Garden City, N.Y.: Doubleday & Co., Inc., 1972.

A "gastronomic autobiography" with recollections of great cooks she has known plus more than 300 easy-to-follow recipes.

Middione, Carlo. *Pasta! Cooking Italian, Loving Italian.* New York: Harper & Row, 1982.

A bewildering variety of sauces and pasta, including bucatini, cappelletti, conchiglie, rotelle, stellini, dried pasta.

Pezzini, Wilma. *The Tuscan Cookbook.* New York: Atheneum, 1978.

Recipes from the heartland of Italy (including Florence) with specialties in fish, cabbage soups, bean soups, roasts, and the coarse, fragrant bread of the region.

Romagnoli, Margaret, and G. Franco. *The Romagnolis' Table. Italian Family Recipes.* Boston: Little, Brown, 1974.

A husband-wife team of Boston public broadcasting fame offers a fine, practical book teeming with genuine recipes.

Ross, Janet, and Michael Waterfield. *Leaves from Our Tuscan Kitchen, or How to Cook Vegetables.* New York: Atheneum, 1974.

A beautifully designed, updated version of a book first published in Great Britain in 1899. It is based on the recipes of Giuseppi Volpi, who served as the chef for the two nineteenth-century Britons who lived in a villa near Florence.

*And, don't overlook*

Hazan, Victor. *Italian Wine.* New York: Knopf, 1982.

Everything you need to know about Italian wine, written in a clear, elegant style.

# Part Four

# CULTURE

## *Enrico Caruso*

Still a legend in opera annals more than sixty years after his death, the famous tenor Enrico Caruso was one of the greatest interpreters of Italian and French opera.

Caruso's life had operatic features of its own. Born in Naples in 1873, he was his parents' eighteenth child—but the first to survive infancy. As a child Caruso learned to sing Neapolitan ballads by ear, and in 1891 he began to study music seriously. By 1894 he had made his opera debut in Naples in *L'Amico Francesco,* and Caruso soon sang roles in *La Traviata, La Favorita, Carmen, Faust, Rigoletto, Aida, Tosca,* and *La Boheme.*

His turning point occurred in 1898 when he landed the tenor lead in the debut of Giordano's *Fedora* in Milan. Favorable critical reception led to roles for Caruso on stages in Moscow, St. Petersburg, and Buenos Aires. By the time of his 1900 debut at Milan's La Scala Opera House in *La Boheme,* he was already a star. But the star shone even brighter after his 1902 London debut in *Rigoletto.* He extended his international fame still further when he sang in America for the first time, performing *Rigoletto* in 1903 with the Metropolitan Opera. Caruso became very wealthy and led a flamboyant life. By the time his career peaked, from about 1908 to 1918, he earned as much as $115,000 a year just from recordings. In 1920, he earned $15,000 for a performance in Mexico City—high now, astronomical then. Caruso's performances were distinguished, among other things, by his ability to interweave dramatic nonsinging lines with melody, and he specialized in a cry that became known as the "Caruso sob." His opportunities in the United States prompted him to remain in New York with the Met until his death in 1921.

I acknowledge that I remember nothing at all about the event, but my parents have told me that I was born at Naples in 1873. My father was a poor man, employed as a working mechanic. He had two sons—myself and a younger boy; and kind relations have been good enough to tell me that, as a youngster, I was unusually lively and noisy, and filled my father's house with the sound of my juvenile voice from morning till night.

When I was eleven years old I already loved singing and had a clear contralto voice. One day the organist of the Church of St. Anna, Naples, heard me singing, and my voice pleased the old musician so much that he engaged me as a member of the choir, and paid me the colossal sum of one lira—twenty cents—every Sunday.

To receive this princely wage caused me intense delight, but when I was confirmed my father attempted to compel me to abandon singing altogether in order to become an iron and steel worker.

In my new work I took but little interest, being indeed more happily occupied in studying mechanical drawings and calligraphy. My dear mother, alas, died when I was only fifteen. Her death seemed to justify me in altering my career while there was yet time, and I therefore announced my intention of abandoning the study of engineering to devote myself entirely to art and music. My father, when he heard this resolution, gave me the choice of continuing to learn to be a mechanic or of starving.

I chose—rashly enough no doubt, to starve—and forthwith I became a wanderer with nothing wherewith to fight the world but a perfect physique and an optimism that, happily, never failed me. Luxury and I were the most absolute strangers at this time—we were not, indeed, even the most frigid of nodding acquaintances—but all the same, I managed to pick up some sort of livelihood at church festivals and private entertainments.

When I was nineteen, the baritone Misciano took me to his master, Vergine, who promptly declared that I was too young for serious study, and that my voice was not sufficiently strong. However, after two trials, he decided to give me lessons regularly, though at this period my voice was so thin that my fellow pupils were wont to declare that it resembled nothing quite so much as "the wind which passes through an open window."

Still I continued to study under Vergine until my work was cut short by military duty, and for a year I wore the uniform of the 18th Regiment of Artillery, being quartered at Rieti.

One morning Major Nagliati of my battery heard me singing as I polished the buttons of my tunic. I sang with an "open throat," and even today I remember how the warm rays of the glorious sun streamed into the room as I polished, polished, polished.

"What is your profession?" Major Nagliati asked sharply, as he entered the room. I stammered out: "I—I—aspire to singing in the opera."

The major said nothing in reply, but quickly walked out of the room. The same evening he informed me that he had found a master for me, and that during the time I remained at Rieti I might continue my lessons.

In 1895, when I was just twenty-two years old, I made my debut at the Teatro Nuovo, Naples, my native city, in an opera by Signor Morelli, entitled *Amico Francesco*.

Neither the opera nor the artists who interpreted it achieved any striking success. For my part, although temporarily discouraged, I was far from deeply downhearted, for in my heart of hearts I believed I had a good voice, and in this belief I was encouraged by my singing master, Signor Guglielmo Vergine, to whose kindly sympathy and unfailing pains to give me the best of teaching I always feel that I owe the deepest debt of gratitude.

It was in Milan, in the Teatro Lirico, under the management of Signor Eduardo Sonsogno, that I made my first real success. I awoke to find that both critics and public were kind enough to say that—well, I had not mistaken my vocation when I took up singing.

After that initial success I continued to receive more offers of engagement than I could possibly accept. Could I have sung for twenty-four hours in the day I should not have been able to carry out all the contracts which have been offered me since that memorable day, Tuesday, November 8, 1898, when I sang the part of Marcello in *La Boheme* of Signor Leoncavallo.

You will, perhaps, permit me to say a few words on singing as a profession. In the first place, experience has taught me that those who decide to adopt the precarious profession of an operatic singer must, to have any realizable hopes of success, above all things possess an exceptionally good voice, to which must be added a robust constitution and a copious capacity for hard work—incessant study; for, believe me, without this advancement is impossible.

It is a matter of the highest importance that the would-be successful singer should have his voice properly produced, and this, I think, can only be done by an efficient teacher. I would point out, however, to prove how mistaken even a first-class master may be as to the suitability of certain parts to the singer who has been his pupil, that when Sonsogno gave me my engagement for Teatro Lirico, Milan, for the autumn season of 1898, he sent me three operas to study: *L'Arlesina*, by Cilea; *Il Voto* or *La Mala Vita*, by Giordano; and *La Boheme*, by Leoncavallo—the last a new work which was looked forward

Enrico Caruso in *Pagliacci* (Courtesy of Culver Pictures)

to with unusual interest, as Puccini had written a successful opera on the same subject—which, by the way, is the work which is now so popular.

When Vergine went through the part of Marcello with me, he bluntly informed me that I could make nothing of it, as the music was not suited to my voice. But immediately on my arrival in Milan, Sonsogno amiably insisted on my studying it.

Accordingly I learned the music, sang it on the first night, and made, to my amazement, such a hit that I pleased the composer and "notched" for myself, I am happy to say, the first step in such reputation as may be mine to-day. But had I not sung that part to oblige Sonsogno I might never have been heard of in England and the United States.

This was, I think I may say, the night which proved the turning point in my career, as from that time onward Fortune has favored me, though I would add that I have not relaxed in any way my desire to attain that perfection which, to the artist, always seems—and is—unattainable.

Naturally the dramatic sentiment is another, all-important accessory to the perfect equipment of an operatic singer. In a large measure, this cannot be acquired, but I am convinced that a good education and a strong literary sympathy are of invaluable assistance in helping the singer to reach a true state of excellence, and on this account I think that a singer should carefully read and re-read the whole libretto, so as to inform himself of the poet's purpose of meaning in the construction of the plot, as well as assimilating to himself as far as he can the composer's idea of how the poetry and the various aspects of mind of the characters should be aptly and effectively interpreted.

All my life I have been a victim of nervousness; but whether or no this has been an advantage or a disadvantage I should not like to say. In any case it has been a trouble, but happily a trouble that I adore when it waylays me on the stage. I am seized with nervousness, and the anguish alone makes my voice what it is. No doubt a keen nervous susceptibility is essential to an opera singer who desires to be eminent, and perhaps it is not too much to say that only a man or woman of highly nervous temperament can succeed as a lyric-dramatic artist.

In the great operas they are portraying love, hate, or revenge—the two latter in a whirlwind, so to speak, of orchestral music and song—they have, the whole time, to watch the conductor, keep time and rhythm, and fail not, at the same time, in reproducing with perfect accuracy the composer's music. In consequence, it should be obvious, even to the merest tyro in singing, that the nervous tension on the operatic artist must be far greater than it is on the actor, who has only to think of his action and his words, while the actor-singer has to think of action, words, and music.

It may be of interest if I say that I neither have a favorite opera nor a favorite part. I love all my operas and my parts.

And now it seems to me that I have little else to say which is likely to interest you. Remembering that your language is one with which I am not too familiar, you will, I hope, pardon me for any shortcomings of which I have been guilty; and if you have perused my story from the beginning to the end, I thank you most sincerely. And now, "Addio."

*The World Magazine, 1909*

# Gian Carlo Menotti

Menotti's unique role as the composer of serious but popular contemporary operas and as the founder of the annual Festival of Two Worlds in Spoleto, Italy, which promotes classical and new music, has placed him in the forefront of musical innovation in the United States and Europe.

Born in Italy in 1911, he came to the United States in 1927 after studying at the Milan Conservatory. Settling first in Philadelphia, where he studied and then later taught at the Curtis Institute, he moved to New York, where he launched a career as a composer, writing symphonic pieces, ballet music, and operas. Menotti's first successful stage work was *Amelia Goes to the Ball* in 1937. Major success came with his 1946 tragic opera *The Medium*, which premiered on Broadway. A satirical short opera, *The Telephone*, followed the next year and established Menotti as a serious composer.

His *Amahl and the Night Visitors*, which premiered on national television on Christmas Eve in 1951, became an annual holiday tradition as a morality play reflecting Christmas themes. Menotti drew on New York's Little Italy for his 1954 *The Saint of Bleecker Street*, which, like his 1950 *The Consul*, won a Pulitzer Prize for opera.

He has remained an operatic innovator, drawing on ancient and contemporary themes for his small-scale yet psychologically rich tales. He uses small instrumental ensembles and English-language libretti.

Menotti's contribution as a musical impresario with the creation of the Spoleto Festival has been equally important. Here, once a year—as well as in Charleston, South Carolina, where he started an American counterpart in 1977—musicians from around the world share their musical experiences by performing together, for each other and for music fans who flock to the concerts annually.

# Arturo Toscanini

Toscanini's name remains synonymous with the very best in symphonic conducting, and it is to his now legendary standards that most classical orchestra conductors have aspired. He dominated the music world for more than half a century and had his greatest impact as head of the now-defunct NBC Symphony Orchestra, with which he was associated for seventeen years, until his retirement in 1954 at age eighty-seven.

He was born in Parma, Italy, in 1867, where his father was a tailor, and it was toward tailoring, not music, that Toscanini was first drawn. But his musical talent as a cellist emerged when he was young, and he began performing professionally immediately after graduating from the Parma Conservatory of Music in 1885.

The role of conducting fell into Toscanini's lap in 1886 when the conductor of a company he was on tour with in Brazil quit. Without looking at the score, Toscanini conducted a performance of Verdi's *Aida* that resulted in a standing ovation. His reputation stuck with him on his return to Italy, and he was soon conducting full time. He introduced Wagner's opera *Götterdämmerung* to Italy in 1895 and made his debut as a symphonic conductor at Milan's La Scala in 1896. Under Toscanini's baton, La Scala was the setting for its first opera—*Die Meistersinger von Nürnberg*—in 1898.

Toscanini came to America in 1908 at the invitation of La Scala's director Giulio Gatti-Casazza, who had been named to head New York's Metropolitan Opera Company. He remained for seven years, then spent World War I conducting orchestras in Italy to benefit injured soldiers, and then returned to the United States to tour with an orchestra he founded. From 1921 to 1929 he was artistic director of La Scala; he became the principal conductor of the New York Philharmonic–Symphony Orchestra in 1928; spent one year as head of the Palestine Symphony Orchestra; then—on the verge of retiring in 1937—accepted the post of director of the newly formed NBC Symphony Orchestra, which he held until he finally did retire in 1954. He died in 1957.

Toscanini was an innovator, willing to introduce music of the modern composers, as well as a superior interpreter of classical and romantic music. But he refused to take credit for his remarkable ability to draw out the best in the orchestras he led, attributing all to the composer whose work he conducted.

ARTURO TOSCANINI

Toscanini by Caruso, Paris 1901 (Courtesy of Culver Pictures)

Arturo Toscanini (Courtesy of Culver Pictures)

# Painting & Sculpture

## Ralph Fasanella

The art world finally "discovered" Ralph Fasanella in the early 1980s and quickly dubbed him "the best American primitive painter since Grandma Moses." Fasanella was almost sixty years old (he was born in 1914) and an attendant at his brother's gasoline station. Like Paul Gauguin, he had been in his thirties and frustrated at another career (as a union organizer) when he turned to painting. Unlike Gauguin, however, whose painting took him far away from banking and French urban life, Fasanella's involvement with New York City, his own Italian background, and the labor movement has steadily deepened through his art.

He brings the crowded, dynamic tenement world of Little Italy, the high energy and excitement of the city, to life on canvas. Again and again he painted family scenes, evoking both the warmth and the struggle of immigrant working-class life through Christ-like images of his father; the church, in its dual character as both refuge and conservative force; his heroes, like Manhattan congressman Vito Marcantonio and the Rosenbergs; neighborhood and factory life, from stickball games to the assembly line. He reduces nature to an occasional shrub, a strip of sky, the sun; instead, the landscape is one of teeming streets, neon, people rushing, the rectilinear patterns of street grids, building facades, rows of windows.

Fasanella did a series of paintings on the mill town of Lawrence, Massachusetts, using the same primitive techniques to convey the oppressive, early industrial environment that made the historic 1912 textile workers' strike there inevitable. Fasanella's work is in the permanent collections of the Hirshhorn and the Textile Museums.

## Mark di Suvero

Sculptor Mark di Suvero's innovative use and combination of industrial materials like wood, rope, chains, nails, and bolts and his monumental works influenced by urban imagery have made him a leading American sculptor in the cubist constructivist tradition.

He was born in Shanghai, China, in 1933, where his father, an Italian of Sephardic Jewish background, worked as a business agent for the Italian government. His mother's roots were Italian and French. The family moved to California in 1941, and di Suvero graduated from the University of California at Berkeley in 1957 as a philosophy major. However, he had been studying sculpture all along and moved to New York after graduation to pursue his artistic goals. He worked as a carpenter to support himself, and despite a nearly crippling accident while working on a construction job in 1960, di Suvero persisted in working with large, heavy materials in his sculpture. Later that year —although temporarily confined to a wheelchair—he completed enough work to have his first one-man show in New York. One art reviewer, calling di Suvero's work "ambitious and intelligent, so raw and clean so noble and accessible," wrote that "from now on nothing will be the same."

Di Suvero moved to Venice in 1971 because of his anti-Vietnam war beliefs and stayed in Europe for four years, exhibiting in France, Germany, and the Netherlands. Returning to New York, he had a major show at New York's Whitney Museum in 1975 of fifty smaller pieces (14 feet or less) while larger pieces were displayed in prominent open spaces in New York.

Later work became both more monumental in size—one of his most famous pieces, *Isis,* weighs 35 tons and measures 43 feet by 65 feet by 33 feet—but sparer in form. One observer noted that di Suvero's work retains its appeal because of its physical accessibility and that the sculptor likes having viewers "participate" in his work by sitting, standing, or even sleeping on it.

# Literature

## Gregory Corso

One of the three best-known Beat writers of the 1950s (the other two are Jack Kerouac and Allen Ginsberg), Corso is a self-taught poet whose early education began in the slums of New York and in prison.

He was born in 1930 in New York's Little Italy to Italian parents, but spent his first thirteen years in orphanages and foster homes when his mother decided to return to Italy without his father. A frequent runaway, Corso got involved in a robbery at age sixteen that led to a three-year jail term. Corso began reading and writing seriously while in prison, and after his release, befriended Ginsberg in Greenwich Village. From 1954 to 1955 he lived in Cambridge, Massachusetts, where he unofficially attended classes at Harvard University and staged one of his plays. In 1956 he followed the "beat" scene to San Francisco, a year after the publication of his first book, *The Vestal Lady on Brattle and Other Poems.*

Supporting himself as a writer and lecturer, Corso travelled extensively and wrote poems whose themes ranged from preoccupations with death and nuclear holocaust to concerns with religious revival and spirituality. Among his titles are *Elegiac Feelings American* (1970), which includes an homage to Kerouac, who died in 1969; *The Night Last Night Was at Its Nightest* (1972); *Way Out: A Poem in Discord* (1974); *Earth Egg* (1974); and *Herald of the Autochtonic Spirit* (1981).

## Lawrence Ferlinghetti

One of the original Beat poets of the 1950s, Ferlinghetti was also a pioneer publisher. His City Lights Bookshop in San Francisco became the meeting ground for the iconoclastic generation of poets and writers who migrated there, including Allen Ginsberg, Gregory Corso, and Jack Kerouac, whose new ideas and often outrageous ways of presenting poetry rocked the American literary establishment. As the publisher in 1956 of *Howl,* Allen Ginsberg's first book of poems, Ferlinghetti was arrested on obscenity charges, but was acquitted in a landmark decision that he chronicled in a prose account called *Howl of the Censor.*

He was born Lawrence Ferling in Yonkers, New York, in 1919, but adopted the original family name in 1954. After Navy service during World War II, Ferlinghetti got an M.A. at Columbia and studied at the Sorbonne for four years. In Paris he met the poet Jacques Prévert, whose work he later translated. In 1951 he moved to San Francisco, where, in addition to operating City Lights Bookshop, he embarked on a prolific writing career of his own. His use of street language and focus on ordinary speech patterns became a trademark of his poetry, which often dealt with surrealistic images or reflected a concern for social and political issues. In all, he has published more than two dozen books, plus a dozen plays since 1955.

### THE OLD ITALIANS DYING

For years the old Italians have been dying
all over America
For years the old Italians in faded felt hats
have been sunning themselves and dying
You have seen them on the benches
in the park in Washington Square
the old Italians in their black high button shoes
the old men in their old felt fedoras
              with stained hatbands
have been dying and dying
                    day by day
You have seen them
every day in Washington Square San Francisco
the slow bell
tolls in the morning
in the Church of Peter & Paul
in the marzipan church on the plaza
toward ten in the morning the slow bell tolls
in the towers of Peter & Paul
and the old men who are still alive
sit sunning themselves in a row
on the wood benches in the park
and watch the processions in and out
funerals in the morning
weddings in the afternoon
slow bell in the morning Fast bell at noon
In one door out the other
the old men sit there in their hats
and watch the coming & going
You have seen them
the ones who feed the pigeons
         cutting the stale bread
            with their thumbs & penknives

*Lawrence Ferlinghetti*
from *Endless Life: Selected Poems*

# Jerre Mangione

The son of Sicilian immigrants, Jerre Gerlando Mangione was born in Rochester, New York, in 1909. He lived in a household in which, at his mother's insistence, no English was spoken. With many of his Sicilian relatives living close by, Mangione grew up listening to stories of Sicily and the adjustment to life in America. These anecdotes and musings form the basis of Mangione's memoir of growing up Italian, *Mount Allegro*, published in 1943. Recently republished for the fourth time, *Mount Allegro* has been called by many critics a classic of American ethnic literature.

From 1937 to 1939 Mangione was national coordinating editor of the Federal Writers' Project. The New Deal project employed over ten thousand writers and would-be writers, publishing collections of folklore, oral histories of ex-slaves, and books on ethnic culture. Its WPA guides to New York, Washington, D.C., and other areas have recently been republished. Mangione's *The Dream and the Deal* (1972) chronicles the history of the WPA project.

During World War II, Mangione was Special Assistant to the Immigration Commission. He moved to Philadelphia and, after several unfulfilling publishing and advertising jobs, joined the University of Pennsylvania English faculty in 1961. He now holds the title of Professor Emeritus of American Literature.

Mangione's interest in his parents' homeland led to two more books, *Reunion in Sicily* (1950), which describes the lives of his Sicilian relatives and their friends, and *A Passion for Sicilians: The World Around Danilo Dolci* (1968), about the "Gandhi of Sicily" who crusades for social and economic justice in western Sicily.

Feeling too few Italian-Americans today know enough about their heritage, Mangione recently wrote what he calls a "Manifesto for Italian-American Culture," in which he suggests Italian-American novels and immigrant memoirs be reprinted and inexpensively distributed and Italian-American studies be encouraged. He is currently at work on a history of the past hundred years of the Italian-Americans.

# Mario Puzo

After years of struggle as a novelist, Puzo struck gold in 1969 with his best-selling epic *The Godfather,* which chronicled several generations in the life of the fictional Corleone crime family. He subsequently collaborated with young film director Francis Ford Coppola in the screenplays of *The Godfather* and *The Godfather, Part II.* Both films—the first in 1972, the second in 1974—won many Oscars, including a shared one for best screenplay for the two men's collaboration.

Born in 1920, one of seven children, Puzo grew up in a crowded tenement in New York's Hell's Kitchen on the far west side of the city, where his father was a laborer for the New York Central Railroad. The neighborhood was poor and crime-ridden, but Puzo found refuge—and a future—in books, reading at the public library and taking advantage of cultural programs at the nearby Hudson Guild Neighborhood Center. He later studied at New York's New School for Social Research and Columbia University.

Puzo supported himself at a variety of jobs, including civil servant and copywriter for male magazines, meanwhile writing at night. His first novel, *The Dark Arena* (1955), set in post–World War II occupied Germany, juxtaposed the plight of a young American soldier returning from war with the plight of a devastated land trying to recover from moral and physical destruction. In *The Fortunate Pilgrim* (1965), Puzo returned to his Italian roots in Hell's Kitchen to chronicle the struggle of an Italian immigrant woman

Jerre Mangione

who seeks the American dream in a house in the suburbs. With the success of *The Godfather* four years later, Puzo realized his own version of the American dream, having attained financial security and fame. Paperback rights for the book were sold for the record sum of $410,000, and he earned more than $1 million from movie sales. An American best-seller, *The Godfather* was also a best-seller in several countries overseas.

Puzo's other books include *The Godfather Papers* (1972), a collection of essays including an autobiographical piece about Italian-American life in Hell's Kitchen, *Inside Las Vegas* (1977), a nonfiction book with photographs about America's gambling mecca, *Fools Die* (1978), a novel set principally in Las Vegas about the corruption of a young American writer, and *The Sicilians* (1985), a sequel to *The Godfather*.

# BUILDING AN ITALIAN-AMERICAN LIBRARY

As a writer and as an Italian-American I have tried to read every Italian-American novel I can find. Libraries are the best sources for obtaining these books, too many of which are out of print. Here is a sampling of the best novelists representing three generations of the Italian-American experience.

*The River Between* by Louis Forgione. 1928.
*The Grand Gennaro* by Garibaldi LaPolla. 1935.
*Wait Until Spring, Bandini* by John Fante. 1938.
*Christ in Concrete* by Pietro Di Donato. 1939.
*Olives on the Apple Tree* by Guido D'Agostino. 1940.
*Mount Allegro* by Jerre Mangione. 1942.
*Golden Wedding* by Jo Pagano. 1943.
*We Ride a White Donkey* by George Panetta. 1944.
*The Fortunate Pilgrim* by Mario Puzo. 1964.
*The Grand Street Collector* by Joseph Arleo. 1970.
*Brotherhood of the Grape* by John Fante. 1980.
*Paper Fish* by Tina DeRosa. 1980.

*Fred L. Gardaphe*

# Books for Children

Angelo, Valenti. *The Golden Gate.* New York: Viking Press, 1939.
 Nino, an immigrant lad, arrives in this country at the beginning of the twentieth century. (Ages 9–12.)
de Paola, Tomie. *Strega Nona.* Englewood Cliffs, N.J.: Prentice-Hall, 1975. (Juvenile.)
 Written and illustrated by de Paola, it tells the story of Strega Nona and her magic pasta pot. Winner of the Caldecott Award.
Grossman, Ronald P. *Italians in America.* Minneapolis: Lerner Publications, 1975. (Young Adult.)
 Discusses the contributions of Italian explorers and immigrants to the history and civilization of the United States.
Kamin, Gloria. *Fiorello.* New York: Atheneum, 1981. (Ages 8 and up.)
 About the colorful Fiorello LaGuardia, former mayor of New York City.
LaGumina, Salvatore John. *An Album of the Italian-American.* New York: Franklin Watts, 1972. (Juvenile to young adult.)
 Pictorial history of Italians in America.
Mangione, Jerre. *America Is Also Italian.* New York: Putnam, 1969. Illustrated. (Young adult.)
 Traces historical causes of Italian immigration to the United States and discusses the cultural and economic contribution of those immigrants to their new homeland.
Marangell, Virginia J. *Gianna Mia.* New York: Dodd, Mead, 1979. (Young adult.)
 The struggle of an immigrant family in Connecticut trying to attain the American dream.

Marinacci, Barbara. *They Came from Italy.* New York: Dodd, Mead, 1967. Illustrated. Famous Italian-Americans.

Panetta, George. *Sea Beach Express.* New York: Harper and Row, 1966. Illustrated by Emily McCully. (Juvenile to young adult.)
A boy and his Italian family have an adventure on the Sea Beach Express and in Coney Island.

Young, Miriam. *Marco's Chance.* Illustrated by Don Sibley. New York: Harcourt Brace Jovanovich, 1959. (Juvenile.)
How a young boy from Sicily moves to New York State and helps his mother adjust to a new life.

*Alex Polner*

# Popular Music

## Tony Bennett

Born Antonio Dominick Benedetto in Astoria, Queens, New York, in 1926, Bennett, a tailor's son, began performing as a singing waiter and originally planned a career in commercial art. He changed his mind after singing with a military band during World War II. When he returned to civilian life, he sang in New York clubs under the name Joe Bari. His first break occurred when he came in second to Rosemary Clooney in Arthur Godfrey's Talent Scouts contest, which led to still more club jobs.

Yet not until 1950 did Bennett make a name for himself—and take on the name by which he is known—when he made his debut at New York's Paramount Theater. The name change is attributed to Bob Hope, who introduced "Tony Bennett" to the New York public—and the name stuck. He soon became a star for his masterful interpretations of the lyrics and music of Irving Berlin, Cole Porter, the Gershwins, Johnny Mercer, and Harold Arlen.

Though Bennett has often said he prefers jazz, his early hits were based on such schmaltzy tunes as "Because of You" and "Cold, Cold Heart," which was a country-western song he adapted to a more popular singing style. By the mid-1950s, however, Bennett's popularity began to wane as stars like Elvis Presley and the rock-and-roll movement commanded the attention of young fans. He reemerged in 1962 with a recording of "I Left My Heart in San Francisco," which not only lit Bennett's star once more, but became his signature piece.

Despite other musical changes since rock-and-roll, Bennett has remained a top-flight club and recording star, often regarded as Frank Sinatra's heir. Much influenced by jazz greats Count Basie and the late Duke Ellington, Bennett has nonetheless not gotten stuck in the past. In the early 1980s, for example, he joined forces with young superstars Stevie Wonder, Billy Joel, and George Benson to produce a contemporary album based on Gershwin themes. By then he had recorded eighty-eight albums.

# Norman Dello Joio

The Pulitzer Prize–winning composer Norman Dello Joio has made major contributions to contemporary American music. An educator as well as a performer, Dello Joio spearheaded a program funded by the Ford Foundation to bring modern music to American public schools.

Dello Joio, born in New York City in 1913 and raised there, came from a family of musicians. His earliest musical influence was his father, who was a church organist. Studying with his father and others, Dello Joio became so accomplished that by age fourteen he was organist for a church on City Island, the Bronx.

Continuing his music studies, Dello Joio retained an interest in liturgical music, but later, at Juilliard, Yale, and Tanglewood, became absorbed in the contemporary American musical scene. Among his mentors was Paul Hindemith, who urged Dello Joio to find his own voice. Because of an early interest in jazz—Dello Joio had his own jazz band in the 1930s—jazz influences became a pervasive element in his music. When his work started reaching wider audiences, a critic praised Dello Joio for the combination of directness and simplicity in his composition, which gave it broad appeal.

He drew on American themes in the early 1940s as musical director for a small ballet company, but as the years progressed—while still writing for ballet—he broadened his range to symphonic music. His 1942 *Magnificat* drew on the Gregorian chants he grew up hearing, yet used a free-form modern format. His *Ricercari*, using musical forms from the Renaissance, was performed by the New York Philharmonic—with Dello Joio on piano—and conducted by George Szell. His *Meditations on Ecclesiastes,* a twelve-section work with theme and variations, again drew on liturgical sources for inspiration and earned the Pulitzer Prize in 1957.


# Chuck Mangione

He defines it as "Mangione music," the mixture of swinging modern jazz, soft rock, and melodious pop as unmistakably identifiable as the trademark narrow-brimmed, feather-banded hat Chuck Mangione always wears in public.

Mangione was born in 1940 to a family in which music was loved. Papa used to take young Chuck and his brother Gaspar ("Gap") to Rochester jazz clubs and invited jazzmen Cannonball Adderley and Dizzy Gillespie to the house for spaghetti, Chianti, and jam sessions with the boys. Mangione considers Gillespie his "musical father."

Mangione entered the Eastman School of Music in Rochester, New York, in 1958. That year Gap, Chuck, and a friend formed the Jazz Brothers, drawing good reviews from a gig at the Half Note in New York City. After graduation from Eastman, Chuck replaced Freddie Hubbard as trumpeter in Art Blakey's Jazz Messengers, staying with the hard-bop group for two and a half years.

Then it was back to Rochester, directing Eastman's jazz ensemble, playing flügelhorn in his own group, and composing. He produced and distributed a recording of his music that he conducted with the Rochester Philharmonic. The album sold well and a record company signed him.

He's been recording top-selling albums since and touring with groups ranging from his quartet to large orchestras. His tune "Feels So Good" is probably the most widely recognized melody of the late 1970s and early 1980s. He was commissioned to write music used in the television coverage of the 1976 Olympics.

Frank Sinatra, 1943 (Courtesy
of Culver Pictures)

(Courtesy of Culver Pictures)

# Frank Sinatra

His life a legend several times over, Sinatra remains one of America's top entertainers and one of the great survivors in the turbulent world of show business.

Francis Albert Sinatra was born in Hoboken, New Jersey, in 1915. His parents were immigrants from Sicily. In 1937, performing with the Hoboken Four, he had his first break as first-prize winner on the famed "Major Bowes' Amateur Hour." This success led to club dates, including contracts for Sinatra with bandleaders Harry James and Tommy Dorsey. Finally Benny Goodman signed him, and at the Paramount Theater on the evening of December 30, 1942, the world discovered Frank Sinatra's talent. The bobby-soxers went nuts. They screamed, moaned, and fainted. The age of the popular ballad singer had begun. *Time* magazine reported, "Not since the days of Rudolph Valentino has American womanhood made such unabashed public love to an entertainer." His piercing blue eyes had a hypnotic quality and his voice had tonal beauty; somehow each member of the audience felt that he was sharing a deep dark secret with them alone. By now a national figure, Sinatra moved to Hollywood, where he made a number of musical films for RKO and MGM, including *On the Town,* with music by Leonard Bernstein, in 1949.

Sinatra's career slumped after his vocal chords hemorrhaged in the early 1950s, but he rebounded in 1953 with his performance as Angelo Maggio in *From Here to Eternity,* for which he won an Oscar for best supporting actor. When he recovered his singing voice, Sinatra alternated live singing performances and recording dates with occasional movie roles. Among the latter were the feature role of Nathan Detroit in *Guys and Dolls* (1955) and the tormented drug addict in *The Man with the Golden Arm* (1956), for which Sinatra got an Oscar nomination.

During the 1960s, Sinatra formed a record company and experimented with new singing styles, relying occasionally on his traditional love ballads and nostalgia, but also singing swing and jazz. In 1971 he retired from performing, only to return two years later to the nightclub and large music hall circuit.

# Lennie Tristano

An innovator of the controversial cool jazz style during the 1940s and early 1950s, jazz pianist Tristano specialized in the development of long, impressionist melodic lines and contrapuntal harmonies that defied the musical and rhythmic structures then in vogue. He pioneered free-form improvisation, which spawned a new generation of jazz performers epitomized by trumpeter Miles Davis's recording "Birth of the Cool."

Tristano was born in 1919 and raised in Chicago. Visually impaired at birth, he became blind by age nine. He studied piano as a child, made his club debut in Chicago at age twelve, and later added clarinet and saxophone to his repertoire of instruments. Although he had some classical training, he was performing jazz, including Dixieland, from the beginning of his professional career in his mid-teens.

Moving to New York in 1946, Tristano formed jazz combos ranging from trios to sextets. Influenced by pianists Art Tatum and Earl Hines, he in turn influenced other performers, including, in addition to Davis, baritone saxophonist Gerry Mulligan, pianist Dave Brubeck, alto saxophonist Lee Konitz, tenor saxophonist Warne Marsh, and guitarist Billy Bauer. Tristano devoted the latter part of his career mainly to teaching and fostering the careers of his better students.

Tristano died of a heart attack in November 1978.

# Film

## Alan Alda

Best-known for his role as the woman-chasing army surgeon Captain Benjamin Franklin "Hawkeye" Pierce through the eleven successful years that "M*A*S*H" ran on television, Alda has forged an acting career on stage and in film. Alda also successfully branched out into directing and screenwriting, garnering Emmy awards for these achievements with "M*A*S*H" as well as for his performances.

Robert Alda, who was twenty-one when his son was born in New York City in 1936, performed often in the Catskills, and son Alan made his unwitting debut when only six months old in one of his father's sketches. By the ripe age of three, Alan Alda (originally Alphonso D'Abruzzo) was a veteran of the burlesque stage. In 1943, the family moved to Hollywood when Robert Alda landed the role of George Gershwin in the film biography *Rhapsody in Blue*, but after seven years the Aldas returned east—and stayed—when Robert Alda performed as Sky Masterson in *Guys and Dolls*.

Although in his teens Alan Alda considered studying medicine (at his father's behest), he instead majored in English at Fordham University and began acting in summer stock. He began making the rounds with Chicago's Second City troupe and taking whatever off-Broadway roles he could get. He made his Broadway debut in a small role in *Only in America* in 1959 and two years later received good notices for his role in *Purlie Victorious*. Yet he couldn't give up cab driving, sales, and other part-time jobs until 1964, when he had his first major success in *The Owl and the Pussycat*. He received a Tony nomination for his role in *The Apple Tree* (1966), but afterward came a string of mediocre film roles. With "M*A*S*H" in 1972, Alda portrayed a character that would become a fixture in American living rooms. Because of the show's theme—it focused on an American field hospital during the Korean War—it often dealt with issues of war, death, and racial animosities. As the role grew—and he grew—Alda began taking more risks, which led to better film roles and the opportunity to write and direct *The Seduction of Joe Tynan* (1979) and *The Four Seasons* (1981).

An outspoken supporter of women's rights and other liberal causes, Alda has often been voted one of America's most popular and respected actors.

## Anne Bancroft

Anne Bancroft's roles as working-class Irish Annie Sullivan and slinky, hip-yet-jaded Mrs. Robinson belie her strong Italian roots. Her real name is Anna Maria Italiano and she was born in 1931 in the East Bronx. Her father was a pattern-maker, her mother a telephone operator. She attended public schools and, at her mother's urging, the American Academy of Dramatic Arts.

Bancroft's career was launched in 1950; she had a regular role in the series "The Goldbergs." She soon signed a contract with 20th Century Fox and chose her stage name from a list submitted to her by producer Darryl Zanuck. However, her film roles with Fox were less than distinctive. Bancroft's fortunes changed in 1958 when she won the lead role of Gittel Mosca in William Gibson's play *Two for the Seesaw*, which told of a Jewish girl from the Bronx who became a ballet dancer living in Greenwich Village—a story not too different from her own. Costarring with Henry Fonda, Bancroft earned rave reviews and a Tony, and was offered the part of Annie Sullivan in *The Miracle Worker*, also written by Gibson. Its debut in October 1959, with Patty Duke as the young Helen Keller, won Bancroft another Tony and propelled her to stardom. She won the Academy Award for best actress for the film version in 1962.

Bancroft's role as Mrs. Robinson in *The Graduate* underscored her versatility. In a tragicomic part, she played the frustrated, bored, and lonely wife of a rich Southern Californian whose daughter is engaged to a young man—Dustin Hoffman in his film debut—whom she seduces. She played other memorable roles in *The Pumpkin Eater* (1964) and *The Turning Point* (1977).

Married to film producer, director, writer, and comedian Mel Brooks, Bancroft has acted in several of his films, including Brooks's remake of the Preston Sturges comic classic *To Be or Not To Be* in 1983.

# Frank Capra

A Sicilian immigrant who became an Academy Award–winning director several times over, Capra made film history in the 1930s with films based on such themes as American patriotism, the triumph of good over evil and hope over cynicism, and the basic goodness of the common man and woman.

Born in Palermo in 1897, Capra came with his parents and six siblings to San Francisco in 1903. His father was an orange picker. As a boy, Capra sold newspapers and played banjo in honky-tonks. After graduating from the California Institute of Technology with a degree in chemical engineering in 1918, he joined the Army.

After his discharge, Capra set his sights on becoming a film director. One of his first jobs was designing gags for the *Our Gang* comedies of Hal Roach. He later wrote for film comedians Mack Sennett and Harry Langdon. In 1927, Capra went to New York to direct his first feature, *For the Love of Mike.* The film was Claudette Colbert's debut—and a flop. However, in 1934 the two collaborated again, this time in *It Happened One Night,* and their fortunes changed; each received an Oscar.

More Oscars followed for Capra with *Mr. Deeds Goes to Town* in 1936 (best film and director) and *You Can't Take It With You* in 1938 (best film). When *Mr. Smith Goes to Washington* was released in 1939, the uproar from Washington politicians was so loud that producer Harry Cohn was sent threatening letters about "punitive legislation." Certain leaders claimed the film gave the impression of a totalitarian government in Washington; they said the movie should not have been released at a time when Nazism was so great a menace. Cohn was advised not to show the film in Europe, but, on Capra's advice, he refused to be cowed.

During World War II, Capra directed an Army documentary series, and in 1942 garnered an Oscar for best documentary for his *Prelude to War.* He made only two major films afterward, *It's a Wonderful Life* and *State of the Union.* After 1946, however, Capra never really recaptured the engaging optimism and the humor of his earlier films, though his *Arsenic and Old Lace, Pocketful of Miracles,* and *Hole in the Head* were outstanding. In a 1971 autobiography, *The Name Above the Title,* Capra reveals that his faith in human goodness had been shattered by his experience of the war.

## Going Home

I drove alone to the Sicilian ghetto I had left fifty years ago. There it was. Mama's three-room house. It seemed smaller, much smaller. And piteously run down. Its roof sagged. Pieces of the porch bannister hung brokenly; half of the once-white picket fence lay flat in the dry weeds. The big spreading pepper tree, whose limbs we climbed and dreamed in, now drooped forlornly under the weight of its scrawny, smog-blackened leaves. And a scruffy shirt-sleeved man and a stout piano-legged woman sat on the porch. They eyed me hostilely as I sat in my car across the street.

How could they know that their run-down house had been built by courage; the courage of two middle-aged, penniless, illiterate peasants who had dared travel halfway around the world to meet the unknown fearful challenges of a strange land, a strange people, and a strange language? And who slaved like oxen and fought like tigers to feed and clothe their children. And who fed them. And clothed them. And one of them became a film director. And became famous. And retired. And now he was belly-aching because he was not needed.

I closed my eyes; thought of Mama, of Papa, of Ben, of my little sister Ann—the youngest and the first to die. I said a prayer for each of them. Out of prayer came peace—

Frank Capra (Courtesy of Culver Pictures)

and impudence. Like Antaeus (whose strength depended upon his touching the ground), I had to return to my roots for a much-needed draught of peasant courage. Out of the refill came a book that is an impertinent try at saying to the discouraged, the doubting, or the despairing what I had been presuming to say in films: "Friend, you are a divine mingle-mangle of guts and stardust. So hang in there! If doors opened for me, they can open for anyone."

*Frank Capra*
*The Name Above the Title*

Producer-director Frank Capra and star Jimmy Stewart on the set of *It's a Wonderful Life* (Courtesy of Culver Pictures)

# Michael Cimino

Part of a new wave of young film directors including Francis Ford Coppola and Martin Scorsese, Cimino made his mark with the 1978 Vietnam epic *The Deerhunter,* which garnered five Oscars, including best director.

He was born in 1943, grew up in New York City and Long Island, and was educated at Yale University. After graduating, he moved to New York, where he worked for a company that produced television commercials and documentaries. By the late 1960s, he had become a director of commercials, while also sharpening his skill as a writer. Moving to Hollywood, he met success with his second screenwriting effort in 1973 as collaborator with John Milius on *Magnum Force,* featuring Clint Eastwood in the first of several film appearances as Harry Callahan.

Cimino's success earned him the role of screenwriter and director of Eastwood's next film, *Thunderbolt and Lightfoot,* in 1974, a western-type story of a bank robbery that combined violence, drama, and low comedy. It also got Cimino the kind of attention he needed to gather momentum for his own projects. Although he spent several frustrating years writing screenplays that were not produced, he was able to get major financing to direct *The Deerhunter,* mainly from British sources.

A film on a grand scale, *The Deerhunter* was shot on locations in Washington state, in milltowns in Pennsylvania, and in Thailand, where Cimino recreated Saigon nightlife and several violent scenes of torture of American prisoners by the Vietcong. When it was shown, it met with critical success and controversy. Historians, politicians, and Vietnam veterans protested Cimino's interpretation of the war, but its imagery and emotional content were widely praised as it explored the impact of going to war on three patriotic, small-town working-class men, their friends, and family.

In 1980 Cimino's *Heaven's Gate* was a colossal failure and was described in Steven Bach's *Final Cut.* (Bach was a United Artists executive.) Five years later, Cimino's *The Year of the Dragon* opened to mixed reviews.

---

## NAME CHANGERS

Can you match these famous people with their given names?

| | | |
|---|---|---|
| 1. Tony Bennett | A. | Angelo Siciliano |
| 2. Anne Bancroft | B. | Michael Gubitosi |
| 3. Mario Lanza | C. | Maria Messina |
| 4. James Darren | D. | Anthony Benedetto |
| 5. Morgana King | E. | Anna Maria Italiano |
| 6. Robert Blake | F. | Salvatore Lombino |
| 7. Bernadette Peters | G. | Bernadette Lazzaro |
| 8. Alan Alda | H. | Alphonso D'Abruzzo |
| 9. Charles Atlas | I. | James Ercolani |
| 10. Evan Hunter | J. | Alfredo Cocozza |

ANSWERS

1.D  2.E  3.J  4.I  5.C  6.B  7.G  8.H  9.A  10.F

# Francis Ford Coppola

Coppola's film career has been one of extreme successes and failures, but above all, he has been a daring innovator and risk taker who has influenced a generation of film-makers.

The son of a composer and musician, Coppola was born in Detroit in 1939 and raised in a New York City suburb. A youthful infatuation with films led him to pursue film studies at UCLA. His first attempts at commercial filmmaking were failures, but in 1967, the prolific film producer Roger Corman gave Coppola the opportunity to direct *You're a Big Boy Now,* and its success opened other doors. His next two directing jobs, *Finian's Rainbow* (1968) and *The Rain People* (1969) were failures, but in 1970 Coppola shared an Academy Award for his script for *Patton.* Two years later he jumped to stardom with the release of *The Godfather,* a film version of Mario Puzo's novel, and won an Oscar for best picture. In 1973, trying his hand at production, Coppola struck gold once more, with *American Graffiti,* directed by newcomer George Lucas, who went on to direct the *Star Wars* trilogy. The following year, Coppola's *The Godfather, Part II* won seven Oscars, including three for him: best picture, best director, and best screenplay (on which he collaborated with Mario Puzo, who shared the Oscar award with him). Coppola's next film, *Apocalypse Now,* released in 1978, was racked with controversy. Costing double the original budget of $12 million and shot on location in the Philippines (where an earthquake destroyed $1 million in sets), the film became Coppola's antiwar saga of mystery in the depths of Vietnam.

In the early 1980s, Coppola did not match his earlier success and was forced to sell his bankrupt Zoetrope American production company, with which he had hoped to do pioneering work in new film techniques. His *One From the Heart,* a romantic, stylized love story, was an experiment—and a financial disaster. Several attempts to produce intelligent films for teenage audiences met with largely lukewarm critical reception and, with the exception of the successful *The Black Stallion* (1979) fared poorly at the box office. In 1985, his new film, *The Cotton Club,* opened after monumental production problems and massive publicity.

# Lou Costello

The short, pudgy half of the famous comedy team Abbott and Costello was born Louis Francis Cristillo in Paterson, New Jersey, in 1906. He spent his early years in odd jobs, including newsboy, soda fountain clerk, and prizefighter before moving to Hollywood in search of a movie career. He found, instead, mainly backstage work as a studio laborer at Warner Brothers and MGM, and occasionally he got stunt jobs. His first foray into show business was in vaudeville and burlesque. In 1931 he teamed up with comedian Bud Abbott, a tall, thin actor who played straight man to Costello's bumbler. In the late 1930s, the pair were featured regularly on radio, and in 1939 starred in a Broadway revue called *Streets of Paris.* During the 1940s and early 1950s their several dozen films made them a leading box-office attraction. While their first feature was a flop, their second film, *Buck Privates* (1941) grossed the then astronomical sum of $10 million. They also had a successful television series. The team broke up in 1957, and Costello died two years later. Abbott died in 1974.

# Robert De Niro

Robert De Niro, once described in a *Newsweek* cover story as "the natural successor to Brando and Dean," grew up in the Little Italy neighborhoods of Greenwich Village and the Lower East Side in New York's Manhattan, where he was born in 1943. He left high school before graduating and became a student of Stella Adler, an eminent teacher of acting. As a result, he learned to "totally submerge into another character and experience life through him," as he once told a *Time* reporter. Often, viewers believe that De Niro has come to be the character he portrays: the ineffectual, undistinguished second-string catcher dying of cancer in *Bang the Drum Slowly* (1973), the psychopathic cab driver in Martin Scorsese's *Taxi Driver* (1976), and the disillusioned heir of a wealthy Italian family in Bertolucci's *1900* (1977) are but three examples.

The extraordinary expressiveness and power of his performances have won him rave reviews for such films as *Mean Streets* (1973), which took place in the very area where he was reared. *The New York Times* described De Niro's role of Johnny Boy as a "bravura performance." De Niro received similar praise for his roles in *The Godfather, Part II* (1974) and in *The Deer Hunter* (1978), in which he played a draftee who was compelled to fight in Vietnam.

Robert De Niro in *Taxi Driver* (Courtesy of Culver Pictures)

# Brian De Palma

Viewed by some critics as a director in the tradition of Alfred Hitchcock, De Palma's filmmaking style combines graphic violence, meticulous and often bizarre storytelling, and a penchant to satirize cultural mores. Until his 1983 remake of the 1932 classic *Scarface*, De Palma was mainly regarded as a cult filmmaker of horror films.

Born in 1941 in Philadelphia, the son of an orthopedic surgeon, De Palma started making movies as an undergraduate at Columbia. His first feature (made in 1967, released in 1969) was *The Wedding Party*, with two unknown actors, Robert De Niro and Jill Clayburgh. De Palma gained national recognition for the 1968 film *Greetings*, which he independently financed. *Hi Mom!* in 1970 was a sequel, starring De Niro as a maladjusted Vietnam veteran who resorts to making pornographic movies and guerrilla theater. De Palma first used the suspense and horror genres with his 1973 *Sisters*, and went a step further in 1976 with *Obsession*, modeled after Hitchcock's classic *Vertigo*, in which a businessman whose life is destroyed when his wife and daughter are murdered by kidnappers finds himself fifteen years later, while in Italy, falling in love with his wife's double. The same year *Obsession* appeared, De Palma had his first commercial hit with *Carrie*, based on the novel by Stephen King.

Subsequent films, including *The Fury* (1978), *Dressed to Kill* (1980), and *Blow Out* (1981), with John Travolta, used such themes as telekinesis and transvestism to draw audiences into the weird and rarified worlds De Palma created, often with the use of special visual and sound effects.

# Jimmy Durante

Renowned for his giant "Schnozzola" (which was insured by Lloyd's of London and impressed in concrete at Grauman's Chinese Theater in Hollywood), Durante endeared himself to millions of Americans during a fifty-year comedy career in nightclubs and films and on radio and television.

James Francis Durante was born in 1893 and raised on New York's Lower East Side. His nose, it was written, was inherited from his mother, Rosa, a native of Salerno. Durante's father, Bartolomeo, owned a barber shop that served many Tammany Hall politicians, and Durante began an apprenticeship there.

It didn't last long. His piano-playing talent overtook even his interest in school, and seemed a better ticket to survival. So, in seventh grade, Durante dropped out and began playing piano in honky-tonk clubs in Manhattan and Brooklyn. By age twenty-three, "Ragtime Jimmy" headed a five-piece band that performed regularly at Harlem's Club Alamo. He soon branched out to Broadway and in 1923 opened the Club Durante, which featured a vaudeville comedian named Lou Clayton. Within a few years, Clayton and Durante, plus singer Eddie Jackson, formed a popular trio that performed in nightclubs and on the Broadway stage, with feature roles in Ziegfeld's *Show Girl* (1929) and Cole Porter's *The New Yorkers* (1930) and in the film *Road House Nights* (1930). In 1931 the team broke up, but Durante's solo career thrived. He starred in numerous films, including the successful *New Adventures of Get-Rich-Quick Wallingford* (1931), with screenplay by Ben Hecht and Charles McArthur. Most of the subsequent films were distinguished only by their mediocrity. On Broadway, he is most remembered as the manager of a one-ring circus in *Jumbo* (1935). In 1936 he costarred with Ethel Merman in *Red, Hot and Blue!* Though Durante's career had waned by the early 1940s, he began a comeback a few years later. By 1950 he had his own radio show, and for the next twenty years was an

Jimmy Durante, 1936 (Courtesy of the National Archives)

international celebrity, appearing frequently in television specials, his performances always characterized by relentless energy and a gentle, if frenetic, wit. He died in 1980.

Among Durante's best-known trademarks were his deliberate use of unrefined (but clean) street language and his sign-off remark, after singing in his raspy voice at the piano: "Good night, Mrs. Calabash, wherever you are." To this day, no one knows who she was.


# Liza Minnelli

She could have been a precocious child relying for a career on the laurels of famous parents. But since her off-Broadway debut at age seventeen and her Broadway debut at nineteen, Liza Minnelli has been a star in her own right, shining as an actress, singer, and dancer.

Minnelli was born in Los Angeles in 1946 to singer/actress Judy Garland and director Vincente Minnelli and raised in Los Angeles and New York. She unwittingly made her movie debut at age two and a half when she crawled on screen while her mother was being filmed. Her New York debut was more official: at age seven, Minnelli danced with her mother during a show at the Palace Theater. Her parents' marriage ended when Minnelli was five.

By 1963 Minnelli was ready to come into her own, and did, to great critical acclaim, when she performed off-Broadway in *Best Foot Forward.* That show enabled her to record her first solo album, *Liza,* the following year, which sold more than a half million copies. In 1965 she starred on Broadway in *Flora, the Red Menace* and garnered a Tony Award, becoming, at nineteen, the youngest recipient to get it.

She attained early success in films as well, exhibiting great dramatic skill as well as comedic acumen. Beginning with *Charlie Bubbles* in 1968 and *The Sterile Cuckoo* in 1969, the latter earning her an Oscar nomination, Minnelli went on to win an Oscar for best actress in 1972 for her performance in *Cabaret.*

Her career has remained a remarkable combination of nightclub performances and acting for film and stage. She won a second Tony in 1978 for her Broadway show *The Act,* which displayed Minnelli at her versatile best, and she returned to Broadway in 1984 to costar with Chita Rivera in the musical *The Rink.* Among the many films in which she performed are *Tell Me That You Love Me, Junie Moon* (1970), directed by Otto Preminger, Martin Scorsese's *New York, New York* (1977), and Blake Edwards's *Arthur* (1982).


# Al Pacino

An intense and emotional actor, Pacino dropped out of New York's High School of Performing Arts to pursue an acting career and has won kudos for stage and film roles ranging from Richard III to Michael Corleone.

An only child, Alberto Pacino was born in 1940 and raised in the South Bronx by his mother and grandmother after his father left the family when his son was only two. His interest in acting was greater than his interest in academia, and at seventeen Pacino worked at a range of odd jobs, saving up to pay for acting classes. Taking whatever off-off-Broadway roles he could get and performing at the avant-garde LaMama Theater and the Living Theater, Pacino gained admission to the prestigious Actors Studio, headed by Lee Strasberg, in 1966. By 1968, he had won recognition—and an Obie award—for his off-Broadway role as a drunken psychotic in Israel Horovitz's *The Indian Wants the Bronx*. In 1969, reaching Broadway at last, he won a Tony for his portrayal of a drug addict in *Does a Tiger Wear a Necktie?* Pacino then ventured into films, where his performance as a junkie in *Panic in Needle Park* (1971) led to his winning the pivotal role of Don Corleone's son and heir-apparent in *The Godfather* (1972) and *The Godfather, Part II* (1974).

In the interim, Pacino showed his versatility as the New York City cop-as-whistleblower in the screen version of Peter Maas's biography *Serpico,* in 1973, and in 1975 played a harried young man who robs a bank to finance a sex-change operation for his transvestite lover in *Dog Day Afternoon.*

Pacino's career has since combined stage and screen. He returned to Broadway in *The Basic Training of Pavlo Hummel,* which earned him a second Tony in 1977, and starred in critically acclaimed performances of *Richard III* and David Mamet's *American Buffalo.* His many film roles have included a controversial movie about homosexuals, *Cruising* (1980), and the lead role in Brian De Palma's 1983 update of the classic *Scarface,* in which Pacino portrays a Cuban-American cocaine smuggler.

Al Pacino in *Scarface* (Courtesy of Culver Pictures)

# Bernadette Peters

In the Ozone Park section of Queens, New York, where she was born in 1949 and grew up, she was known as Bernadette Lazzaro. Today, she is better known as Bernadette Peters, the versatile actress, singer, and dancer who has appeared on Broadway and in movies.

Her father, a first-generation American, drove a bread truck, but Peters's mother, raised in a traditional Italian-American home, had nontraditional ideas for her children. Peters and an older sister were encouraged to pursue their artistic interests, and by 1968 Peters had made it to the off-Broadway stage, appearing to very favorable notices in the musical *Dames at Sea.*

A comedienne, she has been paired with some of the wackiest comic actors and directors. She appeared in Mel Brooks's parody of silent movies called, appropriately, *Silent Movie* (1976), and costarred with Steve Martin in *The Jerk* (1979) and *Pennies from Heaven* (1982), which recreated the 1930s classic of the same name. With manic comic Andy Kaufman, who died in 1984, Peters played a robot in love in *Heartbeeps* (1984).

On the stage, Peters has had serious and comic roles. In 1982 she costarred off-Broadway in *Sally and Marsha,* which examined the tribulations of contemporary women, and in 1984 had the lead female role, opposite Mandy Patinkin as the French painter Georges Seurat, in the Stephen Sondheim/James Lapine Broadway musical *Sunday in the Park with George.*

# Martin Scorsese

As part of a new generation of young filmmakers, and often paired with Francis Ford Coppola, Scorsese has developed a highly personal style of filmmaking, drawing on generational themes of alienation and rootlessness, often spiced with violence. Although his early works drew on the New York of his youth, his later films—some tragic, some tragicomic—branched out into a wider exploration of the purpose of human existence.

Scorsese was born in Queens, New York, in 1942, but spent most of his youth, into his early twenties, in Manhattan's Little Italy. He obtained a master's degree in film at New York University and was an instructor for several years.

His first feature film was *"Who's That Knocking at My Door?* (1968), about a young Italian-American. In the early 1970s, he looked at student life, the antiwar movement, and the counterculture, working in different capacities on the documentaries *Woodstock, Medicine Ball Caravan,* and *Elvis on Tour.*

While honing his editorial, production, and directing skills working on commercials and news broadcasts, Scorsese determined to do his own work, and in 1973 made *Mean Streets,* a chronicle of a small-time hood in Little Italy who cannot raise himself out of the straitjacket of the ghetto. In 1974 Scorsese made a documentary about his family called *Italianamerican,* which featured his mother preparing spaghetti sauce.

Scorsese ventured into other subject matter with his next films: *Alice Doesn't Live Here Anymore* (1975), *Taxi Driver* (1976), and *New York, New York* (1977). *The Last Waltz* (1978) was a rock-concert documentary.

Scorsese's pursuit of realism and his effort to undertand the conflicts and obsessions that drive individuals into accomplishment, or, more often, defeat, have been the common thread of his films of the late 1970s and early 1980s, such as *Raging Bull* (1979) and *King of Comedy* (1983).

(Courtesy of Culver Pictures)

Sylvester Stallone and Talia Shire in *Rocky II* (Courtesy of Culver Pictures)

# Sylvester Stallone

A latter-day exemplar of the American dream, "Sly" Stallone rose from the impoverished background of a broken home to become a top-grossing film star by the time he was thirty.

Born in New York's Hell's Kitchen in 1946, Stallone grew up in New York, Silver Spring, Maryland, and Philadelphia. By his late teens, he had attended fourteen schools in eleven years, but through his athletic prowess he won a scholarship to the American College in Switzerland and also briefly attended the University of Miami. Settling in New York City with the goal of becoming an actor, Stallone took whatever roles he could get, and made his stage debut nude in an off-Broadway play, *Score.* He also performed in low-budget films. In 1974 he starred in *The Lords of Flatbush,* the story of a Brooklyn teenage gang, and in 1975 had a supporting role in *Farewell My Lovely.* The next year, desperate for money, Stallone wrote the screenplay for *Rocky,* the tale of a down-and-out boxer who defeats a champion and finds true love. The script was purportedly written in three and a half days, and he sold it for a relatively low sum to a pair of movie producers, with the condition that *he* play the lead role.

The rest, as most film fans know, is history. *Rocky* became the hit of 1976, earning Oscars for best picture, best director (John Avildsen), and best editing. Stallone was nominated for best actor and best screenplay.

Since then he has continued acting in and directing more Rocky films, culminating in *Rambo* (1985), a mock heroic saga of the Vietnam War—a fantasy of Rocky in uniform that is silly but popular.

# John Travolta

As Tony Manero, a working-class youth from Brooklyn, Travolta danced his way to fame in the 1977 film *Saturday Night Fever,* earning an Academy Award nomination en route. Though his film career since then has been erratic, Travolta, who also starred in the television series "Welcome Back, Kotter," remains a versatile, major young talent.

Born in 1954 and raised in Englewood, New Jersey, where his father owned a tire business and his mother was an acting coach, Travolta studied acting and dancing as a child. At age twelve he joined a local workshop of the Actors Studio, but continued to cultivate his dancing skills. At sixteen, with his family's consent, Travolta left school to act full time, performing in commercials, off-Broadway, and in small television roles. Beginning in 1972, he had a minor role in the national touring company of *Grease,* a musical that depicted American teenage culture of the 1950s, and soon after made his Broadway debut in *Over Here!,* a World War II–inspired musical featuring the two surviving Andrews sisters. Early in his career, Travolta received praise for his acting in a 1976 television drama called "The Boy in the Plastic Bubble," which recounted the true story of a boy whose lack of immunity to disease necessitated his isolation in a plastic-enclosed, antiseptic environment.

Then Travolta got the break that would be the turning point of his career: the role of Vinnie Barbarino, a student at a Brooklyn high school and a member of a local teen gang called the Sweathogs in the TV series "Welcome Back, Kotter." Initially a minor ensemble role, it became a starring role as Travolta's popularity among his preteen viewers mushroomed. The show became Travolta's springboard to an active film career, beginning with a role in Brian De Palma's 1976 horror film *Carrie.* After the huge success of *Saturday Night Fever,* Travolta had starring roles in *Grease* (1978), *Moment by Moment,* a

1978 drama costarring Lily Tomlin, *Urban Cowboy* (1980), in which Debra Winger had her first feature role, and a second De Palma film, *Blow Out* (1981). A 1983 sequel to *Saturday Night Fever* called *Staying Alive* starred Travolta as Tony Manero, disco bum turned Broadway dancer.

## Rudolph Valentino

His life was short, but Valentino's legacy as a romantic leading man has continued to live on in cinema lore.

He was born Rodolpho Alfonzo Raffaelo Pierre Filibert Guglielmi Di Valentina d'Antonguolla, in Castellaneta, Italy, in 1895, the son of an army veterinarian. Soon after his graduation from a military academy, Valentino moved to New York in 1913, where, after a succession of jobs, including landscape gardener, he became a taxi dancer. Valentino next sought opportunities in the burgeoning movie industry, moving in 1917 to Hollywood, where he often worked as an extra. In 1921 he was given the lead role in *The Four Horsemen of the Apocalypse*—and the myth of the Latin lover exploded onto the screen. He was the romantic Apollo who treated women with courtesy and deference but whose eyes promised that behind the deference, and behind the bedroom door, other, more exciting, qualities would emerge. Valentino was pure cinematic magic, sexual magnetism personified, the Italian lover incarnate. Then Valentino made *The Sheik* and millions of women swooned as his menacing eyes stared at Agnes Ayres, preparing for the clinch. Valentino went on to smashing successes, including *Beyond the Rocks* (1922), *Blood and Sand* (1922), considered his best performance, *The Young Rajah* (1922), *Monsieur Beaucaire* (1924), *A Sainted Devil* (1924), *Cobra* (1925), *The Eagle* (1925) and his last film, *The Son of the Sheik* (1926).

In 1926, at the height of his fame, he died of a perforated ulcer. He was only thirty-one. Millions of women who desired to be borne away on Valentino's white Arabian steed mourned his untimely death.

1895

1926

"Rudolph Valentino did not live in vain. He made the most of his gifts, thereby giving happiness to untold thousands throughout the world, devoted admirers who sincerely mourned his passing when death brought to a premature close the greatest career in the history of motion pictures."

"Aspiration"
The Statue to Valentino's Memory
at Hollywood, California

# Rudolph Valentino

"A great artist who mastered the genius that lies in simplicity and restraint."

Rocky Marciano

Phil Esposito

Vince Lombardi

Willie Mosconi

Eddie Arcaro

The Unity Award, which will be presented to the enshrinees upon their induction, was designed by Frank LaMark, especially for the National Italain American Sports Hall of Fame.

Symbolic of the goals of the National Italian American Sports Hall of Fame, the eternal flame indicates the everlasting effect the participants have on the Italian-American community.

Perhaps Hall of Fame sportscaster Jack Brickhouse summed it up best when he tied the name of the award to the goals we are trying to accomplish—"**UNITY**"—it means "**UN**ited **I**talian-**A**merican **T**ribute to **Y**outh."

Each year the National Nominating Committee selects honorees to be inducted into the NIASHF. They are chosen in May and honored with a banquet the following November.

Presently there are 70 NIASHF inductees, including Rocky Marciano, who became the first Italian-American athlete inducted. He was honored posthumously in 1977.

To be eligible for induction, the honoree must have at least one parent of Italian heritage and have participated in their respective sport either professionally or as an amateur.

A screening committee reviews the names submitted to it by the media, sports historians and former players. From this list, 30 names are selected and submitted to the Nominating Committee by March 15 each year.

The Nominating Committee reviews the names and, within 20 days, selects a minimum of four (4) and a maximum of five (5) honorees for induction. Its final selection is based on the player's: a) record in their respective sport; b) ability; c) integrity; d) sportsmanship and e)character or contribution to individual sport if not an athlete.

Mario Andretti

Joe DiMaggio

Hank Luisetti

Donna Caponi

Andy Varipapa

## Inductees

Lou Ambers ● Alan Ameche ● Mario Andretti ● Sammy Angott ● Eddie Arcaro ● Carmen Basilio ● Yogi Berra ● Angelo Bertelli ● Tony Canadeo ● Donna Caponi
Gino Cappelletti ● Primo Carnera ● Phil Cavarretta ● Rocky Colovito ● Tony Conigliaro ● Franco Columbu ● Frank Crosetti ● Alex DelVecchio ● Tony DeMarco
Dom DiMaggio ● Joe DiMaggio ● Angelo Dundee ● Phil Esposito ● Buzz Fazio ● Joey Giardello ● Andy Granatelli ● Rocky Graziano ● Jake LaMotta ● Dante Lavelli
Ernie Lombardi ● Vince Lombardi ● Hank Luisetti ● Sal Maglie ● Gino Marchetti ● Rocky Marciano ● Joey Maxim ● Willie Mosconi ● George Musso ● Leo Nomellini
Willie Pep ● Brian Piccolo ● Phil Rizzuto ● Andy Robustelli ● Ron Santo ● Gene Sarazen ● Joe Torre ● Charlie Trippi ● Andy Varipapa ● Ken Venturi

## Old Timers Group

Ed Abbattichio ● Charles Atlas ● Batt Battalino ● Ping Bodie ● Tony Canzoneri ● Frank Carideo ● Frank Coltiletti ● Young Corbett III ● Ralph DePalma ● Peter DePaolo
Red DiBernardi ● Johnny Dundee ● Pete Herman ● Fidel LaBarba ● Tony Lazzeri ● Lou Little ● Sammy Mandel ● Hank Marino ● Pat Pazzetti ● Babe Pinelli ● Johnny Wilson

**NATIONAL ITALIAN AMERICAN SPORTS HALL OF FAME•7906 W. GRAND AVE., ELMWOOD PARK, ILLINOIS 60635•(312) 452-4812**

## *Eddie Arcaro*

One of only two jockeys to ride five Kentucky Derby winners, Arcaro also won six Preaknesses, six Belmonts, and two Triple Crowns, riding Whirlaway in 1941 and Citation in 1948. By 1962, his mounts had earned over $30 million in purses, making Arcaro the then top-grossing jockey in history.

Born in Cincinnati in 1916, George Edward Arcaro weighed only three pounds at birth, and at adulthood stood 5'2", weighing 114 pounds. As a child he wished to play baseball, but was always excluded when his classmates chose teams.

Arcaro began riding in the late 1920s, and rode his first race in 1931. He had 45 losses until his first victory in early 1933. In 1938, he won his first Kentucky Derby—by only one length. He continued riding until 1962, when he retired to become a sports commentator. By then, Arcaro had become a millionaire several times over.

## *Yogi Berra*

Lawrence Peter Berra was born in St. Louis, Missouri, in 1925, where his immigrant father was a bricklayer. Among his childhood friends was another up-and-coming baseball pro, Joe Garagiola. Berra left school in eighth grade to work as a factory laborer and truck driver, but he always harbored a desire to play ball and spent his free time on the field. He earned his nickname from a friend named Jack Maguire, who played with Berra on a local team and briefly for the New York Giants.

In 1942 Berra tried out for the St. Louis Cardinals, but was told he had no future in the major leagues. Not one to give up, Berra got a minor league contract with the New York Yankees, thanks to a former umpire who knew his catching and hitting skills. In 1943 Berra played with the Norfolk (Virginia) Tars and slowly rose through the ranks of the minors. By 1946 he was promoted to the Yankees, and in an auspicious debut hit a home run his first time at bat.

An unlikely figure—Berra is short and squat—he nonetheless was an outstanding runner and catcher. He played on the American League All-Star Team from 1948 through 1962 and was named Most Valuable Player in 1951, 1954, and 1955. In nineteen years, he played in 2,120 games, had 2,150 hits, 358 home runs, and a lifetime batting average of .285. He was also an exceptionally able catcher. He retired from playing in 1963, managed the New York Mets, and was elected to the Baseball Hall of Fame in 1971. Berra held several career records, including most World Series games played (75) and most World Series hits (71). He was manager of the Yankees in 1964 and again in 1984–85.

Joe DiMaggio (Courtesy of Culver Pictures)

# Joe DiMaggio

DiMaggio was named the greatest living baseball player in a 1969 poll for the baseball centennial.

The son of immigrants from Isola della Femina off the Sicilian coast, Joseph Paul DiMaggio was born in Martinez, California, in 1914 and raised in San Francisco, where his father was a fisherman. He was the eighth of nine children, two of whom, Vince and Dom, also played professional baseball. In 1932, when Vince was playing in the minors, he recommended Joe as a shortstop for the San Francisco Seals of the Pacific Coast League. In only three games Joe managed to exhibit the talents that would make him a star; on his first day out, for example, he hit a double and a triple. The next year he played a full season in the Pacific Coast League, breaking a record when he hit safely in 61 consecutive games. Despite a knee injury, he was bought by the Yankees in 1934, spending two years playing for their minor league teams.

In his rookie year, 1936, the record breaking continued. He batted .323 and tied for first place for the most triples. In his second season he hit 46 home runs and became the American League leader. His outstanding records in home runs, runs scored, hits, stolen bases, and batting average earned him Most Valuable Player status in 1939, 1941, and 1947, and he played on every American League All-Star Team every year of his pro career from 1936 until he retired in 1951. Moreover, he was in the World Series every prewar year except 1940 and on a winning team every subsequent year except 1942. He excelled as a center fielder. His greatest major league feat was hitting safely in 56 consecutive games in 1941.

In 1949, DiMaggio—also known as the "Yankee Clipper"—was the first baseball player to command the astronomical salary of $100,000. He was elected to the Baseball Hall of Fame in 1955.

# Tom Lasorda

In the 1950s the Dodgers called their young pitcher Tommy Lasorda "a little short," meaning in ball-playing talent. But the organization hung onto him, because they knew then, as everybody knows now, that Tom Lasorda is long on loyalty, competitiveness, and showmanship. He became the Dodgers' manager in 1976.

Lasorda's hamminess and his friendliness with show-biz people such as Frank Sinatra and Don Rickles have completed the Dodgers' uprooting from Brooklyn and planted them firmly in Hollywood.

That sense of loyalty probably started with what Lasorda describes as a very close family life. He was born in 1927, in Norristown, Pennsylvania, not far from Philadelphia. His father, Sam, who came from the town of Tolla in the Chieti province of Italy, worked as a truck driver in a stone quarry.

Tom started with the Dodgers as a minor league pitcher in 1951. He played in the majors from 1954 to 1956—and then was moved back to the minors. Lasorda stopped playing in 1960, but the Dodgers kept him on as a scout.

In 1974, Lasorda went to Italy to instruct Italian baseball coaches at the request of the Italian Baseball Federation. He says he wouldn't accept any money, telling the federation, "Italy gave me the greatest gift I ever received, my father. Now I want to give something back to Italy."

# Rocky Marciano

Born Rocco Francis Marchegiano, Marciano became world heavyweight champion in 1952 when he defeated Jersey Joe Walcott. By then he had had an undefeated record in his previous 44 professional bouts, and he had ended the ring career of black boxer Joe Louis with a knockout in 1951.

The son of an immigrant factory worker, Marciano was born in 1924 and grew up in Brockton, Massachusetts. He set his sights on college and a football career. But his educational prospects were short-circuited when he dropped out of high school to help support his family, working in a string of odd jobs while cultivating an emerging boxing talent.

Marciano began serious training in the Army during World War II. Yet his hopes were elsewhere when he was discharged. Aiming to play pro baseball, Marciano went as far as qualifying for a farm team of the Chicago Cubs. But his weak fielding spelled the end before his career really began, so he turned to boxing seriously, and in July 1948 fought his first pro bout. He soon began amassing steady victories, but his initial opponents were regarded as second-string boxers. Matched against Roland LaStarza, who had an undefeated record in 37 matches, Marciano won a split decision.

By 1951, Marciano was a starring name in boxing, and that October he knocked out an aging Joe Louis, who was trying to make a comeback after retiring. His 1952 match against Walcott propelled him to the top, and he remained there as world heavyweight champion until he retired in 1956. By then he was undefeated, with 49 straight wins, including 43 by knockout. He died in 1969.

# Vincent Lombardi

Credited for coining the phrase "Winning isn't the main thing; it's the only thing," Lombardi took the faltering Green Bay Packers from a steady losing record to one of dominance in the National Football League. Today he is recalled as the "Miracle Man of Football."

Born in 1913 and raised in Brooklyn, Lombardi was the son of an Italian immigrant meat wholesaler. He had planned to be a priest, but his outstanding performance on Fordham University's fabled "Seven Blocks of Granite" football team as a 5'11", 200-pound guard in the mid-1930s led him to focus on football coaching. He did it first as a sideline, working full time as an insurance investigator, then turned to coaching full time at a Catholic high school in New Jersey. In 1947 he returned to Fordham as its freshman coach. From 1948 to 1954 he coached at the U.S. Military Academy and then moved to the pros in 1954 as an assistant coach of offense with the New York Giants. In 1956 the Giants won their first NFL championship since 1938.

1959 was a turning point for Lombardi. That year he became head coach of the Green Bay Packers, a team that in 1958 had had its worst record yet: 1-10-0. In his initial meeting with the Packer players, Lombardi announced: "I have never been on a losing team, gentlemen, and I do not intend to start now!" Thereafter, the club did not have a losing season while he was coach. Demanding full control of the team, he had a winning season of 7–5 after his first year. In 1960 the Packers became Western Conference champions, and in 1961, 1962, 1965, 1966, and 1967 they were NFL champions. Lombardi made further history with the Packers in 1967 and 1968 when he led the team to victory in Super Bowl I and II.

In 1969 Lombardi left the Packers to rebuild another ailing team, the Washington Redskins, and led it to a 7-5-2 record—its first winning season in fourteen years. He died of cancer in 1970.

# *Billy Martin*

Martin's volatile personality and career—he seems to be kicked out of jobs as regularly as the swallows return to Capistrano—mark him as one of baseball's most controversial managers.

Born in 1928 in Berkeley, California, Alfred Manuel Pesano was raised by his Italian-speaking maternal grandmother. His playing talent emerged while he was in grade school, and by 1946 Martin was playing in the minor leagues. In 1947 he was spotted by Casey Stengel, whom Martin would later describe as his mentor. Stengel then managed in the Pacific Coast League, and recruited Martin to play for his Oakland Oaks. When Stengel moved up to the Yankees, he called Martin up with him, and from 1950 through 1957 Martin played for the team (his longest stint in one place).

Martin's off-the-field hitting didn't make him valuable, however. Two fights involving Martin prompted the Yankees to trade him, and from 1957 through 1962 he played for seven different teams, amassing several lawsuits in the process. Over the next six years his career waned; he worked in a series of second-string coaching and scouting jobs. His turnaround began in 1968, when Martin became a minor league manager, and from 1971 through 1973 he returned to the majors to lead the previously troubled Detroit Tigers through three good seasons. But friction with team owners led to Martin's being booted out. He next led the last-place Texas Rangers to second place in their division in 1974, an effort that earned Martin recognition as Manager of the Year.

Martin's return to the Yankees in 1975 propelled him to the limelight. In 1976, he brought the poorly playing team to an Eastern Division title in the American League; by 1978 the team swung from a poor start to a dramatic World Series triumph, in which, in one historic game, Reggie Jackson hit three home runs. Martin remained with the Yankees through 1979; in 1980 he became field manager with the Oakland Athletics. In the three years following, his tumultuous love-hate relationship with Yankee owner George Steinbrenner brought Martin in and out of the Yankee clubhouse and earned the two of them much criticism in the press and among fans. But the two took it in stride— and earned money in the process—by recreating their enmities in televised beer advertisements. In 1983, Martin made headlines when he successfully contested a home run by Kansas City Royal batter George Brett, claiming Brett's bat had an illegal amount of pine tar. The league president later overturned the ruling. After that season, Martin left the Yankees as manager, though his much-touted contract still had two years left, and became a consultant to the ball club. He returned as manager in 1985.

# Phil Rizzuto

Though popular conceptions of what a baseball player should be made the 5′6″, 150-pound Rizzuto an unlikely prospect for major league ball, he excelled for most of the thirteen seasons he played with the New York Yankees, earning Most Valuable Player honors in 1950. Many believe he was one of baseball's great shortstops.

Born in the Ridgewood section of Brooklyn, New York, in 1918, to immigrants from the same town in Italy—who met in Ridgewood—Rizzuto grew up in Queens. His father was a dockworker. In high school he played quarterback on the football team and was captain of his baseball team. He was offered athletic scholarships to both Columbia and Fordham universities, but turned them down to gamble on a professional sports career.

He tried out first for the Brooklyn Dodgers, but was rejected. The Yankees accepted him, however, and in 1938 sent him to play for its Class-D team in Norfolk, Virginia. His excellent hitting and fielding there led to his promotion to the Piedmont League and eventually to the American Association, a top minor league level, where he continued to play outstanding ball. In 1940 he was named Minor League Player of the Year by *Sporting News* for his batting average of .347 and fielding average of .994. He also had a record number of stolen bases.

In 1941, Rizzuto finally made it to the majors and combined with Joe Gordon to lead the American League in double plays. From 1942 to 1945 he served in the Navy and returned to the Yankees in 1946. A perennial All-Star, the sure-handed shortstop was a mainstay in the Yankees' defense up the middle for the next decade and appeared in nine World Series with the Yankees. He ranks fourth overall in walks (30) and stolen bases (10) in World Series play. In his MVP season, 1950, Rizzuto amassed 200 hits and batted .324.

Retiring from pro ball in 1956, Rizzuto—also called "the Scooter"—went immediately into broadcasting for the Yankees, never hiding his pro-Yankee bias. In 1984, when former Brooklyn Dodger Pee Wee Reese, a Rizzuto contemporary, was admitted to the Hall of Fame, many sportswriters and fans complained that Rizzuto should also have been admitted. Still, many expect him to be voted in before too long.

## PIONEER

The first baseball player of Italian ancestry to play in the major leagues was Francesco Stephano Pezzolo. Facing discrimination, he changed his name to the unlikely Ping Bodie. Born October 8, 1887, in San Francisco, he was 5′8″ and weighed 195 pounds. A right-handed batter and outfielder, Bodie played from 1911 to 1917 with the Chicago White Sox and from 1918 to 1921 with the New York Yankees. His lifetime batting average was a respectable .275. Long forgotten, he died in his native city on December 17, 1961.

Italian Athletic Club Baseball Team, Barre, Vermont, 1909 (Courtesy of Aldrich, Vermont, Public Library)

*Part Five*

# HISTORY

# The Italian Heritage

In the fourteen centuries between the collapse of the Roman Empire in A.D. 476 and the reunification of Italy (1859–70), Italian life was characterized by localism, religiousness, and, especially in the *mezzogiorno* (south) and Sicily, extreme poverty.

In part, Italian localism can be traced to the centuries of poverty, population decline, and lawlessness that characterized the Middle Ages in Italy; in part, too, it resulted from the growth of city-states beginning in the twelfth century. Italians also turned inward to village and family life in reaction to the frequent foreign invasions of Europe's "boot" (as Italy was known) by the Spanish (1525–1700), Austrian Hapsburgs (1700–1796; 1814–59), and French (1796–1814).

In the nineteenth century, Giuseppe Mazzini and other patriots called for the liberation of Italy from foreign rule and its unification under a republican government. This renaissance in Italian nationalism, called the *risorgimento,* produced several abortive revolts in the 1820s, 1830s and 1840s.

The Italian states, principalities, and duchies were finally united in the period from 1859 to 1870. This was accomplished under the leadership of two men; Count Cavour of Piedmont, who, through adept diplomacy involving alliances with France, Great Britain, and Prussia, and through military initiatives during the Crimean and Austro-Prussian wars (1853–56 and 1866, respectively), liberated the north (except for papal territory) from Hapsburg control. At the same time, the radical republican Giuseppe Garibaldi liberated Sicily and the south from Bourbon rule.

After unification, Italy slowly became industrialized, gained a number of African colonies (notably Libya and Ethiopia), and began to be respected as a Western European power that would have to be reckoned with.

Yet so strong did the localist tradition remain that the story is told of the patriot who, exuberant at the first stage of Italian unification, rode through a village in 1861 shouting "Viva l'Italia!" Thinking a new queen had been crowned, a villager hearing the patriot turned to a friend and asked, "Who's Italia?"

Historians came to call this localist tradition, which was strong in the *mezzogiorno* and Sicily (from which most immigrants to America came), *campanilismo.* The *campanile* was the village belltower, and the term refers to those who trusted and interacted almost exclusively with others who were within the range of its peals. It implies a certain provincialism, the narrow world view of a peasant society. Italy's geography, particularly its hilly terrain, which made communication difficult from one valley to the next (until the advent of railroads and the telephone during the last half of the nineteenth century), reinforced *campanilismo.*

At the core of *campanilismo* values is loyalty to one's *paesani* (fellow townspeople) and family. According to Rudolph Vecoli, in *Italian American Radicalism,* "When foreign armies overran parts of Italy during the 16th and 19th centuries, Southern Italians knew that though they could not count on their own armies to rout the invaders, they could at least count on their own townsmen to make sure that individual results were not without their price. Similarly, when local scandals ruined reputations—or threatened to do so—it was understood that families would rally to uphold honor. The code of behavior that developed was an intricate one, placing high value on the use of vendetta and a code of silence. Insults and transgressions, clearly defined, received traditional punishment. Family not only became the most important possession to protect—it was also the means of that protection."

The family was very much an extended rather than a nuclear one. It included blood relatives, relatives by marriage, and godparents. In some villages, all the inhabitants were related by blood or marriage. Whatever the hardships of village life, Italians came to revere *la via vecchia,* "the old way," centered on family life and loyalty.

In the villages, male and female roles were sharply delineated. Men were expected to be virile, aggressive, and better educated than women, as well as being the exclusive breadwinners. Women were seen as subordinate to men and were expected to raise many children and to lead a domestic life. Until well into the twentieth century, when modern urban culture reached rural Italy via highways, the telephone, radio, films, and television, parent-arranged marriages sometimes took place between young people in their teens. (While a few such marriages still take place in some of the remotest rural regions, they are rare today.)

Because the heart of the Roman Catholic Church is in Italy, the country has always had a deep religious tradition. The Church added color and ceremony to village life through rituals and holidays, including the annual *festa* (a day celebrating the memory of the village patron saint). But the life of the southern peasant was influenced at least as much by folk religion—the belief in the evil eye, the Black Madonna, and the power of curses— as by Catholic dogma and ritual. The influence of folk religion antedated the Church, and this influence was strengthened in the nineteenth century because priests were frequently allied with wealthy absentee landowners who opposed change. So pervasive is this folk religion that one historian has written, "Italians may not keep the Sabbath day, may not go to Church but once in a whole life, may despise and reject the teachings of the Church and yet be religious."

Religious fatalism was also offset by the Italian penchant for taking maximum enjoyment in the present moment, particularly through celebrations, eating, drinking, loving, or even fighting. The rituals of the meal—the selection and preparation of food, eating with large numbers of people—were at the center of Italian social life and they have the same importance today for many Italians. This combination of religiousness and epicureanism tended to make Italians both stoic and adaptable, able to cope with difficult situations but unwilling to try to change them. Although their lives were harsh, Italian peasants lived with vigor.

The Italians who emigrated also tended to be products of grinding rural poverty. Much of the land in the south was hilly, difficult to cultivate, and, because of inadequate water supplies, barely arable. Often the better soil was overworked.

Few of the *contadini* (peasants) owned land; almost all were tenant farmers or sharecroppers for absentee landowners. These landowners included wealthy noblemen and the church. The peasants customarily began work at sunrise by walking several miles from their homes to their small plots, and they did not finish until sunset. Most lived their entire lives within a few miles of the villages in which they were born.

During and after the unification period, some large landholdings of the nobles and the church were distributed among proprietors and peasants. But during the late nineteenth and early twentieth century, a real land redistribution was thwarted by fraud, exorbitant taxes, which overwhelmed the poorer peasants, and priests who promised divine retribution if the old ways were disturbed.

While railroads, better roads, and factories were built in the north, the south was sorely neglected; it gave the central government much more in produce and taxes than it took in subsidies or development aid. Thus, while the north modernized, the south remained essentially a peasant-based society until the advent of fascism (1922).

In some provinces, as the number of absentee proprietors actually increased and the number of landholders declined, the tenants and day laborers remained as bad off as they were in the preunification period. Barely able to eke out a living and feeling enslaved to the estate owners for whom they worked, the peasants began to consider migrating to other countries.

## Italians in America

In the half-century between the beginning of Italian immigration and the institution of American immigration quotas (1870–1924), the trickle of immigrants became a torrent. Most were Southern Italian peasants desperate to escape severe and worsening economic conditions.

Since 1860 no less than 12.5 million Italians emigrated permanently and, of this number, approximately 5 million (40 percent) settled in the United States. The lure of America increased steadily: only about one in twelve Italians who emigrated in 1881 settled here, but two decades later, the ratio rose to one in four and, by 1904, two out of three Italian emigrants came to these shores. During the peak period of immigration, 1907–1914, the approximately 1.3 million Italian immigrants constituted 25 to 30 percent of all immigrants to the United States.

Approximately a third came as sojourners; they intended to accumulate enough money to return home and buy land. Others who stayed were influenced by the sojourners' mentality, a yearning for their *paese* (village), which made these newcomers resist becoming integrated into American society (either by learning English or by becoming citizens).

More than any other ethnic group, with the exception of the Jews, they were an urban people. Over 80 percent settled in the 450-mile stretch of the East Coast between Boston and Baltimore—particularly in such crowded Italian enclaves as Boston's West End, New York's south Brooklyn, and Philadelphia's South Side (there were also substantial Italian communities in a number of Midwestern cities, notably Chicago, Detroit, and Cleveland). By 1910, New York had the largest Italian community by far (over 340,000 Italian residents), with large communities in Philadelphia and Chicago (45,000 each), Boston (31,000), San Francisco (17,000), and New Orleans (18,000). The Italian communities in the latter two cities were more middle class (and prosperous) than the Italian communities in the other cities.

In these cities' Little Italies—tenements and neighborhoods where immigrants found relatives and friends from their regions—there weren't Italians so much as subcommunities of Palermans, Calabrians, Venetians, etc. The rural localism of the old country—dialects, folkways, and foods—was preserved in the urban ghettos of the new country. (Sociologist Herbert Gans has referred to this first generation of Italian-Americans as "urban villagers.")

When Italian-Americans came to New York at the turn of the century, they found, of course, that the streets were not paved with gold; instead, they were expected to do the paving. A large number were common laborers who helped build city streets, sewers, subways, and office buildings. They also worked in the garment industry, the steel factories, and in meat plants. Frequently they were exploited—forced to work long hours at subsistence wages. Around 1900, some Italian workers labored twelve hours or more a day, six days a week, for a grand salary of $1.50 a day. (They might save a third of that.)

Their lives often were controlled by *padroni*, Italian-Americans who had immigrated earlier and who served as contractors for, and liaisons between, the new Italian immigrants and prospective employers. Critics charged that they controlled the workers' lives and that the padrone system was all too liable to corruption. Its defenders claimed

An Italian family sits for its portrait in Chicago tenement, 1910 (Photo by Lewis W. Hine, Courtesy of the New York Public Library)

Tenement (Photo by Lewis W. Hine, Courtesy of the International Museum of Photography, Rochester, New York)

Italian track-walker on Pennsylvania Railroad, near New York City, 1930 (Photo by Lewis W. Hine, Courtesy of the New York Public Library)

padroni played a necessary and useful role in helping new immigrants get on their feet economically.

At a time when industry was unregulated and capitalism exploitative, and there were increasing conflicts between native workers and management, the new immigrants often were viewed as wage-cutters by American workers. There were frequent outbreaks of violence against them. Employers, in turn, used many different ethnic groups to maintain control, keeping the laborers divided and incapable of organizing on their own behalf.

As the number of Italians continued to grow, particularly in the cities, people already there began to feel a threat to their own economic positions and social status. In principle, they were committed to an America where people from different backgrounds came together and contributed to the good of the entire society. They reconciled this ideology with their fear of newcomers by simply branding the new immigrants "inferior" and "dangerous" to society.

Even within their own religion, Italians faced prejudice from the Irish-dominated Catholic church. The immigrants brought their own brand of Catholicism to this country. Many from the north tended to be anticlerical and radical, while many from the south were indifferent and practiced their faith with a mixture of superstition and festiveness. As one Italian-American priest put it, "When we Italian-Americans celebrate a saint's day there must be music, dancing, eating, drinking, and fireworks. It's our way of praying." These practices peeved the Irish Catholic clergy, who were more authoritarian and self-sacrificing. The Italians saw the Irish as fanatics, and the Irish viewed the Italians as ignorant and superstitious.

At the end of the nineteenth century, genetic and psychological theories reinforced the supposed superiority of Nordic intelligence and culture over that of Mediterranean and black groups. This gave "scientific" justification for prejudice and discriminatory acts.

In short, Italians, along with other immigrants, were victims of what Michael Novak calls the white racism of that time: they were portrayed as socially disorganized and lacking in freedom and responsibility. Italians were also seen as swarthy, unstable Mediterraneans and as part of a papist plot to control America.

This kind of bigotry was especially prevalent in the South and the West where, unlike the situation in the East, there were few Italian communities. At times, prejudice even exploded into violence. During a labor dispute in 1891, for example, eleven Italians were lynched in New Orleans, and in 1904, six Italian workers were murdered during a strike in the coal fields of Colorado.

Italian-Americans survived and coped with these adversities in the same way their ancestors withstood hundreds of years of corrupt government, foreign invaders, and natural disasters. They clustered together and—sustained by a common language and traditions—developed mutual aid organizations. In 1910 there were two thousand Italian-American mutual aid societies in New York City. These helped the immigrants find refuge from a hostile society. The first generation also developed its own economic and social services: there were Italian food stores, doctors, lawyers, banks, sports clubs, and charities.

### The Second Generation, 1920–1950

During the next three decades, the children of the immigrants continued to suffer prejudice and discrimination. With the advent of Prohibition—some Italians were active in bootlegging—Italians came to be associated with criminality and such secret criminal organizations as the Mafia. This stereotype has persisted to the present day.

Italian-Americans also suffered because of the isolationism and xenophobia of the interwar period. The overt bigotry manifested against two Italian immigrants accused of a 1920 murder in South Braintree, Massachusetts—Nicola Sacco and Bartolomeo Vanzetti—drew worldwide attention and protests.

Yet despite prejudice and discrimination, Italian-Americans slowly achieved greater social mobility. This was harshly interrupted by the Depression, but resumed with the advent of the second Roosevelt Administration (1937) and, especially, the war boom.

This period also saw the rapid Americanization of the second generation of Italian-Americans. Children of immigrant parents often clashed with, or grew distant from, their parents, as the children adapted to American culture. In America, parental authority was weaker, while peer pressure was often stronger. Some women worked. Socializing networks, including schools, settlement houses, and clubs, existed outside one's immediate neighborhood, and the popular culture—newspapers and magazines, films and radio (and, later, television)—promoted Anglo-Saxon Protestant values. Thus, many second-generation Italian-Americans considered the Italian way of life as being low in social status. This view was reinforced by the entrenched prejudice and discrimination they faced.

## The Third and Fourth Generations, 1951–1985

During the past three decades, the third and fourth generations of Italian-Americans have increasingly moved from blue-collar to white-collar jobs. But given their national heritage and their parents' and grandparents' occupations, today's Italian men still take more pride in physical work than do men in many other ethnic groups. Most have moved from Little Italies to more mixed urban neighborhoods or to the suburbs. As a result, many of today's Italian-Americans have looser ties to Italy as well as to the Italian language and culture. According to Richard Alba, a sociologist, of Italian-Americans under the age of thirty, 72 percent of the men and 64 percent of the women marry someone with no Italian background. His conclusion, based on the 1980 census, also indicates that 70 percent of Italian-Americans born after 1970 were children of an intermarriage.

As they became less blue collar, many third-generation Italian-Americans also overcame their people's traditional skepticism toward higher education. Before 1945, Italian-Americans sent fewer young people to college than most other ethnic groups; today college attendance for Italian-Americans is just above the national average. And a significant number of Italian-American women in their thirties and forties are attending college for the first time. A professor at a branch of the City University of New York observes, "Just count up the names of the older women in your classes—you'll see they're mostly Italians, the wives of construction workers and sanitation men."

With the immigration of large numbers of Hispanic-Americans and the ongoing northern immigration of blacks, inner-city Italian-Americans have sometimes engaged in turf struggles with these groups. Often during the 1970s and early 1980s Italians have struggled to preserve the character of their neighborhoods. At times, however, poverty, unemployment, and a tight housing market have resulted in prejudice, racism, and fear on both sides. The tragedy is that Italians, blacks, Puerto Ricans, and other urban minorities all are "victims of a corrupt, manipulated real estate market" (Rudolph Vecoli), as well as of utterly inadequate social services. In the late 1960s and 1970s, many young Italian-Americans began showing a new interest in their heritage. With other ethnic groups, Italian-Americans played a key role in defining the new ethnicity of the 1970s.

Italian coal miner with grandchild, West Virginia, 1939 (Photo by Vadron)

Italian shoe repairman, New York City, 1943 (Courtesy of the National Archives)

Children playing in Palumbo Yard, Cleveland, Ohio, ca. 1920 (Courtesy of the Western Reserve Historical Society)

Flag-raising ceremony for local boys in U.S. Army, Mott Street, New York City, 1942 (Photo by Marjory Collins, Courtesy of *Il Progresso*)

Welcome for a soldier home from World War II (Photo by Todd Webb, Courtesy of Museum of the City of New York)

New Year's presents suggested for our newly arrived Italian immigrants.
*Leslie's Weekly*, January 18, 1873. (Culver Pictures)

Husband and wife reading a letter from their son in U.S. Army, 1943 (Photo by Marjory Collins, Courtesy of *Il Progresso*)

Organ grinder and wife, New York City, 1897 (Photo by Elizabeth Alice Austen)

As they became more conscious of their influence and power in America, third-generation Italian-Americans acted on a number of fronts with a new assertiveness and unpredictability. Long underrepresented in the American church hierarchy, they began to voice their grievances on this matter until, in 1968, Francis Mugavero, a son of Sicilian immigrants, was named Bishop of the Diocese of Brooklyn. In 1983 Archbishop Joseph L. Bernardin of Chicago, the son of an immigrant stonecutter from the Torrentino region, was elevated to Cardinal. (However, Irish-Americans continue to dominate high church positions in America, while Italians have been appointed to bishoprics in only a relatively small number of sees).

According to the Center for Migration Studies, 95 percent of Italians are Catholic, and this group constitutes about 24 percent of the total Catholic population in the United States. Italians today—those in the third and fourth generations—still maintain deep religious feelings but reject formal church going. They are also more inclined to disagree with the Church's stand on papal infallibility, divorce, and abortion.

## From the Melting Pot to the New Pluralism

The prejudice, discrimination, and violence that were directed at first-generation Italian-Americans are not present today. The melting-pot idea, which encouraged all immigrants to give up their heritage and blend into a homogeneous society, was put to rest in the 1960s. We know today that this goal was based on a myth, and that the hope that America's ethnic groups would give up their distinctive languages and customs could never work.

Instead, American life today is characterized by the "new pluralism," as described by Irving M. Levine of the Institute for American Pluralism. Levine notes that the theory of cultural pluralism, which was popular in the early part of the century, meant that individuals ought to be able to maintain their identity and group pride, while at the same time identifying themselves primarily as Americans and contributing to a common culture. The new pluralism, Levine points out, takes this concept one step further. It acknowledges that there are such things as group identity and interests, group status, and group power—as well as intergroup rivalry and conflicts. According to Levine, individuals have a right to use their group as a political vehicle even though they have no right to believe that it should dominate other groups.

Today, there is a more tolerant atmosphere, which encourages Italian-Americans to openly identify with their heritage. Italian-Americans, as well as other ethnic groups, are also asking American institutions to be more sensitive to their particular values and lifestyles.

One area where such sensitivity is particularly needed is in education. Working with Italian youngsters in Chicago, Jane Addams stated in 1897 that a primary aim of education is to use in a positive way the child's own cultural experience. She concluded that American education failed the children of foreign-born peasants, particularly Italians, by not drawing upon this experience.

What Jane Addams said in 1897 is still applicable today. Many Italian-American children still have trouble in school, with the result that in a number of cities there is a sizable Italian dropout rate in high school.

Yet, by no means is the Italian-American story over. Since the liberalization of American immigration laws in 1965, an average of 25,000 Italians have immigrated to this country each year.

Often there are tensions between the newly arrived Italians and those who have been here a generation or longer. The former tend to see American influences as destructive of traditional Italian values. The latter see these influences as a way to improve their socioeconomic position. Both wonder: What will endure of the Italian tradition? And what will be the emerging characteristics of Italian-Americans in the future?

The Italian language will probably not endure in this country. Only a diminishing minority of Italian-Americans speak Italian (in the same way that a fraction of the children and grandchildren of Eastern European Jewish immigrants still speak Yiddish). And while there is a growing interest in "Italianata" (the history and culture of the old country), and a few colleges offer "Italian studies" programs, only a small number of intellectuals are engaged in such activities.

For most Italian-Americans, what has endured and what is likely to continue to endure are certain core values. Primary among these are the primacy of personal relationships (particularly close relationships with family and friends), enjoyment of home life, and respect for authority.

While Italian-Americans strive to close the gap separating them from other ethnic groups, they are also committed to preserving those aspects of their heritage that are uniquely Italian. Not for them the mores of "rugged individualism" or the "cult of narcissism." For the Italian-American, the pulse of life is found largely in the strong social bonds of his or her extended family, neighborhood, and ethnic group.

*Joseph Giordano*

## Amadeo Peter Giannini

A vegetable merchant turned banker, Giannini pioneered the concept of interstate banking and turned his Bank of Italy, which he founded in San Francisco in 1904, into the Bank of America, at one time the world's largest private bank.

The son of immigrants from Genoa, Giannini was born in 1870 in San Jose, California, and left school at age thirteen to work in his stepfather's wholesale produce business. He became a partner in six years, built up the business, and sold out his share in 1901. He became interested in banking, and in 1904 formed the Bank of Italy, which specialized in lending mainly to small farmers, merchants, and laborers. Though self-educated and regarded as an outsider by the banking establishment, Giannini was an astute business-man. When other banks were wiped out during the earthquake and fire of 1906 that ravaged San Francisco, his bank survived: he had run in and recovered more than $2 million in gold and securities in the vault, which he then hid under piles of vegetables in a horse-drawn cart. Subsequently, during the rebuilding of the city he was the only banker around who could make loans.

Giannini fostered the concept of branch banking in 1907 when he opened a second Bank of Italy office in San Francisco, and he began buying banks in other cities—often meeting anti-Italian sentiment in the process. Undaunted, he moved beyond California borders when, in 1919, he took over the East River National Bank in New York. Since interstate banking was then illegal, he made the purchase through a holding company called Bancitaly Corporation. By 1927 Giannini's composite holdings represented the largest banking entity outside New York. Within New York, it grew still larger when, in 1928, Bancitaly acquired the Bank of America in New York. That year, Giannini dis-solved Bancitaly and created a new holding company called Transamerica. In 1930, the Bank of Italy was renamed the Bank of America National Trust and Savings Association. It took a leading role in lending to motion picture pioneers Charlie Chaplin, Mack

Sennett, and Darryl Zanuck when that industry was still new and risky, and it also made loans to Broadway producer and entrepreneur Florenz Ziegfeld.

By 1948, Bank of America was the largest private bank in the world and the largest bank in the United States. Giannini died in 1949.

# Enrico Fermi

Fermi's pioneering work in experimental physics while he lived in Italy paved the way for the creation of the atom bomb. When the A-bomb was actually designed in America, he was among its chief architects.

A prodigy, Fermi was born in 1901 in Rome and became entranced with mathematics and physics as a youth. He read so much on his own that by age seventeen he had absorbed even more than was required for a doctorate in theoretical physics, which he received in 1922 from the University of Pisa. In 1924 he was appointed lecturer at the University of Florence, where his studies in theoretical physics attained wide notice in the academic community, and in 1927 he became a professor at the University of Rome, where he remained for eleven years.

In 1934 Fermi began his most important work, which occurred when he left the realm of theoretical physics for experimental physics. He bombarded all the chemical elements with neutrons, the beginnings of the process that would lead to the atomic bomb. In so doing, he became the first person to split the uranium atom, but he didn't recognize that he had achieved nuclear fission. In 1938, in recognition of his work with neutrons, Fermi received the Nobel Prize.

From Stockholm, after accepting the prize, Fermi and his wife, who was Jewish, fled the fascist regime in Italy and came to the United States, where he was appointed professor of physics at Columbia University. In 1939, he consulted with federal officials about the possibility of atomic weapons. When the government embarked on a project to develop a bomb, Fermi was called to the University of Chicago, where, in 1942, he was part of a scientific team that created the first nuclear chain reaction. He shortly thereafter became chief of the advanced physics laboratory at Los Alamos, New Mexico, working under the overall supervision of J. Robert Oppenheimer.

In 1945, the year Fermi became an American citizen, he returned to Chicago as a full professor in its newly created Institute for Nuclear Research and finished his career there. He died in 1954.

# A. Bartlett Giamatti

Giamatti's 1978 appointment as president of Yale University marked the first time in Yale's history that a man not wholly of Anglo-Saxon origin had risen to the post. In addition, he is the youngest Yale president since the 1700s.

A professor of Renaissance history, Angelo Bartlett Giamatti was born in Boston in 1938. His paternal grandfather had emigrated from Italy in 1900 and settled in New Haven. His father, Valentine, graduated from Yale in 1932 and taught Romance languages and Italian literature at Mount Holyoke College.

Giamatti attended Phillips Academy in Andover, Massachusetts, and Yale College, graduating magna cum laude in 1960. Four years later, he received a Ph.D. in compara-

Enrico Fermi (Courtesy of the National Archives)

tive literature. Giamatti taught for two years at Princeton University, then returned to Yale to teach. By age thirty-three he was a full professor.

As president of Yale, he proved a surprisingly successful fund-raiser, bringing Yale its first balanced budget in ten years when he had been president for only two. Giamatti also beefed up the undergraduate academic program at Yale, instituting an intensive writing program and abolishing pass-fail grades. He improved faculty morale by raising their pay.

His tenure hasn't been problem-free. He angered some alumni—while pleasing others—by his outspoken criticism of the Moral Majority and other conservative groups, whom he accused of being "peddlers of coercion," in a 1981 speech to freshmen. He also crticized the Reagan administration's policies of heavy defense spending at the expense of educational programs. And Giamatti spearheaded the historic sale of Yale's Brasher Doubloon for $650,000 to partially finance a new library. In 1985 he announced his plans to retire from Yale.

# Lee A. Iacocca

As president of Chrysler Corporation Iacocca steered the failing automobile giant to a new lease on life when, in 1979, he obtained congressional help in landmark legislation to avert the company's bankruptcy. In the years since, Iacocca has become a folk hero to America's workers as an example of a self-made millionaire who never lost sight of his roots.

The son of an immigrant from Southern Italy who built up an auto-rental business, Lido Anthony Iacocca was born in 1924 and grew up in Allentown, Pennsylvania. He graduated from Lehigh University and obtained a master's degree in engineering from Princeton University. In 1946, he joined the Ford Motor Company as an engineer, but soon switched to sales, where he seemed to have a natural talent. He was named president of the company in 1970. He introduced the Mustang as a sleek, sexy compact, as well as the classy Continental Mark III.

In 1978 Iacocca was fired in a dispute with company directors and joined Chrysler, which was then verging on crisis. Between 1978 and 1981, Chrysler had lost nearly $3.5 billion. The ensuing and controversial bailout through a pioneering congressional loan arrangement enabled Chrysler to survive, although some facilities had to be shut down and some workers laid off. By 1982 the company made a modest profit, mainly through having closed its tank division, and since then has become a design leader, recognized for its "K-car" and for successfully reintroducing the convertible sedan with the Chrysler LeBaron. In 1984 Chrysler introduced a minivan, which offered many design and space features of full-sized vans, yet was compact in other respects. It became a hot seller and was imitated by other automobile makers.

Iacocca, whose name has cropped up from time to time as a possible Democratic cabinet appointee, also broke from the tradition of executive aloofness by appearing in many Chrysler advertisements. Observers have often attributed Chrysler's survival to Iacocca's inordinate gutsiness and powers of persuasion.

Lee Iacocca (Courtesy of the Bettman Archive)

# Eleanor Cutri Smeal

Eleanor Cutri Smeal has been a leader in the women's movement since 1970, when the National Organization for Women (NOW) was being formed. From 1977 through 1982, she was NOW's president.

Born in 1939 in Ashtabula, Ohio, to an Italian-born father and a first-generation Italian-American mother, Eleanor Cutri was raised to think independently, because, she says, her mother wanted her daughter to feel freer than she herself had felt as a child. Cutri attended public schools although the family was devout Roman Catholic and then enrolled at Duke University in North Carolina, where she was active politically and graduated Phi Beta Kappa. Her outspoken support of racial integration was a controversial stance to take on this Southern campus.

Cutri's plans to get a doctorate were cut short by illness. By then married, the mother of two, and forced to stay home, she realized the difficulties mothers have without the ready availability of day care or disability insurance. During this period, she and her husband, who shared many of the homemaking duties, became converts to the burgeoning women's movement. When NOW was being formed in 1970, she joined, and the next year helped found and then became president of a chapter in the Pittsburgh suburb where she lived. From 1972 to 1975 she was president of Pennsylvania NOW and focused her energies on the fight for educational equity for women, especially in access to sports scholarships for college students.

Smeal joined the national board of directors of NOW in 1973 and by 1975 was its chairperson. Her most important achievement—election as national president in 1977—was accompanied by another milestone she had fought for. For the first time, the job of NOW president was salaried, which meant, importantly, that a woman seeking to devote herself full-time to feminist causes did not need an independent income. During Smeal's first year on the job, she balanced the organization's budget, which, when she was elected, had run up a $120,000 deficit.

Smeal served on the National Advisory Committee for Women in 1978 under President Carter. After she left office, she remained a vocal and respected proponent of women's rights and wrote *Why Women Will Elect the President in 1984*. She was reelected NOW's president in 1985.

# Historical Highlights: A Selective Chronology of Italians in America, 1492–1985

**1492**   Christopher Columbus left the port of Palos, Spain, on August 3; after long, uncertain days and nights, he sighted the Island of San Salvador (one of the Caribbean islands), the date being October 12, 1492. Columbus was attempting a new route—by sea rather than by land, to the West rather than to the East—to the rich markets of India and China. In fact, Columbus carried with him a letter from King Ferdinand of Spain to his "Royal Brother," the Emperor of China.

**1493**   Christopher Columbus, realizing that his progress to the Orient had been interrupted by an unchartered landmass, made three other voyages to the new world, all in an attempt to bypass the landmass and reach the East. The dates of the later voyages were 1493, 1498, and 1502.

**1496**   John Cabot (Giovanni Caboto), an Italian, probably of Genoa, received from King Henry VII, of England, on March 5, 1496, letters-patent to find a short, high-latitude route to the Orient for trade purposes but especially for spices, such as pepper, cloves, and nutmeg, necessities in days of no refrigeration. Henry had turned down Columbus's request; he was not going to lose this opportunity for a faster, northern route to the land of trade and take title to lands that might be discovered.

**1497**   Amerigo Vespucci, a noble Florentine, was sent by the Bank of the Medici to Spain where he helped to outfit the ships for Columbus's second voyage in 1493. Vespucci made four voyages himself to the new world, the first two under the flags of Spain, in 1497 and 1499, the last two for Portugal in 1501 and 1503. In the course of these voyages, Vespucci followed the coastline of South America, made maps and astronomical observations such as to estimate the circumference of the earth, which he did with amazing accuracy. He also noted, for the first time, that the new land was a continent, not many small islands. These descriptions were so numerous and popular, so the story goes, that a German mapmaker, publishing the writings of Vespucci, said "Now a fourth part [of the world] has been found by Amerigo Vespucci, and I do not see why we should be prevented from calling it Amerige or America." Thus the name of America.

**1506**   Christopher Columbus died a very much saddened and disappointed man. S. E. Morison records a wry observation: "As a literary wit remarked, America was discovered by accident, not wanted when found, and early explorations were directed to finding a way through or around it."

**1524**   Giovanni da Verrazano, a Florentine explorer and humanist, was the first European to sail into New York Bay, record its exact position on a map, and give it a name, Angouleme, the family name of Francis I, King of France, under whose flag he sailed. Like Columbus and his other predecessors, Verrazano set out for the new world with the same purpose in mind.

**1524**   Verrazano's letter to Francis I, his official report of his discoveries, is a classic and a landmark in history. Like the narrative of Columbus, the report is first-hand, personal documentation on the exploration and description of the Atlantic coast of the United States and Canada—from the Carolinas to Newfoundland. The narrative is rich in detail of animals, trees, grasses, and wild flowers and a vivid eyewitness account of the American Indians. It is the earliest geographical, typographical, and ethnological survey of the previously undescribed coastline from Florida to Newfoundland.

**1539**   Friar Marco Da Nizza traveled the border of a desert, now known as the southern boundary of Arizona; crossing the desert he reached what is now the Gila Valley; and from the valley he touched the present region of Phoenix, Arizona.

**1639**   Peter Caesar Alberto is described in the historical archives of Kings County (New York) as "the Italian." He is regarded as the first Italian to reside in Brooklyn, then known as New Amsterdam. There is persuasive evidence that he later developed a large tobacco plantation in Wallabout Bay.

**1678**   Henri de Tonti, "the Man with the Iron Hand," arrived in America to serve with La Salle, the famous explorer, whose great aspiration it was to travel the full length of the Mississippi River from the Great Lakes down to the Gulf of Mexico and claim it all for the King of France. To pay for this venture, the fur trade had to be exploited to the full, and means of transportation had to be devised. Thus, Tonti built the first crude sailing vessel to sail on the Great Lakes.

**1682**   Henri de Tonti and La Salle, after torturous travel and heartbreaking hardships, explored the entire length of the Mississippi River to its delta where it empties into the Gulf of Mexico. They took possession in the name of Louis, King of France, and named the southern section Louisiana, after the King.

**1686**   Henri de Tonti built a fort and set up a trading post at the Arkansas River, the first European settlement in the state. Hence, Tonti is sometimes called the "father of Arkansas," and the Arkansas River was known for a while as La Riviere de Tonti (Tonti's River).

**1773**   Philip Mazzei arrived in Virginia. His revolutionary spirit and strong ideals of democracy quickly bound him by hoops of steel to Jefferson. Mazzei and Jefferson collaborated on a series of articles espousing political freedom. Mazzei's profound statement that "All men are by nature equally free and independent. This equality is essential to the establishment of a liberal government. . . . A truly republican form of government cannot exist except where all men—from the very rich to the very poor—are perfectly equal in natural rights" was the fierce conviction shared by Jefferson and Mazzei and was reflected in so much of the American constitutional theory. Mazzei's agricultural experimentation and introduction of new strains of flowers, fruits, and vegetables produced new eating patterns. Jefferson, a horticulturalist in his own right, admired Mazzei's skills and abilities with the soil. He was so impressed with the qualities of Mazzei's workers that he proposed expanded immigration from Italy.

**1774**   Giuseppe Maria Francesco Vigo, frontiersman and hero of the American Revolution, arrived in New Orleans, Louisiana, from Italy. Vigo was a shrewd fur trader whose wealth and knowledge of the forest trails and the Indian tribes substantially contributed to the conquest of the Northwest Territory. His financial contribution was so exhaustive that he died impoverished. Many years later the United States Supreme Court acknowledged $49,898.60 as compensation to his heirs for his contribution to the war.

**1776**   William Paca, as a member of the Continental Congress, signed the American Declaration of Independence. Prior to this, Paca had served in the Maryland legislature.

**1791**   Alessandro Malaspina headed a scientific expedition, surveying the Pacific coast from Alaska to Mexico.

**1801** Father Charles Constantine Pise was the first priest born in America (Maryland) of Italian extraction.

**1805** Lorenzo Da Ponte, of Italian-Jewish ancestry, came to America at age fifty-six. Father Da Ponte was a priest, linguist, and musician. He became the first teacher of Italian in New York City in 1806, and in 1825 he received an appointment as the first professor of Italian language and literature at Columbia College (now Columbia University) without benefit of any stipend. Da Ponte also wrote libretti for several of Mozart's operas.

**1819** Charles Botta wrote the first history of the American Revolution in Italian. A four-volume work, it was translated in 1834, under the title *A History of the War of Independence,* by Nathan Whiting, New Haven, Connecticut.

**1825** *Barber of Seville* was the first Italian opera to be sung at the Park Theatre in New York City.

**1829** Father Charles Constantine Pise wrote the first Catholic novel, entitled *Father Rowland, A North American Tale.*

**1835** Antonio Meucci, alleged to be the true inventor of the telephone, arrived in Cuba from Italy to become Superintendent of Mechanism and Scenic Designer of the Tacon Theatre (he was a mechanical engineer). While experimenting with electricity, by sheer chance, he heard a voice transmitted through an electric wire. To be near a source of technical equipment, he moved to New York in 1850.

**1837** John Phinizy probably was the first son of an Italian immigrant (Ferdinando Finizzi) to serve as mayor of an American city, Augusta, Georgia.

**1838** Philip Traetta, musician and composer from Venice, a friend of Presidents Madison and Monroe, established a conservatory of music in Boston, Massachusetts, and later established a second one in Philadelphia, Pennsylvania. He composed several musical works and was the author of *An Introduction to the Art and Science of Music* (1829) and *Vocal Exercises and Rudiments of the Art of Singing,* 2 vols. (1841–43).

**1850** Giuseppe Garibaldi arrived in New York as a political refugee. He lived with Antonio Meucci in Rosebank, Staten Island. They eked out a living by hunting, fishing, and making candles.

**1850** An Italian consulate was opened in San Francisco, California, headed by Colonel Leonetto Cipriani, to care for Italians on the West Coast.

**1854** The New York Academy of Music opened on Fourteenth Street at Third Avenue in Manhattan. Here opera found a permanent home and during its brilliant existence it hosted the most gifted artists of the day. Its inadequacy of size made imperative the Metropolitan Opera House in 1883.

**1855** Constantino Brumidi, the "Michelangelo of the United States Capitol," was employed by the Superintendent of the Capitol, Captain Montgomery C. Meigs, to decorate the Agriculture Committee room. This was the first example of fresco in America. Indeed, Brumidi's work was so magnificent that he was retained for the remainder of his life, a period of twenty-five years. During that time he decorated practically every important area of the Capitol, from the various rooms and chambers to the Capitol rotunda containing a frescoed frieze of fifteen historical groupings and capped by the huge frescoed canopy in the eye of the Capitol dome, measuring 4,664 square feet. A tragic near fall while working on the high scaffolding up in the rotunda terminated his work. He died shortly thereafter in 1880.

**1859**  St. Anthony of Padua Roman Catholic Church (located on Sullivan Street, New York City) was founded by the Franciscan Fathers to serve the Italian immigrants living in the lower Manhattan district. It is a well-known landmark which still attracts thousands of visitors.

**1861**  Gaetano Lanza founded the Massachusetts Institute of Technology and for twenty-nine years was head of the Department of Mechanical Engineering.

**1872**  Antonio Meucci tried to interest New York District Telegraph (branch of Western Union) in making an experimental trial of his telephone on their wires. They accepted his models and papers, but they gave him one excuse after the other for over two years. When in disgust he asked for his models, they simply stated they had lost them. In 1876, Alexander Graham Bell filed for the same idea. Meucci appealed to the Patent Office in Washington, D.C. The answer: all papers related to the "Speaking Telegraph" had disappeared from the file.

**1880**  *Il Progresso,* the first Italian daily newspaper in New York City and the United States, was established by Charles Barsotti, editor.

**1883**  The Metropolitan Opera House opened its doors to the thousands of opera lovers of New York City and indeed of the world.

**1887**  Francis B. Spinola, a Democrat, was the first Italian-American congressman from New York and the first Italian-American congressman in the United States.

**1889**  Mother Frances Cabrini arrived in America with six nuns to begin her apostolate among the Italian immigrants of New York. Her first work was to establish an orphanage with the help of Countess Di Cesnola.

**1891**  Scalabrinian Fathers started the Society of St. Raphael for Italian immigrants in New York City.

**1892**  Mother Frances Cabrini opened Columbus Hospital in New York City, which is still considered one of the finest hospitals today.

**1893**  Dr. E. O. Fenzi, horticulturist, also known as Dr. Franceschi, came to Santa Barbara, California, to cultivate the nearly barren soil of that area. He introduced many foreign and exotic plants and was successful in growing them in that very arid territory.

**1894**  Dr. Maria Montessori was the first woman in Italy to receive a medical degree. She developed methods of teaching children that emphasized the child's initiative and freedom of expression. Her methods have influenced teaching practices for three to six year olds all over the world. Her books include *The Montessori Method, Spontaneous Activity in Education, The Montessori Elementary Material,* and *Dr. Montessori's Own Handbook.*

**1897**  Luigi Amedeo Duca Delgi Abruzzi, explorer and mountain climber, led the first ascent of Mt. Elias in Alaska.

**1900**  Andrew Houston Longino was elected Governor of the State of Mississippi.

**1903**  Probably the most famous tenor of all times, Enrico Caruso, made his American debut on November 23, 1903, when he sang the first of 607 performances at the Met. His roles as Canio in *Pagliacci* and Radames in *Aida* made his fame worldwide.

**1903** Mother Frances Cabrini opened hospitals in Chicago, Seattle, Colorado, and Southern California.

**1904** Amadeo Giannini, banker and businessman, was the founder of the Bank of Italy in California. It is now called the Bank of America, the largest banking institution in the world.

**1905** Charles J. Bonaparte served as Secretary of the Navy under President Theodore Roosevelt, and was appointed Attorney General in 1906.

**1906** Amedeo Obici, businessman, was the founder of the Planters Peanuts enterprises in Virginia. He is known as the Peanut King of America.

**1908** Charles J. Bonaparte founded the Federal Bureau of Investigation. He died in 1921.

**1908** Arturo Toscanini opened the 1908 season of the Metropolitan Opera House on November 16 with *Aida.* The response was overwhelming. His preeminence as a conductor was established.

**1908** Giulio Gatti-Casazza (from La Scala) became general manager of the Metropolitan Opera Company and remained director until retirement in 1934. He introduced 110 works novel to the Metropolitan.

**1915** *Il Caroccio,* published in New York City from 1915 to 1935, a monthly bilingual cultural magazine dealing with social and political problems of Italian-Americans in America, was cofounded by Agostino De Biasi.

**1916** Fiorello H. La Guardia became a member of Congress, as Representative from the 14th Congressional District of Manhattan and was reelected in 1918 while in active service in the Air Force. He reentered Congress in 1922 as Representative from the 20th Congressional District, where he remained until 1932.

**1916** Giovanni Schiavo came to America from his native Italy. He probably did more to promote the Italian name than any other single person. His volumes speak for themselves: *Italians in Chicago,* 1928; *Italians in Missouri,* 1929; *Italians in America before the Civil War,* 1934; *Italian-American History,* 2 vols., 1947 and 1949.

**1921** After World War I, Congress hurriedly passed a new frankly restrictive law based on the principle of ethnic quotas. It limited immigrants of each nationality to 3 percent of the number of that nationality resident in the United States according to the census of 1910; and cut the total annual number of quota aliens to 357,000. The majority of immigrants from Southeastern Europe came too late to be recorded in the 1910 census. This was admittedly a discriminatory measure in favor of the Nordic migration.

**1924** The notorious National Origins law was passed. It reduced the quotas of the previous law of 1921 from 3 percent to 2 percent, and openly discriminated against Southern and Eastern Europeans by making the census of 1890 (rather than that of 1910 or 1920) the basis for its quotas. It also limited total immigration to 150,000 persons annually.

**1926** Arturo Toscanini's second career emerged when, as conductor of the Philharmonic Symphony Society of New York, from 1926 to 1936, he produced an orchestra which has since been unrivaled.

**1928** Alfred Emanuel ("Al") Smith, four-time governor of New York State, became the first Roman Catholic candidate to run for the highest office in the land.

**1933**  Fiorello H. La Guardia was elected Mayor of New York City. On news of his election, the Italians of New York City danced in the streets.

**1937**  Arturo Toscanini conducted the NBC Symphony Orchestra until 1954, at which time his farewell performance produced a sensational outburst of admiration, joy, and sorrow.

**1938**  Enrico Fermi received the Nobel Prize for his experiments with radioactivity. The citation read as follows: "To Enrico Fermi of Rome for his identification of new radioactive elements produced by neutron bombardment and his discovery made in connection with this work, of nuclear reactions effected by slow neutrons."

**1941**  Enrico Fermi became involved in the all-out effort to produce the atomic bomb. In 1942 he relocated to Chicago with the rest of the team working on the bomb. In 1943 the operation was moved to Los Alamos in New Mexico. On July 15, 1945, the first atomic bomb was exploded at Alamogordo (White Sands), New Mexico.

**1942**  Charles Poletti, Lieutenant Governor of New York State, became governor when Herbert Lehman was elected to the United States Senate.

**1943**  Sergeant John Basilone, World War II Marine hero, was the first enlisted Marine in World War II to receive the Congressional Medal of Honor. He was killed on the first day of the invasion of Iwo Jima in 1944. He was awarded the Navy Cross posthumously. General MacArthur called him a "one-man army."

**1946**  Mother Frances Xavier Cabrini, a United States citizen, was canonized by Pope Pius XII.

**1948**  The Italian Historical Society of America was founded by John La Corte to promote and foster the Italian heritage and its contributions to American civilization. La Corte was the person most instrumental in having the Narrows Span called the Verrazano Bridge.

**1950**  John O. Pastore, of Rhode Island, was elected United States Senator, the highest elective office to date achieved by anyone of Italian lineage.

**1950**  In this election year four Italian-Americans ran for the office of Mayor of the City of New York, Vincent Impelliteri, Ferdinand Pecora, Edward Corsi, and Vito Marcantonio. Impelliteri, an Independent, won. He was the second Italian-American to hold the highest executive position in the City of New York.

**1952**  John J. Muccio was appointed Ambassador Extraordinary to Korea. Prior to that time, at the end of World War II, he served as political advisor to the Supreme Allied Command in Germany.

**1956**  Alberto D. Rosselini was elected Governor of the State of Washington.

**1956**  John J. Marchi was elected to the New York State Senate.

**1956**  Foster Furcolo, a liberal Democrat, was elected Governor of Massachusetts.

**1958**  Michael V. Di Salle was elected Governor of Ohio.

**1959**  Emilio Segrè, physicist, was awarded the Nobel Prize. He was a pupil, close friend, and collaborator with Enrico Fermi during most of Fermi's active years as a scientist.

**1961**  John Anthony Volpe was elected Governor of Massachusetts and re-elected in 1965.

**1961**    The Mutual Educational and Cultural Exchange Act was enacted. This law promoted cultural and educational programs with every country in the world. As it affected the Italians in America, however, during its first seven years of existence, the act appropriated grants to 1,660 Italian students, teachers, specialists, lecturers, and research scholars to come to the United States. For the same period, 1,470 American students, teachers, lecturers, researchers, and specialists received grants to go to Italy. This was one of a multitude of cultural exchanges effected under the act.

**1963**    President John F. Kennedy, by special message to Congress, urged total revision of the anachronistic immigration legislation. He asked for a law which would reflect "in every detail the principle of equality and human dignity, to which our nation subscribes."

**1964**    Ralph J. Menconi, sculptor, designed the John F. Kennedy Memorial Medal and the President Lyndon B. Johnson Medal. He produced more than 300 medallion portraits including those of fourteen Presidents.

**1965**    Following the strong pleas of four presidents—Truman, Eisenhower, Kennedy, and Johnson—Congress passed the Immigration and Nationality Amendments of 1965. Said President Johnson, as he signed the bill into law, this "corrects a cruel and enduring wrong in the conduct of the American nation. . . . Those who come will come because of what they are—not because of the land from which they spring." The amendments provided for the gradual elimination of the national origins formula over a period of three years.

**1965**    Peter W. Rodino, United States Congressman from New Jersey, was instrumental in removing discriminatory national quotas and in humanizing the country's immigration program by introducing a bill to amend the Immigration and Nationality Act.

**1965**    Michael Musmanno, lawyer, judge and author, wrote *The Italians in America.* He was one of a team of lawyers defending Sacco and Vanzetti in the murder trial of 1927. He wrote a strong plea in their defense in his book *After Twelve Years,* 1939. President Harry S. Truman appointed him one of the presiding judges at the International War Crimes Trials in Nuremberg in 1946. He also authored his minority opinions while on the Pennsylvania bench, appropriately titled *Musmanno Dissents,* 1939.

**1965**    The Center for Migration Studies, Staten Island, New York, was formed to house and preserve documents, photographs, memoirs, and private papers of organizations and individuals reflecting the experience of Italians in the United States. The center is open to researchers and graduate students interested in the history and sociology of the Italians in America.

**1967**    Peter W. Rodino, United States Congressman from New Jersey, succeeded in making Columbus Day a national holiday.

**1968**    Francis J. Mugavero was ordained Bishop of the Diocese of Brooklyn, New York. Bishop Mugavero was the first ecclesiastic of Italian extraction to achieve the highest office of one of the greatest dioceses in the world.

**1969**    Salvador Luria, biologist, was the corecipient of the Nobel Prize for Medicine for discoveries concerning the replication mechanism and the genetic structure of viruses.

**1975**    Renato Dulbecco (with David Baltimore and Howard Martin Temin) was awarded the Nobel Prize for medical research in genetics.

**1977**  Michael Cristofer was awarded the Pulitzer Prize for drama for *The Shadow Box.*

**1978**  Ella Grasso was elected Governor of Connecticut.

**1978**  A. Bartlett Giamatti was appointed President of Yale University.

**1982**  Mario Cuomo was elected Governor of New York.

**1982**  Joseph Bernardin was appointed Cardinal of Chicago.

**1984**  Geraldine Ferraro was nominated to be the Democratic Party candidate for Vice President, the first woman chosen as a major party nominee and the first Italian-American ever to run for national office (unless one counts Al Smith, whose maternal grandfather was Italian).

# The Immigrant Experience

## Ellis Island

The ferry eased into the boat slip. Fifty-eight years after my father stepped ashore there, and more than six decades after my maternal grandparents, I set foot on Ellis Island. Historians refer to it as the "Golden Door" or "The Gate of Freedom," but to immigrants it was—in many languages—"the Island of Tears."

My father—accompanied by my grandfather—had come through Ellis Island at the age of thirteen. Once in New York, he went to work nights in a bakery; during the day, he assisted my grandfather, a tailor. They brought over my father's three sisters, one by one. Only my father's brother, four years old when the rest of the family left Palermo, never made it to America.

Today, Ellis Island's French Renaissance-style buildings, of red brick and white stone, look almost new—at least from the outside. Not much different from the many photographs of them I'd seen all my life. But there is a strangeness about the place. A few feet away, the hull of the old ferry boat, *Ellis Island,* rests motionless at the bottom of a shallow slip. In fifty years of service, shuttling the one mile between the Island and the lower tip of Manhattan, it had logged a total of forty million miles. Its skeletal, sun-bleached upper deck is above water and still shows hints of its distinctive white paint. It lists hard to one side, its single, rusted, black funnel tilting crazily toward the Island's hospital.

But most unsettling of all was the forlorn quiet of the Island, emptied of its "huddled masses" of rag-tag immigrants, rope-tied bundles filling their arms, burdening their backs, numbered tags gripped between their teeth.

The first building I entered was the cavernous baggage room. Immigrants were urged to leave their parcels there for convenience. Few consented to abandon their possessions. They were permitted to bring into the country only what they could carry. Every-

Waiting for the boat in Naples

Naples

Italian family at Ellis Island ca. 1910 (Joseph Kossuth Dixon Collection)

thing they owned was in those boxes, baskets, and sacks, and hard experience had taught them never to let them out of their sight. Most of the arrivals, weary and often sick from the journey in the foul steerage of ships, carried everything with them throughout the long, slow, snaking march through the "processing" buildings.

Now the U.S. National Park Service has charge of the Island, and I listened as earnest college-age guides in Smokey the Bear hats tried to conjure up for us visitors the desperation of people as they were subjected to the Island's inspections and interrogations. I glanced around at the other tourists. How could we understand the threat of being sent back to grinding poverty in Italy, or to conscription into the czar's armies in Eastern Europe, or to a famine-stricken Ireland under British domination?

Mario La Mastro remembers the Island in its busiest time. He came in 1919, from Teano, near Naples, on the French ship *Patria*. (In the late 1940s Mario read in a newspaper that the same ship had been sunk while carrying illegal Jewish immigrants to Palestine.) He was thirteen at the time, traveling with his mother, eighty-six-year-old grandmother, uncle, and three of his uncle's family. They had been sent for by Mario's father, who had come to the United States and labored for seven years to bring over his family. Mario's father was a skilled shoemaker, but his trade had provided less than a living in Teano. Those few who bought shoes usually paid in goods. In Campania, the province surrounding Naples, unemployment ran as high as 65 percent, and a barter system replaced cash business. In later years, Mario's mother was to say, "Better to be dead in America than alive in Italy."

The *Patria* took sixteen days to cross the Atlantic. Mario spent them in the men's section of the steerage hold, his bunk on the top of five tiers. He hung on with both hands as the ship pitched and rolled through the November Atlantic weather. Once in New York harbor, the ship was quarantined for two days because of sickness on board.

Finally the La Mastro family was ferried to Ellis Island, carrying wool stuffing from their mattresses in Teano, a luxurious possession in Italy. Mario remembers meeting an Italian woman in her eighties on the Island. She was dressed in black, traveling alone. The officials tied a tag around her neck. On it they wrote her destination: California. She would go to the Island's "railroad room" where she could buy a rail ticket and from which she would be ferried to the mainland rail lines in New Jersey.

A tag was tied to Mario's wrist, and he settled down on a bench with his family to await his father. "There were bars all over the place," he recalls. His father arrived, recognizable to Mario only through pictures. The La Mastro family stood anxiously before a high, round desk while his father proved to an official that he had a job and enough income to support his family. After a lengthy questioning, they were admitted to the United States and went to the lodgings Mario's father had rented for them at 506 Metropolitan Avenue in Brooklyn—a converted stable, with horses just beyond their wall next door.

Mario grows pensive for a moment. "You know," he says, "this is the first time I have talked about Ellis Island since I arrived there exactly sixty years ago this month. I guess for us, we wanted to forget it."

Maria Baccili has not forgotten Ellis Island, where she arrived, at age twenty-one, in September 1927, carrying her eighteen-month-old son in her arms. Her husband, Pietro, had come earlier and had sent for them. He had a history of migrations. Born in Brazil, where his Italian parents had gone seeking a better life, he went to Italy at the age of nineteen. He met Maria in a small village near Lucca, and they were married in 1923. Pietro found a job in a marble quarry. "There was just enough work to keep going," Maria remembers. They decided to try their luck in America.

Maria and her son were detained on Ellis Island for two days and nights—first, because they had arrived on a holiday weekend, and second, because they were suspected of

Teaching immigrant students the Constitution (Photo by Dorothea Lange, Courtesy of the National Archives)

having an infectious skin disease. (Actually, the "disease" turned out to be inflamed insect bites, a souvenir of the ship.)

"It was a harsh place," Maria says, gesturing emphatically with her hands. *Severo* is the word she repeats again and again in describing it. "All the walls were covered with white tiles. The guards didn't speak Italian, and they never smiled." At night she, her baby, and another woman were locked into a detention room by a guard with a huge ring of keys. Maria was ill from an intestinal disorder. And scared. Her baggage, containing all her possessions in the New World, had been taken from her.

On Monday, the Island's staff returned to work and Pietro was able to take his wife and son off the Island. The area in the Bronx where Maria and Pietro settled was farmland, cultivated by Italian immigrants, mostly Neapolitans, who grew all sorts of vegetables. Goats wandered on Gun Hill Road, now one of the busiest thoroughfares in New York City. Maria worked in a laundry with Pietro until the birth of their second child; she then quit and began making money by knitting sweaters and embroidering infants' wear at home.

Would she still make the trip to America if she had to do it over? Maria's twinkling eyes and cheerful face become serious. "I don't know how to answer that," she says. "My children are here, but my brother, sister, and *nipoti* are still in Italy." How many nieces and nephews? She counts for a moment. "Fourteen," she laughs. She pauses again. "But the Church of the Immaculate Conception on Gun Hill Road . . . the Italians were already building it when we came. We finished it in 1930. It's beautiful. Bella!"

The interiors of Ellis Island's buildings today are not belli. They are in terrible disrepair. They haven't received any maintenance, any heat in winter or ventilation in summer, in twenty-five years. Paint and plaster bubble and peel hideously. Whole sections of ceilings and interior walls have fallen, leaving huge rotting cavities. The large staircase which led from the baggage area up to the great halls has been dismantled. Every one of the immigrants who came through the Island climbed those steps. Unbeknownst to them, they were taking the Island's first medical examination.

Doctors stood at the top of the stairs. Their eyes searched out anyone having difficulty, anyone breathing too hard, limping, or sweating too much. Such people were pulled from the procession. Their clothing was marked with white chalk—an L for lame, an H for heart and lungs. (Tuberculosis, then unarrestable, was the leading disease causing death in the United States at the turn of the century.) They were escorted by uniformed officials—and they feared uniforms with Old-World dread—to steel-mesh cages that lined both sides of the Great Hall. All the H's, all the L's, and so forth, were put together, detained for extensive examination and observation.

The Great Hall is 200 feet long, 100 feet wide, and its vaulted ceiling is 56 feet high. Its floor was divided by iron fences into a maze of narrow passages through which the immigrants shuffled up and down to the various examinations. Five thousand people every day. Uniformed officials sat behind desks at points along the line. The desks were high, like those of court judges, which was fitting because the new arrivals depended on those officials for acceptance or rejection to the new land. Translators shouted their rapid-fire questions over a veritable babel of noise.

"They would try to trick us," a woman recalled. A few minutes after answering that she had never been married, the interpreter asked casually, "What was your husband's first name again?"

An official wrote the response in a file envelope. A wrong or suspicious response would lead to his calling one of the guards who roamed the hall. He would take the person out of the line, chalk an SI on his clothes for "Special Inquiry," and lock him or her in a cage with other SI's. Later, each SI would face a board of interrogators seated at a table in an inquiry room. A particularly tricky question for single women was "Who sent for you?" If she answered, "My fiancé," she was detained until he showed up. Frequently, officials required that a marriage ceremony be performed on Ellis Island before they would allow the woman to enter the country.

The remaining immigrants moved along to another medical exam—of the face, neck, hair, and hands. Those with lice or possible infectious skin diseases were sent into cages. The next exam was the "mental" one, to discover the "feebleminded." It consisted of being asked "common-sense questions." For example, literate immigrants might be shown a watch and asked to tell the time.

There was still more interrogation at the next desk. Two of the most troublesome questions for Italians were "Do you have a job waiting?" and "Who paid your passage?" Being the poorest of the large national groups immigrating, Italians often could not pay the cost of their passage. Many signed labor contracts, agreeing, in return for a ticket, to work for a boss (*padrone*) in the United States—for exploitative wages and a length of time set by the padrone. The problem: the U.S. Congress had made the practice illegal, forcing many Italians to become liars on entering their new country.

The most dreaded exam for many was the "buttonhook exam" for trachoma, a highly contagious disease, then incurable, which caused blindness. A doctor took an ordinary iron hook used to lace up the high, buttoned shoes of the era and now used for ice-skate laces. He would, when he didn't forget to do so, dip it in an antiseptic solution. Then he would place it over the eyelid of the immigrant, and pull the lid all the way back.

People balked. Children screamed and fought. The exam was the bottleneck in the processing.

All in all, the work of the Island was awesome. During its peak period, one million arrivals per year came through it. (Its present buildings, opened in 1900, were made to handle at most a half million a year.) The former supervising historian of the National Park Service, Thomas M. Pitkin, wrote in his excellent 1975 study that the history of Ellis Island was "plagued by corruption, swindling, brutality, and exploitation, on the Island and near it (con men and thugs waited for the successful immigrants to land in Manhattan's Battery); attacks from restrictionists and antirestrictionists alike; misunderstanding with distant superiors who were often subjected to powerful lobby pressure; increasingly complex legislation to be applied at once to exhausted human beings, and enormous numbers of people to be sifted through inadequate facilities as quickly as possible." The Island's superintendent in 1907, Robert Watchorn, was moved to complain, "A saint from heaven actuated by all his saintliness would fail to give satisfaction in this place."

The U.S. government, using incomplete records, claims that 80 percent of the immigrants passed all exams and were off the Island in one day, leaving the other 20 percent behind. For Italians, padrone-linked and frequently diseased because of poor living conditions at home, the percentage of detainees was undoubtedly higher. Before the lucky ones could board the ferry for Manhattan, they were taken to the Island's money exchange. There, as often as not, they were cheated. At one point cigar coupons were distributed as U.S. currency. Although the Italian government bombastically spoke of its "subjects" in its "American colonies," it provided no real protection for them on the Island; American officials did little better. Scandal after scandal marks the Island's record. In October 1921, *Outlook* magazine commented that Ellis Island was "one of the most efficient factories in the world for the production of hatred for America and American institutions." Around the same time, New York City's Commissioner of Health inspected the Island. He found that five times more doctors were needed to handle the medical problems there. A pile of vermin-infested blankets had been used the night before by immigrants sleeping on the floor. Moreover, there was a backlog of fifteen thousand immigrants locked in the steerage holds of ships in the harbor, waiting to be taken to the Island. The Newspaper Enterprise Association investigated Ellis Island and found:

• Immigrants herded like cattle in the ill-ventilated, fetid detention rooms.

• Vermin on the walls and floors of detention rooms and dormitories.

• Immigrants forced to sleep indiscriminately two in a bed or on the floor.

• Only 1,100 beds, though the overnight population averaged from 2,000 to 3,000 and went as high as 4,500.

• No mattresses for beds—only blankets spread over strips of steel; bunks built in tiers, three high.

• Only six bathtubs for use of all women and small children.

• No bathtubs for men; thousands forced to use sixteen showers.

• Lavatories so inadequate that they were a menace to health.

• Many washbasins on upper floors without water.

• Only two pumps, with low water pressure, inadequate against fire.

• Many immigrants forced to wait weeks because affidavits and money sent by relatives had been lost.

Appropriately, on Ellis Island one has a fine view of the nearby Statue of Liberty. But of Miss Liberty's back. Only those admitted to Manhattan would see her face.

*Richard Gambino*

THE SOCIETY FOR THE PROTECTION OF ITALIAN IMMIGRANTS

Entrance to the City from the Ellis Island Boat at Battery.

Here "Runners" formerly fleeced the Newcomers.

OFFICE,

17 PEARL STREET, NEW YORK.

TELEPHONE, 3641 BROAD.

# Advice for Those Who Intend to Emigrate to North America

If real necessity urges you to quit your native land, before undergoing any expense, enter into communication with the Society for Protection established in Italy. Explain your case to them, seek their advice, whether or not it will be profitable for you to come to America.

Remember that the aged, the deformed, the blind, deaf mutes, and all suffering from contagious diseases, mental aberration, or any other infirmities, are inexorably excluded from American soil. Likewise are they excluded who have at any time been condemned to prison for crime, or come here bound by contract to some determined work previously agreed upon by the employer. I might add here by way of advice, that bookkeepers, clerks, amanuenses, teachers, students who have interrupted their dreams and relying on their talents, felt sure that in a short time they would have amassed a fortune. But a few weeks in America sufficed to show them the true state of affairs, and unwilling to beg, they were obliged to take up the pick-axe and shovel. This they continued but a few days when, with swollen and lacerated hands, tattered clothing, and almost shoeless, they had recourse to me as a last resort. Many of this class have been provided by the Society with the means to return to Italy.

If you are advised to leave Italy for America, procure from the Committee of Patronage or their correspondents a ticket of recommendation. Procure likewise the exact address of relatives and friends, if you have any in America. Before leaving the vessel, see that you receive a brass check for each parcel of your baggage; otherwise you will experience great difficulty in securing it after you land.

*St. Raphael's Italian Benevolent Society, 1891*

# The Trial of Sacco and Vanzetti

On April 15, 1920, in the small town of South Braintree, Massachusetts, two employees of a shoe factory were shot and killed, and a payroll of over $15,000 was stolen by the murderers. Nicola Sacco, shoemaker, and Bartolomeo Vanzetti, fish peddler, were arrested, tried, and in 1921 were convicted of the crime in Dedham, Massachusetts. They were executed six years later, on August 23, 1927. During their years in prison all appeals and motions for a new trial were denied, and controversy over their innocence or guilt stirred the country and the world.

The trial took place during the period of a Red scare in which U.S. Attorney General A. Mitchell Palmer waged a vigorous and undoubtedly unconstitutional war against aliens and radicals. Mass arrests, invasions of homes, and the holding of persons without hearings or trials became known as the Palmer raids.

Sacco and Vanzetti were Italian-born anarchists who had continued their radical activity among the Italian colony in eastern Massachusetts. Because of their opposition to the war, both had evaded the draft in 1917 by going to Mexico. Millions believed that

Sacco and Vanzetti (Lithograph by Ben Shahn, 1959)

they were convicted less because of the evidence, which was wholly circumstantial, than because of their political philosophy. The trial judge, Webster Thayer, was thought to be biased; the cross-examination, especially of Sacco, highly improper; and various witnesses for the prosecution unworthy of belief.

When Judge Thayer imposed the sentence of death on April 9, 1927, there was a great public outcry for a new trial. Protest meetings were held throughout the nation and appeals were made to Governor Alvan T. Fuller. A remarkable array of American and world intellectuals joined the protests: Sherwood Anderson, Romain Rolland. H. G. Wells, Edna St. Vincent Millay, Sinclair Lewis, Albert Einstein, and Thomas Mann, to name a few. Felix Frankfurter, then a Harvard law professor, wrote an article in the *Atlantic Monthly* pointing out Thayer's prejudices and errors, as well as the contradictions in the prosecution's case.

During the last months of appeals, demonstrations and strikes took place in Belgrade, Buenos Aires, Berlin, Moscow, Havana, and cities in Asia, Africa, and Australia.

In response to the mounting protests, Governor Fuller appointed a committee of three to advise him: A. Lawrence Lowell, president of Harvard; Samuel Stratton, president of M.I.T.; and Judge Robert Grant. The committee found that the judicial procedure had been correct. The committee was then also accused of contradictions, errors, and suppression of evidence. It seemed that public opinion had placed American justice and the justice of the Commonwealth of Massachusetts on trial.

Although proof of Sacco and Vanzetti's innocence or guilt can never be established, it can be unequivocally stated that they were not given a fair trial due to the atmosphere of prejudice and hostility that prevailed in the courtroom. This fact was officially recognized fifty years after their execution in a proclamation issued by the governor of Massachusetts, Michael S. Dukakis, designating August 23, 1977, "Nicola Sacco and Bartolomeo Vanzetti Memorial Day" and declaring that "any stigma and disgrace should be forever removed from the names of Nicola Sacco and Bartolomeo Vanzetti, from the names of their families and descendents, and so, from the name of the Commonwealth of Massachusetts. . . ."

*Armand V. Mauro*

# The Mafia: Setting the Myth Straight

*Mafia is a term that has plagued Italian-Americans from the moment they arrived in this country. And despite the fact that more and more Italians are upright and educated citizens, the fantasy continues that we are somehow linked inextricably to criminals and violence. Indeed, by now the Mafia has become part of American folklore and will never be entirely erased from prevailing mythology.*

*How did this cruel stereotype originate? How much of it is a reality? How much a distortion? Professor William Helmreich, a sociologist at the City University of New York, explores these questions.*

The beginnings of the Mafia go back at least as far as the thirteenth century, when the Sicilian Vespers tried to drive the French out of Sicily. The word itself is of uncertain origin. Some claim it is an acronym for *Morte alla Francia Italia anela* (Italy desires France's death). Others attribute it to a slogan used in the days when Giuseppe Mazzini was battling the Bourbons—Mazzini Autorizza Furti, Incendi, Avvelenamenti (Mazzini authorizes thievery, arson, and poisoning). Over the centuries numerous secret organizations were established to fight against foreign domination. Gradually these groups

Edward G. Robinson in the film classic *Little Caesar*

became a permanent feature of Southern Italy. The term Mafia came into common use during the nineteenth century, when the organization—actually a loose confederation of many societies—greatly expanded its operations, particularly in western Sicily. Sometimes they were nothing more than extortionists and thieves, while at other times they were vanguard members of political movements fighting against either the landowners or the peasants. By the twentieth century, however, the Mafia in Italy had become synonymous with greed and corruption, as its members sought only to increase their power and maximize their profits.

The term mafia, when not capitalized, had a different connotation among Italians. It was an adjective used to describe someone who commanded respect, who knew how to "take care of things" without running to the authorities. It referred to an individual who had both power and dignity while also inspiring fear. He was, most importantly, a person whom one could approach when in need. Thus, such a term might be applied to a family patriarch who had no connection with the organization known as the Mafia. Such values were deeply rooted in the culture and heritage of Southern Italian peasant society. All too often Americans who heard this term used by the newcomers when conversing among themselves confused the adjective with the noun.

Although they were only a small minority of the immigrant population, the stereotype that all Italian-Americans from Southern Italy belonged to the Mafia was quite popular in this country around the turn of the century. Two incidents were highly instrumental in the development of this attitude. The first took place in 1890 in New Orleans, where eleven Italians were lynched by an angry mob after the police chief, David Hennessy, was murdered. Although a court failed to find anyone guilty, the prevalent belief was that the Mafia had been behind it. (Hennessy had been investigating extortion in the local Italian community.) The second incident concerned a New York City police lieutenant who was killed by a Mafia chieftain in Palermo, Sicily, where he had gone to look into possible connections between organized crime in America and Sicily. The attendant publicity greatly heightened the suspicion and hostility with which Americans viewed Southern Italians.

When the fascists came to power in Italy during the 1920s and began a campaign against the Mafia, many came to the United States hoping to get rich quickly. Their optimism was justified, for this was the era of Prohibition, when qualities such as ruthlessness, lust for power, and a tightly knit organization paid off. The Mafia established itself in American crime circles and has remained there ever since. True, the Jews and the Irish had their gangs too—actually, the Irish got started long before the Italians—but neither group had a history of criminal activity that stretched back for centuries. What all three groups did have in common was a willingness to use crime as a vehicle for economic betterment. The Irish were influential in politics and, of course, they had always controlled the Catholic Church hierarchy in the United States. As for the Jews, their strong belief in education, as well as their experience in commerce, helped them immeasurably in their efforts at raising their status. The Italian-Americans had none of these advantages, and subsequent to Prohibition many became involved in gambling, prostitution, contract murder, and loan-sharking. The majority, it should be added, were law-abiding citizens who were nonetheless stigmatized as criminals by the larger society.

While hardly anyone today would deny the existence of a Mafia organization made up almost solely of Italian-Americans (not to mention a very active one in Italy), relatively few Italian-Americans belong to it. In a 1967 article that appeared in *Life* magazine, writer Sandy Smith put the number of Mafia or Cosa Nostra (Our Thing or Our Affair, a synonym for Mafia) members at about five thousand. In *Blood of My Blood* author Richard Gambino estimated the membership at approximately five to six thousand, a small figure when one considers that there are over twenty million Italian-Americans in the United States. Why, then, has the stereotype survived? For one thing, the Mafia makes excellent copy and entertainment. With its Black Hand symbol, its code of *omertà* (requiring silence, which is actually part of Italian culture in general), and its unique customs and rituals, it has provided material for countless books, movies, and television programs. . . .

Helped by TV series such as "The Untouchables" and "The F.B.I.," plus movies like *The Godfather* and books such as *Honor Thy Father,* by Gay Talese, the term Mafia has become synonymous with crime of every sort. Thus people will talk about a "Mafia-type organization" that has no Italian members, or they will accuse someone of "Mafia tactics," which both perpetuates the stereotype and demonstrates how pervasive it is. The popularity of the term makes it harder to deal with the stereotype because whenever the word is uttered the speaker is almost always aware of its Italian origin. . . .

The Mafia's days as a criminal organization are numbered despite its long though not so venerable history. The main factor is competition from Latins and blacks, who have the same economic needs and lack of legitimate opportunities that faced their ethnic forbears of sixty years ago. In some cases actual wars have erupted, while in others, such as New York's East Harlem, the area has simply been "leased" to others, who then "work the neighborhood." Government efforts to destroy the syndicates have also sapped its strength. Finally, the increased opportunities for upward mobility that await young Italians means that fewer and fewer will see crime as an attractive alternative. The extinction of this stereotype will come as a great relief to most Italians, for never have so few been given credit for being so many.

# Politics

## Luigi Antonini

Luigi Antonini was probably the most prominent Italian-American labor leader in the history of American trade unionism.

Born in Vallata in Southern Italy in 1883, Antonini came to New York City in 1908 and worked as a presser in the dress industry. He soon became active in the International Ladies Garment Workers' Union. The conditions of the garment workers at the time were deplorable; they came to public attention as a result of the tragic Triangle fire in New York City, in which 147 working women lost their lives.

In 1916 he became a paid union official. He was instrumental in the formation of an independent local of Italian dressmakers in 1919. The local, of which he was manager until his death, took the charter number 89 after the ideals of the French Revolution—liberty, fraternity, and equality—symbolized by the storming of the Bastille in 1789.

In the early 1920s Antonini fought both communist and fascist infiltration of Local 89. Through his weekly radio talks on the "Voice of 89," he promoted democracy and progressive trade unionism among the Italian-American community. By 1933, Local 89 had forty thousand members and had become the largest local in Italian-American labor. Antonini also became the New York State chairman of the American Labor Party, which in the late 1930s and early 1940s became an important factor in local, state, and national elections.

Luigi Antonini died in 1968. He is remembered for his courage and devotion to the cause of democracy and to decency in political life and the workplace.

# Mario Cuomo

Cuomo's election in 1982 as New York's fifty-second governor was a triumph for the son of an immigrant grocer and the first time an Italian-surnamed candidate had attained that job by election (Lieutenant Governor Charles Poletti had briefly been governor in the 1940s). Representing the liberal wing of the Democratic Party, he brought to the job a wealth of experience in law and public service.

Cuomo was born in 1932 in Queens, New York, to natives of Salerno. His father was a ditchdigger and pushcart peddler before opening an Italian-American grocery. Cuomo attended St. John's University on an athletic scholarship and went on to St. John's Law School. He practiced law in a Brooklyn firm where he eventually became partner.

He also taught at St. John's and represented community groups. He was involved in a heated controversy in the middle-class neighborhood of Forest Hills, Queens, where city planners wanted to construct low-income housing. Negotiating a plan in which the density and number of housing units were significantly reduced, Cuomo was able to resolve what had verged on being a major crisis; later he published *Forest Hills Diary: The Crisis of Low-Income Housing.*

As secretary of state under Governor Hugh Carey from 1974 to 1978, Cuomo led a major investigation of nursing home scandals, leading to the appointment of a special prosecutor.

After serving as lieutenant governor with Carey from 1978 to 1982, Cuomo made his own bid to become governor during the next election and won. He garnered national acclaim with his brilliant opening speech at the Democratic National Convention in 1984.

### Cuomo's 1984 Gubernatorial Inauguration Address

Like everyone in this room today, and everyone in this state today, I am the offspring of immigrants.

My parents came some sixty years ago from another part of this world, driven by deprivation, without funds, without education, without skills.

When my mother arrived at Ellis Island, she was alone and afraid. She carried little more than a suitcase and a piece of paper with the address of a laborer husband who had preceded her looking for work. She passed through all the small indignities visited on immigrants everywhere always. She was subjected to the hurried condescension of those who decide if others are good enough to enter, or at least not bad enough to be kept out.

Like millions of others, my mother and father came here with very little more than a willingness to spend all their effort in honest toil. They asked only for the opportunity to work and for some protection in those moments when they would not be able to protect themselves.

Thanks to a government that was wise enough to help without stifling them, and strong enough to provide with opportunities to earn their own bread, they survived. They remained a people of modest means. But that they were able to build a family, and live in dignity, and see one of their children go from behind their little grocery store in South Jamaica where he was born to the highest seat in the greatest state, in the greatest nation.

That by itself is an almost ineffably beautiful commentary on this magnificent system of American democracy. But this is not a personal story. This is the story of all of us.

What our imperfect but peerless system of government has done for those two frightened immigrants from Europe, it has done for millions of others in different ways. That experience is a source of pride and gratitude, but it has to be much more. It must serve as a challenge to all of us, as we face the future. The achievements of our past impose upon us the obligation to do at least as much for those who come after us.

It would be a terrible desecration of our history to allow the difficulties of the moment, which pale when compared to those faced by our ancestors to excuse our obligation to produce government that excels at doing what government is supposed to do. We need not fear the challenge. Underlying everything I believe about our government is an unshakable conviction that it is good enough to do what must be done and more.

Through all of our present travail . . . the deficits, the hordes of homeless, unemployed and victimized, the loss of spirit and belief. . . . I believe that we are wise enough to address our deficits without taxing ourselves into bankruptcy, strong enough to reconcile order with justice, brave enough to bring opportunity and hope to those who have neither. We can, and we will, refuse to settle for just survival and certainly not just survival of the fittest.

I believe we can balance our lives and our society even as we balance our books. We can. To those who today stand on platforms built by their forebears' pain and are warmed by applause earned by their forebears' courage, remember who we are, and where we came from and what we have been taught.

Those who made our history taught us above all things the idea of family, mutuality, the sharing of benefits and burdens fairly for the good of all. There's an ideal essential to our success and no family that favored its strong children or that in the name of evenhandedness failed to help its vulnerable ones would be worthy of the name. And no state or nation that chooses to ignore its troubled regions and people, while watching others thrive, can call itself justified.

We must be the family of New York. Feeling one another's pain, sharing one another's blessings equitably, honestly, fairly, without respect to geography or race or political affiliation. Those who made our history taught us more. By a willingness to sweat for a lifetime just to give their children something better, they taught us the virtue of hard work. These things, then, I pledge as I begin my term.

But I have learned what they had to teach. That if we do not succeed, it will not be because we have divided one part of this state from another, or dealt unfairly with any region, or any group of people or forgotten that we are a family.

Nor will it be because we have failed to expend the strength and effort that we might have. This will be a government as hard working and realistic as the thousands of families and businesses struggling to survive a national economy that is more distressed at this moment than at any time since the 1930s.

I have no illusions about how difficult this will be. It will require that we pass a fierce test of our resolve. But if the risks we face are greater, the resources we command are greater still.

A rich good earth; water that ties us together, replenishes us, feeds our capacity to grow; an education system matched by few other states, indeed even nations, anywhere in the world; an irreplaceable weave of roads and rails; the world's largest banks and financial institutions, communications systems and markets.

And more than all of this, our marvelous people, the offspring of native Americans, Africans, Europeans, Asians, people from the North and people from the South, the children of those who refused to stop reaching, stop building, stop believing, the children of those who refused to believe it could not be done. We are the sons and daughters of giants, and we have been born to their greatness.

We begin to meet our obligation today, all of us together. So good people of the Empire State, I ask all of you, whatever your political beliefs, whatever your region, whatever you think of me as an individual, to help me keep the moving and awesome oath that I just swore before you and before God.

Pray that we all see New York for the family that it is. That all of us sworn into office today give New York the leadership it deserves. That I might be the state's good servant and God's, too. And Pop, wherever you are, and I think I know, for all the "cerimonie" and the big house and the pomp and circumstance, please don't let me forget.

Thank you and God bless you.

# *Geraldine Anne Ferraro*

Largely unknown outside Queens political circles when first elected to the House of Representatives in 1978, Democratic Congresswoman Geraldine A. Ferraro quickly established a reputation as a moderate to liberal pragmatic politician. She is concerned with events that profoundly affect her conservative working- and middle-class district.

Ferraro was born in 1935 in Newburgh, New York, the daughter of an Italian immigrant father who died in 1943. She went to Marymount School in Tarrytown on a scholarship and then to Marymount College.

Later, Ferraro attended Fordham University School of Law at night, teaching during the day in public schools in Astoria, Queens. Today she lives in Queens with her husband, John Zaccaro (Ferraro kept her maiden name, she says, out of respect for her mother), and their three children. Before being elected to Congress, she worked as a prosecutor in the Queens County District Attorney's office.

In Congress, she focused on issues of interest to women, including the Economic Equity Act, which seeks to explore and remedy economic problems faced by working women and homemakers. A Roman Catholic, Geraldine Ferraro describes herself as personally opposed to abortion, but she also says she would not impose her beliefs in the making of public policy.

In 1984, she was named Walter Mondale's Vice-Presidential running mate, the first woman ever to be chosen for this office by a major party.

# Ella Grasso

Grasso's election as Connecticut's governor in 1974 marked the first time a woman reached that office in her own right rather than as the spouse of a previous incumbent. Her tenure—cut short during her second term by death from cancer in 1980—was marked by a progressive administration noted for its personal concern for the constituency and by Grasso's accessibility.

She was born Ella Tambussi in 1919 in Windsor Locks, Connecticut, to Italian immigrant parents (her father was a baker) from Tortona near the Piedmont. She attended Mount Holyoke College, where she received bachelor's and master's degrees in economics and sociology.

An activist from her youth, Grasso worked for Democratic state party chairman John Bailey, becoming his protégée, and in 1952 won her first electoral race as state assemblywoman. Even then an aggressive legislator—she worked to streamline the county government system statewide—she went on in 1958 to be elected secretary of state. At the same time she chaired the Democratic State Platform Committee, which led to involvement on a national level with the development of party platforms. In 1968, she was among a minority of committee members whose stance against the war in Vietnam prompted them to leave the Democratic National Convention in Chicago, where police had used violent tactics against antiwar demonstrators.

Grasso's next move was a successful run for Congress in 1970, and she was reelected in 1972. There she established a mainly liberal voting record and received wide labor support. Becoming Connecticut's leading Democrat, she ran in the state's primary for governor, and, victorious, went on to be elected by a comfortable margin in 1974. As governor, she kept a promise to maintain an open government and instigated a series of "right-to-know" laws that made files available to private citizens. Despite her ties to party leaders, she often went outside the mainstream of party regulars to fill important jobs.

# Fiorello H. La Guardia

Rarely has a political person inspired the kind of respect and affection that Fiorello La Guardia did. Few who lived in New York City during his terms in office as mayor (1933–45) will forget the spunky figure with the big western hat and high-pitched voice, ever visible not only at required ceremonial events but at fires and accidents, conducting at public concerts, and giving consumer information to housewives and reading comics to children on radio during a newspaper deliverers' strike.

The "Little Flower," as he became affectionately known because of his first name, was born in 1882 in Greenwich Village to an Italian father, Achille La Guardia, a musician and bandmaster from Foggia, and a Jewish mother, Irene Luzzato Coen, from Trieste.

Fiorello spent most of his boyhood in Arizona, and went to Trieste with his family in 1898. He worked in the American consular service in Budapest and Fiume, acquiring fluency in a number of languages—an asset to his political career in ethnic New York City. He returned to New York City in 1906 and went to law school at New York University, mostly in the evening while working as an interpreter at Ellis Island. He was admitted to the bar in 1910 and established a legal-aid bureau. He soon decided that he wanted a career in public service.

Fiorello La Guardia (Courtesy of the National Archives)

He successfully ran for Congress in the 14th Congressional District on the Republican ticket in 1916. In his autobiography, La Guardia states that his strong aversion to Tammany Hall and the Democratic machine boss rule led to his joining the Republican Party. During World War I, he joined the Aviation Section of the Signal Corps and was commander of all American combat pilots in Italy.

Back in New York City, La Guardia resumed his political life. He was elected to the House of Representatives again in 1922, where he served until 1932 as one of its most influential Republican Progressives. He fought for child-labor laws and women's suffrage, against Prohibition and pork-barrel legislation, and exposed graft in the judiciary. His greatest accomplishment was his coauthorship of the 1932 Norris–La Guardia Anti-Injunction Act, a landmark in American labor legislation. The act outlawed the yellow dog contract, under which workers had to agree not to join a union as a condition of employment, and generally forbade federal courts from issuing an injunction against legal strikes.

Unseated in 1932, La Guardia successfully ran for mayor on a reform-fusion ticket, and became New York City's first mayor of Italian descent in 1933. As mayor, La Guardia made his mark as a reformer of unimpeachable honesty and integrity. He balanced the budget and brought about the adoption of a new city charter. He supported an extensive public works program: bridges, tunnels, parkways, playgrounds, and slum clearance projects proliferated during his administration.

La Guardia served as mayor for three consecutive terms, but chose not to run in 1945. He served briefly as director general of the United Nations Relief and Rehabilitation Administration in 1946 before his death from cancer in 1947. The "insurgent," as he termed himself in his autobiography, left an indelible mark on the city he loved.

# John J. Sirica

A former federal judge in Washington, D.C., Sirica became a national figure in 1973 for his astute handling of one of America's most dramatic cases: the trial of the Watergate burglars and, soon after, of several of President Nixon's top aides.

Sirica was born in Waterbury, Connecticut, in 1904, to an immigrant barber from a village near Naples and to an American-born mother. He graduated from George Washington Law School in 1926. Starting a private practice, he became a trial lawyer.

Sirica was an assistant U.S. attorney from 1930 to 1934. In 1949 he became chief trial lawyer at a prestigious Washington firm, remaining there until he was appointed to the federal bench by President Eisenhower in 1957.

Sirica's judicial career reflected the variety of one of the country's busiest courts, combining complex criminal, antitrust, and other cases. He was known as a law-and-order judge who often gave maximum sentences and who also saw many of his judgments reversed on appeal. But the climax of his career began in early 1973, shortly before his planned retirement. By then the court's chief judge—a title earned by seniority—Sirica decided to preside over the trial of seven defendants accused of breaking into the Democratic National Committee headquarters in the Watergate building complex the year before. He took the case because he had fewer active cases and because he felt that as a Republican, he could not be accused of letting political biases interfere with judicial fairness.

The revelation that people higher up in the Nixon administration were involved in the break-in led to the appointment of a special prosecutor to investigate the crimes, culminating in Nixon's resignation while impeachment proceedings were under way. Sirica made the historic ruling that executive privilege did not take precedence over Constitutional requirements and forced Nixon to hand over tapes and other material subpoenaed by a grand jury. After presiding over the trial of the seven burglars, Sirica heard the cases of top Nixon aides John Ehrlichmann, H. R. Haldeman, and Attorney General John Mitchell. All were found guilty and were sentenced to prison terms ranging from twenty months to five years. Though some critics felt Sirica had overstepped his judicial role in the trials, he was generally hailed for his fairness. He was named *Time* magazine's 1973 Man of the Year.

In a news article called "Lessons from Watergate," he wrote,
There is always a tendency to search out heroes and point to individual acts of courage and responsibility in analyzing historical events. . . . But in the end, justice was done not by any individual or any particular decision, but by our Constitutional system itself. . . . The greatest lesson we have gained is that our Constitutional system works the way the Founding Fathers intended and that it is able to reaffirm its fundamental principle of our form of government—that no individual is greater than the law and all individuals must stand equal before it.

Judge John Sirica (Courtesy of *Time* magazine)

# Choosing a Dream: Italians in Hell's Kitchen

As a child and in my adolescence, living in the heart of New York's Neapolitan ghetto, I never heard an Italian singing. None of the grown-ups I knew were charming or loving or understanding. Rather they seemed coarse, vulgar, and insulting. And so later in my life when I was exposed to all the clichés of lovable Italians, singing Italians, happy-go-lucky Italians, I wondered where the hell the moviemakers and storywriters got all their ideas from.

At a very early age I decided to escape these uncongenial folk by becoming an artist, a writer. It seemed then an impossible dream. My father and mother were illiterate, as were their parents before them. But practising my art I tried to view the adults with a more charitable eye and so came to the conclusion that their only fault lay in their being foreigners; I was an American. This didn't really help because I was only half right. I was the foreigner. They were already more "American" than I could ever become.

But it did seem then that the Italian immigrants, all the fathers and mothers that I knew, were a grim lot; always shouting, always angry, quicker to quarrel than embrace. I did not understand that their lives were a long labor to earn their daily bread and that physical fatigue does not sweeten human natures.

And so even as a very small child I dreaded growing up to be like the adults around me. I heard them saying too many cruel things about their dearest friends, saw too many of their false embraces with those they had just maligned, observed with horror their paranoiac anger at some small slight or a fancied injury to their pride. They were, always, too unforgiving. In short, they did not have the careless magnanimity of children.

In my youth I was contemptuous of my elders, including a few under thirty. I thought my contempt special to their circumstances. Later when I wrote about these illiterate men and women, when I thought I understood them, I felt a condescending pity. After all, they had suffered, they had labored all the days of their lives. They had never tasted luxury, knew little more economic security than those ancient Roman slaves who might have been their ancestors. And alas, I thought, with new-found artistic insight, they were cut off from their children because of the strange American tongue, alien to them, native to their sons and daughters.

Already an artist but not yet a husband or father, I pondered omnisciently on their tragedy, again thinking it special circumstance rather than a constant in the human condition. I did not yet understand why these men and women were willing to settle for less than they deserved in life and think that "less" quite a bargain. I did not understand that they simply could not afford to dream, I myself had a hundred dreams from which to choose. For I was already sure that I would make my escape, that I was one of the chosen. I would be rich, famous, happy. I would master my destiny.

And so it was perhaps natural that as a child, with my father gone, my mother the family chief, I, like all the children in all the ghettos of America, became locked in a bitter struggle with the adults responsible for me. It was inevitable that my mother and I became enemies.

As a child I had the usual dreams. I wanted to be handsome, specifically as cowboy stars in movies were handsome. I wanted to be a killer hero in a world-wide war. Or if no wars came along (our teachers told us another was impossible), I wanted at the very least to be a footloose adventurer. Then I branched out and thought of being a great artist, and then, getting ever more sophisticated, a great criminal.

My mother, however, wanted me to be a railroad clerk. And that was her *highest* ambition; she would have settled for less. At the age of sixteen when I let everybody know that I was going to be a great writer, my friends and family took the news quite calmly, my mother included. She did not become angry. She quite simply assumed that I had gone off my nut. She was illiterate and her peasant life in Italy made her believe that only a son of the nobility could possibly be a writer. Artistic beauty after all could spring only from the seedbed of fine clothes, fine food, luxurious living. So then how was it possible for a son of hers to be an artist? She was not too convinced she was wrong even after my first two books were published many years later. It was only after the commercial success of my third novel that she gave me the title of poet.

My family and I grew up together on Tenth Avenue, between Thirtieth and Thirty-first streets, part of the area called Hell's Kitchen. This particular neighborhood could have been a movie set for one of the Dead End Kid flicks or for the social drama of the East Side in which John Garfield played the hero. Our tenements were the western wall of the city. Beneath our windows were the vast black iron gardens of the New York Central Railroad, absolutely blooming with stinking boxcars freshly unloaded of cattle and pigs for the city slaughterhouse. Steers sometimes escaped and loped through the heart of the neighborhood followed by astonished young boys who had never seen a live cow.

The railroad yards stretched down to the Hudson River, beyond whose garbagey waters rose the rocky Palisades of New Jersey. There were railroad tracks running downtown on Tenth Avenue itself to another freight station called St. Johns Park. Because of this, because these trains cut off one side of the street from the other, there was a wooden bridge over Tenth Avenue, a romantic-looking bridge despite the fact that no sparkling water, no silver flying fish darted beneath it; only heavy dray carts drawn by tired horses, some flat-boarded trucks, tin lizzie automobiles and, of course, long strings of freight cars drawn by black, ugly engines.

What was really great, truly magical, was sitting on the bridge, feet dangling down, and letting the engine under you blow up clouds of steam that made you disappear, then reappear all damp and smelling of fresh ironing. When I was seven years old I fell in love for the first time with the tough little girl who held my hand and disappeared with me in that magical cloud of steam. This experience was probably more traumatic and damaging to my later relationships with women than one of those ugly childhood adventures Freudian novelists use to explain why their hero has gone bad.

My father supported his wife and seven children by working as a track man laborer for the New York Central Railroad. My oldest brother worked for the railroad as a brakeman, another brother was a railroad shipping clerk in the freight office. Eventually I spent some of the worst months of my life as the railroad's worst messenger boy.

My oldest sister was just as unhappy as a dressmaker in the garment industry. She wanted to be a school teacher. At one time or another my other two brothers also worked for the railroad—it got all six males in the family. The two girls and my mother escaped, though my mother felt it her duty to send all our bosses a gallon of homemade wine on Christmas. But everybody hated their jobs except my oldest brother who had a night shift and spent most of his working hours sleeping in freight cars. My father finally got fired because the foreman told him to get a bucket of water for the crew and not to take all day. My father took the bucket and disappeared forever.

Nearly all the Italian men living on Tenth Avenue supported their large families by working on the railroad. Their children also earned pocket money by stealing ice from the refrigerator cars in summer and coal from the open stoking cars in the winter. Sometimes an older lad would break the seal of a freight car and take a look inside. But this usually brought down the "Bulls," the special railroad police. And usually the freight was "heavy" stuff, too much work to cart away and sell, something like fresh produce or boxes of cheap candy that nobody would buy.

The older boys, the ones just approaching voting age, made their easy money by hijacking silk trucks that loaded up at the garment factory on Thirty-first Street. They would then sell the expensive dresses door to door, at bargain prices no discount house could match. From this some graduated into organized crime, whose talent scouts alertly tapped young boys versed in strong-arm. Yet despite all this, most of the kids grew up honest, content with fifty bucks a week as truck drivers, deliverymen, and white-collar clerks in the civil service.

I had every desire to go wrong but I never had a chance. The Italian family structure was too formidable.

I never came home to an empty house; there was always the smell of supper cooking. My mother was always there to greet me, sometimes with a policeman's club in her hand (nobody ever knew how she acquired it). But she was always there, or her authorized deputy, my older sister, who preferred throwing empty milk bottles at the heads of her little brothers when they got bad marks on their report cards. During the great Depression of the 1930s, though we were the poorest of the poor, I never remember not dining well. Many years later as a guest of a millionaire's club, I realized that our poor family on home relief ate better than some of the richest people in America.

My mother would never dream of using anything but the finest imported olive oil, the best Italian cheeses. My father had access to the fruits coming off ships, the produce from railroad cars, all before it went through the stale process of middlemen; and my mother, like most Italian women, was a fine cook in the peasant style.

My mother was as formidable a personage as she was a cook. She was not to be treated cavalierly. My oldest brother at age sixteen had his own tin lizzie Ford and used it to further his career as the Don Juan of Tenth Avenue. One day my mother asked him to drive her to the market on Ninth Avenue and Fortieth Street, no more than a five-minute trip. My brother had other plans and claimed he was going to work on a new shift on the railroad. Work was an acceptable excuse even for funerals. But an hour later when my mother came out of the door of the tenement she saw the tin lizzie loaded with three pretty neighborhood girls, my Don Juan brother about to drive them off. Unfortunately there was a cobblestone lying loose in the gutter. My mother dropped her black leather shopping bag and picked up the stone with both hands. As we all watched in horror, she brought the boulder down on the nearest fender of the tin lizzie, demolishing it. Then she picked up her bag and marched off to Ninth Avenue to do her shopping. To this day, forty years later, my brother's voice still has a surprised horror and shock when he tells the story. He still doesn't understand how she could have done it.

My mother had her own legends and myths on how to amass a fortune. There was one of our uncles who worked as an assistant chef in a famous Italian-style restaurant. Every day, six days a week, this uncle brought home, under his shirt, six eggs, a stick of butter, and a small bag of flour. By doing this for thirty years he was able to save enough money to buy a fifteen-thousand-dollar house on Long Island and two smaller houses for his son and daughter. Another cousin, blessed with a college degree, worked as a chemist in a large manufacturing firm. By using the firm's raw materials and equipment he concocted a superior floor wax which he sold door to door in his spare time. It was a great floor wax and with his low overhead, the price was right. My mother and her friends did not think this stealing. They thought of it as being thrifty.

The wax-selling cousin eventually destroyed his reputation for thrift by buying a sailboat; this was roughly equivalent to the son of a Boston brahmin spending a hundred grand in a whorehouse.

As rich men escape their wives by going to their club, I finally escaped my mother by going to the Hudson Guild Settlement House. Most people do not know that a settlement house is really a club combined with social services. The Hudson Guild, a five-story field of joy for slum kids, had ping pong rooms and billiard rooms, a shop in which to make lamps, a theater for putting on amateur plays, a gym to box and play basketball in. And then there were individual rooms where your particular club could meet in privacy. The Hudson Guild even suspended your membership for improper behavior or failure to pay the tiny dues. It was a heady experience for a slum kid to see his name posted on the billboard to the effect that he was suspended by the Board of Governors.

There were young men who guided us as counselors whom I remember with fondness to this day. They were more like friends than adults assigned to watch over us. I still remember one helping us eat a box of stolen chocolates rather than reproaching us. Which was exactly the right thing for him to do; we trusted him after that. The Hudson Guild kept more kids out of jail than a thousand policemen. It still exists today, functioning for the new immigrants, the blacks, and the Puerto Ricans.

There was a night when the rich people of New York, including the Ethical Culture Society, attended a social function at the Hudson Guild in order to be conned into contributing huge sums of money for the settlement house program. I think it was a dinner and amateur theater presentation that was costing them a hundred bucks a head. Their chauffeurs parked the limousines all along the curbs of Twenty-seventh Street and Tenth Avenue. Us deprived kids, myself the leader, spent the night letting the air out of our benefactors' tires. *Noblesse oblige.*

But we weren't all bad. In our public schools one year an appeal was made to every child to try to bring a can of food to fill Thanksgiving baskets for the poor. The teachers didn't seem to realize *we* were the poor. We didn't either. Every kid in that public school, out of the goodness of his heart, went out and stole a can of food from a local grocery store. Our school had the best contributor record of any school in the city.

Some of the most exciting days in my life were spent at the Hudson Guild. At the age of eleven I became captain of my club football team for seven years, and president of the Star Club, an office I held for five. I enjoyed that success more than any other in my life. And learned a great deal from it. At the age of fifteen I was as thoroughly corrupted by power as any dictator until I was overthrown by a coalition of votes; my best friends joining my enemies to depose me. It was a rare lesson to learn at fifteen.

The Star Club was made up of boys my own age, a gang, really, which had been pacified by the Hudson Guild Settlement House. We had a football team, a baseball team, a basketball team. We had a yearbook. We had our own room, where we could meet, and a guidance counselor, usually a college boy. We had one named Ray Dooley whom I remember with affection to this day. He took us for outings in the country, to the Hudson Guild Farm in New Jersey for winter weekends where we hitched our sleds to his car, towed at thirty miles an hour. We repaid him by throwing lye into his face and almost blinding him. We thought it was flour. He never reproached us and it wound up OK. We idolized him after that. I liked him because he never tried to usurp my power, not so that I could notice.

The Hudson Guild was also responsible for absolutely the happiest times of my childhood. When I was about nine or ten they sent me away as a Fresh Air Fund kid. This was a program where slum children were boarded on private families in places like New Hampshire for two weeks.

As a child I knew only the stone city. I had no conception of what the countryside could be. When I got to New Hampshire, when I smelled grass and flowers and trees, when I ran barefoot along the dirt country roads, when I drove the cows home from pasture, when I darted through fields of corn and waded through clear brooks, when I gathered warm brown speckled eggs in the henhouse, when I drove a hay wagon drawn by two great horses—when I did all these things—I nearly went crazy with the joy of it. It was quite simply a fairy tale come true.

The family that took me in, a middle-aged man and woman, childless, were Baptists and observed Sunday so religiously that even checker playing was not allowed on the Lord's day of rest. We went to church on Sunday for a good three hours, counting Bible class, then again at night. On Thursday evenings we went to prayer meetings. My guardians, out of religious scruple, had never seen a movie. They disapproved of dancing, they were no doubt political reactionaries; they were everything that I came later to fight against.

And yet they gave me those magical times children never forget. For two weeks every summer from the time I was nine to fifteen I was happier than I have ever been before or since. The man was good with tools and built me a little playground with swings, sliding ponds, seesaws. The woman had a beautiful flower and vegetable garden and let me pick from it. A cucumber or strawberry in the earth was a miracle. And then when they saw how much I loved picnics, the sizzling frankfurters on a stick over the wood fire, the yellow roasted corn, they drove me out on Sunday afternoons to a lovely green grass mountainside. Only on Sundays it was never called a picnic, it was called "taking our lunch outside." I found it then—and now—a sweet hypocrisy.

The Baptist preacher lived in the house a hundred yards away and sometimes he, too, took his lunch "out" with us on a Sunday afternoon, he and his wife and children. Outside of his church he was a jolly fat man, a repressed comedian. Also a fond father, he bought his children a great many toys. I borrowed those toys and on one late August day I sailed his son's huge motor launch down a quiet, winding brook and when it nosed into a wet mossy bank I buried the toy there to have the following year when I came back. But I never found it.

There came a time, I was fifteen, when I was told I was too old to be sent away to the country as a Fresh Air Fund kid. It was the first real warning that I must enter the adult world, ready or not. But I always remembered that man and woman with affection, perhaps more. They always bought me clothing during my visits, my very first pajamas. They sent me presents at Christmastime, and when I was about to go into the army I visited them as a young man of twenty-one. The young were excessively grateful then, so I did not smoke in their house nor did I follow up on a local maid who seemed promising.

I believed then, as a child, that the State of New Hampshire had some sort of gates at which all thieves and bad guys were screened out. I believed this, I think, because the house was left unlocked when we went to church on Sundays and Thursday nights. I believed it because I never heard anyone curse or quarrel with raised voices. I believed it because it was beautiful to believe.

When I returned home from these summer vacations I had a new trick. I said grace with bowed head before eating the familiar spaghetti and meat balls. My mother always tolerated this for the few days it lasted. After all, the two weeks' vacation from her most troublesome child was well worth a Baptist prayer.

From this Paradise I was flung into Hell. That is, I had to help support my family by working on the railroad. After school hours of course. This was the same railroad that had supplied free coal and free ice to the whole Tenth Avenue when I was young enough to steal with impunity. After school finished at 3 P.M. I went to work in the freight office as a messenger. I also worked Saturdays and Sundays when there was work available.

I hated it. One of my first short stories was about how I hated that job. But of course what I really hated was entering the adult world. To me the adult world was a dark enchantment, unnatural. As unnatural to the human dream as death. And as inevitable.

The young are impatient about change because they cannot grasp the power of time itself; not only as the enemy of flesh, the very germ of death, but time as a benign cancer. As the young cannot grasp really that love must be a victim of time, so too they cannot grasp that injustices, the economic and family traps of living, can also fall victim to time.

And so I really thought that I would spend the rest of my life as a railroad clerk. That I would never be a writer. That I would be married and have children and go to christenings and funerals and visit my mother on a Sunday afternoon. That I would never own an automobile or a house. That I would never see Europe, the Paris and Rome and Greece I was reading about in books from the public library. That I was hopelessly trapped by my family, by society, by my lack of skills and education.

But I escaped again. At the age of eighteen I started dreaming about the happiness of my childhood. As later at the age of thirty I would dream about the joys of my lost adolescence, as at the age of thirty-five I was to dream about the wonderful time I had in the army which I had hated being in. As at the age of forty-five I dreamed about the happy, struggling years of being a devoted husband and loving father. I had the most valuable of human gifts, that of retrospective falsification: remembering the good and not the bad.

I still dreamed of future glory. I still wrote short stories, one or two a year. I still KNEW I would be a great writer but I was beginning to realize that accidents could happen and my second choice, that of being a great criminal, was coming up fast. But for the young everything goes so slowly, I could wait it out. The world would wait for me. I could still spin out my life with dreams.

In the summertime I was one of the great Tenth Avenue athletes but in the wintertime I became a sissy. I read books. At a very early age I discovered libraries, the one in the Hudson Guild and the public ones. I loved reading in the Hudson Guild where the librarian became a friend. I loved Joseph Altsheler's (I don't even have to look up his name) tales about the wars of the New York State Indian tribes, the Senecas and the Iroquois. I discovered Doc Savage and the Shadow and then the great Sabatini. Part of my character to this day is Scaramouche, I like to think. And then maybe at the age of fourteen or fifteen or sixteen I discovered Dostoevsky. I read the books, all of them I could get. I wept for Prince Myshkin in *The Idiot*, I was as guilty as Raskolnikov. And when I finished *The Brothers Karamazov* I understood for the first time what was really happening to me and the people around me. I had always hated religion even as a child but now I became a true believer. I believed in art. A belief that has helped me as well as any other.

My mother looked on all this reading with a fishy Latin eye. She saw no profit in it but since all her children were great readers she was a good enough general to know she could not fight so pervasive an insubordination. And there may have been some envy. If she had been able to she would have been the greatest reader of us all.

My direct ancestors for a thousand years have most probably been illiterate. Italy, the golden land, so loving to vacationing Englishmen, so majestic in its language and cultural treasures (they call it, I think, the cradle of civilization), has never cared for its poor people. My father and mother were both illiterates. Both grew up on rocky, hilly farms in the countryside adjoining Naples. My mother remembers never being able to taste the ham from the pig they slaughtered every year. It brought too high a price in the marketplace and cash was needed. My mother was also told the family could not afford the traditional family gift of linens when she married and it was this that decided her to emigrate to America to marry her first husband, a man she barely knew. When he died in a tragic work accident on the docks, she married my father, who assumed responsibility for a widow and her four children perhaps out of ignorance, perhaps out of compassion, perhaps out of love. Nobody ever knew. He was a mystery, a Southern Italian with blue eyes who departed from the family scene three children later when I was twelve. But he cursed Italy even more than my mother did. Then again, he wasn't too pleased with America either. My mother never heard of Michelangelo; the great deeds of the Caesars had not yet reached her ears. She never heard the great music of her native land. She could not sign her name.

And so it was hard for my mother to believe that her son could become an artist. After all, her one dream in coming to America had been to earn her daily bread, a wild dream in itself. And looking back she was dead right. Her son an artist? To this day she shakes her head. I shake mine with her.

America may be a fascistic, warmongering, racially prejudiced country today. It may deserve the hatred of its revolutionary young. But what a miracle it once was! What has happened here has never happened in any other country in any other time. The poor who had been poor for centuries—hell, since the beginning of Christ—whose children had inherited their poverty, their illiteracy, their hopelessness, achieved some economic dignity and freedom. You didn't get it for nothing, you had to pay a price in tears, in suffering, but why not? And some even became artists.

Not even my gift for retrospective falsification can make my eighteenth to twenty-first years seem like a happy time. I hated my life. I was being dragged into the trap I feared and had foreseen even as a child. It was all there, the steady job, the nice girl who would eventually get knocked up, and then the marriage and fighting over counting pennies to make ends meet. I noticed myself acting more unheroic all the time. I had to tell lies in pure self-defense, I did not forgive so easily.

But I was delivered. When World War II broke out I was delighted. There is no other word, terrible as it may sound. My country called. I was delivered from my mother, my family, the girl I was loving passionately but did not love. And delivered WITHOUT GUILT. Heroically. My country called, ordered me to defend it. I must have been one of millions, sons, husbands, fathers, lovers, making their innocent getaway from baffled loved ones. And what an escape it was. The war made all my dreams come true. I drove a jeep, toured Europe, had love affairs, found a wife, and lived the material for my first novel. But of course that was a just war as Vietnam is not, and so today it is perhaps for the best that the revolutionary young make their escape by attacking their own rulers.

Then why five years later did I walk back into the trap with a wife and child and a civil service job I was glad to get? After five years of the life I had dreamed about, plenty of women, plenty of booze, plenty of money, hardly any work, interesting companions, travel, etc., why did I walk back into that cage of family and duty and a steady job?

For the simple reason, of course, that I had never really escaped, not my mother, not my family, not the moral pressures of our society. Time again had done its work. I was back in my cage and I was, I think, happy. In the next twenty years I wrote three novels. Two of them were critical successes but I didn't make much money. The third novel, not as good as the others, made me rich. And free at last. Or so I thought.

Then why do I dream of those immigrant Italian peasants as having been happy? I remember how they spoke of their forebears, who spent all their lives farming the arid mountain slopes of Southern Italy. "He died in that house in which he was born," they say enviously. "He was never more than an hour from his village, not in all his life," they sigh. And what would they make of a phrase like "retrospective falsification"?

No, really, we are all happier now. It is a better life. And after all, as my mother always said, "Never mind about being happy. Be glad you're alive."

When I came to my "autobiographical novel," the one every writer does about himself, I planned to make myself the sensitive, misunderstood hero, much put upon by his mother and family. To my astonishment my mother took over the book and instead of my revenge I got another comeuppance. But it is, I think, my best book. And all those old-style grim conservative Italians whom I hated, then pitied so patronizingly, they also turned out to be heroes. Through no desire of mine. I was surprised. The thing that amazed me most was their courage. Where were their Congressional Medals of Honor? Their Distinguished Service Crosses? How did they ever have the balls to get married, have kids, go out to earn a living in a strange land, with no skills, not even knowing the language? They made it without tranquillizers, without sleeping pills, without psychiatrists, without even a dream. Heroes. Heroes all around me. I never saw them.

But how could I? They wore lumpy work clothes and handlebar moustaches, they blew their noses on their fingers and they were so short that their high-school children towered over them. They spoke a laughable broken English and the furthest limit of their horizon was their daily bread. Brave men, brave women, they fought to live their lives without dreams. Bent on survival they narrowed their minds to the thinnest line of existence.

It is no wonder that in my youth I found them contemptible. And yet they had left Italy and sailed the ocean to come to a new land and leave their sweated bones in America. Illiterate Colombos, they dared to seek the promised land. And so they, too, dreamed a dream.

Forty years ago, in 1930, when I was ten, I remember gas light, spooky, making the tenement halls and rooms alive with ghosts.

We had the best apartment on Tenth Avenue, a whole top floor of six rooms, with the hall as our storage cellar and the roof as our patio. Two views, one of the railroad yards backed by the Jersey shore, the other of a backyard teeming with tomcats everybody shot at with BB guns. In between these two rooms with a view were three bedrooms without windows—the classic railroad flat pattern. The kitchen had a fire escape that I used to sneak out at night. I liked that apartment though it had no central heating, only a coal stove at one end and an oil stove at the other. I remember it as comfortable, slum or not.

My older brothers listened to a crystal radio on homemade headsets. I hitched a ride on the backs of horses and wagons, my elders daringly rode the trolley cars. Only forty years ago in calendar time, it is really a thousand years in terms of change in our physical world. There are the jets, TV, penicillin for syphilis, cobalt for cancer, equal sex for single girls; yet still always the contempt of the young for their elders.

But maybe the young are on the right track this time. Maybe they know that the dreams of our fathers were malignant. Perhaps it is true that the only real escape is in the blood magic of drugs. All the Italians I knew and grew up with have escaped, have made their success. We are all Americans now, we are all successes now. And yet the most successful Italian man I know admits that though the one human act he never could understand was suicide, he understood it when he became a success. Not that he ever would do such a thing; no man with Italian blood ever commits suicide or becomes a homosexual in his belief. But suicide has crossed his mind. And so to what avail the finding of the dream? He went back to Italy and tried to live like a peasant again. But he can never again be unaware of more subtle traps than poverty and hunger.

There is a difference between having a good time in life and being happy. My mother's life was a terrible struggle and yet I think it was a happy life. One tentative proof is that at the age of eighty-two she is positively indignant at the thought that death dares approach her. But it's not for everybody that kind of life.

Thinking back I wonder why I became a writer. Was it the poverty or the books I read? Who traumatized me, my mother or the Brothers Karamazov? Being Italian? Or the girl sitting with me on the bridge as the engine steam deliciously made us vanish? Did it make any difference that I grew up Italian rather than Irish or black?

No matter. The good times are beginning, I am another Italian success story. Not as great as DiMaggio or Sinatra but quite enough. It will serve. Yet I can escape again. I have my retrospective falsification (how I love that phrase). I can dream now about how happy I was in my childhood, in my tenement, playing in those dirty but magical streets —living in the poverty that made my mother weep. True, I was a deposed dictator at fifteen but they never hanged me. And now I remember, all those impossible dreams strung out before me, waiting for me to choose, not knowing that the life I was living then, as a child, would become my final dream.

*Mario Puzo*

## Part Six

# ITALY

# In Search of My Sicilian Heritage

I can still see the sun-browned hands fumbling dry yellowed pages of the hand-written registries labeled *Indice di Morti*. A swarm of five clerks, ostensibly the full staff of the rickety municipal building, hovered over these annals of their dead *paesani*. They chattered rapidly in dialect, a sound as familiar to me as birds chirping, its full meaning just as elusive.

Occasionally Jimmy Latona, the one English-speaking employee (he had lived in Bayonne, New Jersey, for many years, only to return here to his native Sicilian village), looked up at me and posed questions. "What year did your paternal grandfather die?" "Did your father's mother's first husband die very young?" "How many sisters did she have?" I shrugged my shoulders, exasperated with my ignorance of the answers.

It was 1976, the year most of my compatriots were celebrating the American bicentennial. But I'd been studying in southern France and was more interested in finding and celebrating my own roots. In midsummer of that year I traveled a culture-filled, circuitous route down through Italy to the sunny mountainous island of Sicily.

I had subliminally noted the changes from the north to the south of Italy but it was only when I stood helpless in Cammarata's deserted train station nestled nine kilometers from the village proper that I succumbed to apprehensions about my great idea. Fortunately, an inquisitive family came to my rescue. The Gennaros led me to their home and lodged, fed, and protected me from what seemed to be many unseen dangers.

That evening another quirk of fate worked in my favor and I met Jimmy Latona in a caffé-bar. I was walking the village with Carmela and Mimi Gennaro while they asked villagers if anyone knew of my relatives. Jimmy was eager to help and told the girls to bring *l'american'* to Cammarata's municipal building next morning.

In my crude Italian I told the City Hall clerks all I knew: my grandparents' paternal and maternal names were Cusumano-Federico and Catalano-Franciamore, respectively. Other than that all I knew was that Cammarata, a name I'd heard often at home in America, was the birthplace of my paternal grandfather. His wife, my grandmother, was from a neighboring village.

After an hour or so of paging through three or four oversized registries and several false discoveries, I wanted to give up, to move on to Greece, my next destination. The dogged determination of the clerks to satisfy my request didn't match my waning interest.

"We will call your father in America and ask him some questions," said Jimmy.

"Really, it's not necessary; perhaps there are no relatives," I replied, not anxious to involve my parents in this whimsical endeavor.

As my eyes followed the clerk's finger down the ancient pages I could see that my family name appeared many times in the registries' lefthand columns with the names of deceased Cammaratesi; in the older nineteenth-century records it was written in a fancy script as *Cufumano*. But none of these, it seemed, were kinfolk to me.

What would I say to my relatives anyway, I wondered; would they be hostile or hospitable? What would they think? I was a jean-skirted, tee-shirted student with few belongings in my knapsack. I had little money then, and I brought no gifts of greeting. Would they kiss me and send me on my way?

I gazed through the window at the yellow stucco medieval castle gracing one of Cammarata's promontories, having no idea that shortly these questions would all be answered. Seeing the heady mix of Arab, Norman, and Byzantine architecture in Cammarata was stirring.

The varied structural design reminded me of my father's oft-told tales of Sicily's many plundering tribes. Phoenicians, Greeks, Carthaginians, Romans, Saracens, Byzantines, Normans, Germans, French, and Spaniards had all ruled here. If I never found my relatives, I did not regret coming here just to witness this ancient legacy I'd only imagined.

I was looking at a somber twelfth-century church on a hill below the Cammarata castle when one of the clerks nudged me firmly. I had to look down to respond to the short, fat, red-headed, severely club-footed woman.

*"Ven acá, talé"* ("Come here, look"). How often I'd heard these commands from my grandparents.

Jimmy had had a hunch. ("Sicilians have a genius for giving order to chaos," Luigi Barzini once wrote.) He was phoning one of the persons whose family name appeared in the registry. He spoke briefly, then hung up and smiled at me. Less than two minutes passed. All eyes turned to the shortish swarthy man who appeared in the doorway. Except for his height he resembled my brothers. His continuous outpouring of speech was musical and uplifting, but too fast for me to comprehend.

Jimmy turned to me. "Did your father work for the post office?"

"Yes . . ." My ears strained to translate the exchange between Jimmy and the man.

"This is your cousin: go into his home."

If I had any reservations they were put to rest when the man produced a color snapshot of my father's sister and mother.

I'd come on impulse to this village of more than eight thousand inhabitants, armed with a paltry knowledge of the language and facts of my relatives' background and now, miraculously, I was hugging my father's first cousin, Toto Tuzzolino (Toto's father, Nicolo, was first cousin to my father through Nicolo's mother, Nazarena Cusumano). Toto indeed took me into his family's home, a rather primitive thirteen-room stone *albergo* just five doors up the cobbled street from the municipal building.

Seven years after that first visit I returned to Sicily. I had changed a hundred times over from the impoverished student with audacious ideas—but it was thanks to that audacity that I was making a return visit to Cammarata, this time announced, with money and gifts, a better grip on the language, and established in a career. I was returning, not only for the infinite warmth of the people and the captivating mystery of the entire island, but to pursue the incomplete knowledge of my ancestry: Who were they? From which exotic lands did they come? What did they do throughout history? Was there, perhaps a Pirandello, or even a famous bandit such as Turiddu Giuliano among them?

I had spoken so little Italian the first time, and only Toto's sister Rena, several years younger than I, spoke a little English since she was studying to be a teacher. Trite as it sounds, we did not need words—we were bonded by gestures, touching, and the enigmatic knowledge of a blood tie. I had met members of five families, all first cousins to my father. There were many other relations, but three families—the Tuzzolinos, Coniglios, and Saccos—monopolized my time.

Bridging the gap of a generation, silent for so long, was exhilarating, but there were many cultural differences to reckon on the way. Most immediate was my status as a single and independent woman. In a land where the family is the irreducible social unit and celibacy or clerical life the only alternative to marriage, my marital status aroused discreet curiosity. I sensed that I was a bold *ragazza* (girl) in their eyes for traveling *tutta*

*sola*—alone. The older Sicilians, steadfast and single-minded in their beliefs, were rarely interested in discussing American cultural differences or lifestyles. They drew their own conclusions, which they did not share with me. Only Colletta, a twenty-seven-year-old mother of three, counseled me to marry as soon as possible, as I was becoming *vecchia* (old).

My cousins' ways surprised me no less than mine surprised them. Rena Tuzzolino and her boyfriend, Enzo, both twenty-five years old and dating for five years, had not met each other's parents. Nor did they talk to their parents about each other. Only when they announced plans to marry would the parents acknowledge the courtship. Rena's brothers Gino and Mario, both very handsome and in their twenties, would also slip out of the *albergo* each night to spend time with their respective girlfriends.

Culture shock could come when I least expected it. My first night in the Albergo Letizia (where the Tuzzolinos lived and worked together) we sat down to dinner as usual at 10 P.M. Everyone became mesmerized by the television. During my first visit to Cammarata my cousins had proudly shown me the hideous metal sculpture on top of the mountain, the television transmitting tower that brought them closer to the mainland as well as the outside world. Below us loomed the truly glorious monuments of antiquity, but perhaps they represented only a trampled past.

Nicolo would often come late for dinner because someone always had to wait until there were no more customers in the *albergo's* caffé-bar. He would spit on the floor and sometimes snuff out his cigarette in someone's empty dinner plate. He did not ask if I minded his cigarette smoke. Everyone else seemed comfortable with his manners. How well I knew that the Sicilian father was king in his home.

Nicolo, suave and attractive with shiny jet black hair, resembled my father in physique and mentality. He combed his hair exactly as my father did and had the same stern demeanor that had kept my father's ten children from stepping out of line. Nicolo's and my father's oldest sons had, coincidentally, become chemists.

"Am I not your *papà* when you are here?" Nicolo interrogated me one day, a twinkle betraying his granite stare.

"*Si,* you are *mio papà siciliano,*" I agreed.

"Then, I must know where you are at all times, *capisce?*"

"*Capisco,* Nicolo." At thirty-two I would no more disagree with him than I would have with my own strict father years ago.

This land "knows no mean between sensuous slackness and hellish drought" wrote the Sicilian Giuseppe di Lampedusa. The land around Cammarata is indeed a mosaic of sun-seared fields and lush, irrigated farms. The grotesque and sensual motifs seemed to abound everywhere in the land and in the people, young and old, whose minds are formed by its atmosphere, climate, and landscape. The imagery is rich—from the colorful *Vucciria* market in nearby Palermo to the daily rituals in Cammarata: My cousin Nazarena Sacco dries a crimson mass of tomato paste on a board out on her sun-drenched balcony, heedless of the swarming flies. Nicoletta, her mother, pulls a tasty loaf of bread from her stone hearth oven and hands me a warm wedge she breaks off with her dirty hand. A heart-warming topaz-colored liqueur is offered to me by Carmela, Nicolo's seventy-eight-year-old sister, a large woman with glaucous eyes that are as dolorous as a burro's. Breathing heavily, she tells me she will be angry if I refuse the drink, even though it is before noon.

Some of my most enjoyable moments in Cammarata were spent when I was allowed to wander alone (a hard-won victory only achieved on my second visit) observing the village's landscape and historical character. I still remember the sights and scents: the

Francesco Tuzzolino turns toward home after his daily toil on the Cammarata farm where he has worked most of his life with his brother Nicolo. (Photo by Camille Cusumano)

Rena Tuzzolino proudly dangles the fruit of the vine, the result of her father's intense labor. (Photo by Camille Cusumano)

A Sicilian woman listens to the good and bad news that passes through the Tuzzolinos' albergo. (Photo by Camille Cusumano)

screaming magenta of bougainvillea climbing stone walls, the honey sweetness of snowy jasmine or licorice aroma of crushed feathery *carosella*, Sicilian wild fennel.

Like other medieval Sicilian villages, Cammarata was carved into a mountainside so that powerful overlords could house their serfs and defend their land. With much of that feudal town still intact, the many cars that attempt to climb alleys and cobbled streets built for animals seem more out of place than do the donkey-driven carts and the black-clad women.

Sicilian food underscores and is a direct manifestation of the land's sensuality. "An Italian meal," notes the great cook Marcella Hazan, "is a story told from nature, taking its rhythms, its humors, its bounty and turning them into episodes for the senses."

Despite the absence of the stereotyped adornments one might expect, the food my relatives regaled me with was simple, sumptuous, always fresh, and a true extension, not only of the cook's love, but of the grower's love too. The grain-fattened chicken and rabbit, the string beans, potatoes, *cucuzze*, onions, and the slithering amber puddles of olive oil in the intensely flavored broth, the wheat for bread and pasta, the plum tomatoes for *sugo* and pizza, were all the fruit of Nicolo's daily toil on their hundred acres of farmland.

The Tuzzolino family and I visited their rolling farmland, which feeds them but leaves nothing left over for profit. As we strolled past grapevines, purple for the *vino nero* or frosty green sweet ones, everyone fed me fruit—bunches of grapes, black raspberries, peaches, oranges, mandarins, pomegranates, figs, all plump, ripe, and ready for picking.

The Tuzzolino family were inseparable, and living and working together as they did, were an anomaly. A friend, Concetta, filled her apron, a wicker basket, and a plastic bag as we walked, Toto handing her *fagiolini* or plum tomatoes, Rena the eggplants, Mario the peaches, *cucuzze*, and its greens for the evening's dinner.

At last the day arrived when Toto Tuzzolino could take me to the municipal building to unearth all the genealogical information about my heritage. Two carabinieri had done most of the research. They had put together a family tree that went back to my great-great-great-grandfather, who died before 1871. This *capostipite* was Calogero Cusumano, like my father. Calogero's son Nicolo had a son, also Calogero, who died in 1895. This Calogero, my father's grandfather, sired nine children, five of whom died within two years of birth. One of the surviving sons, Vincenzo Cusumano (my father's father), migrated around 1920 to the United States, where he died at the age of fifty-one, leaving my grandmother a thirty-five-year-old widow. In America my father named his first son Vincent and his second son Charles (for Calogero), continuing the tradition of filial duty to the father and the grandfather.

Nazarena Cusumano, my paternal grandfather's sister, had married Salvatore Tuzzolino and bore ten children, the youngest of whom was Nicolo.

The carabinieri were puzzled when I asked for more information. What were the professions of all these people? Where did they come from? Rena answered, "Farmers, they were all farmers, just poor peasants."

I realized then that if there were anything to learn it was only by an oral tradition, for this knowledge was not filed somewhere that I could have a librarian pull from a shelf. I would have to stay months, even years, and master the intricacies of the language and the culture. And then, perhaps, I could become privy to part of the past that was mine.

After my second visit I realized this: my family and I had learned a few things about one another; even so, there were hundreds of unanswered questions. And though the blood running through my veins was no less Sicilian than theirs, living in America had placed us light-years apart. Who was ahead and who was behind was, and still is, debatable.

*Camille Cusumano*

# The Family Tree

For most Americans, until a few years ago, history went along with teachers' dirty looks, and both were best ignored. Then along came *Roots*—first a best-selling book, then a widely acclaimed television series—and suddenly Americans began to see the past as intimately connected to their own present. Out came photo albums, heirloom Bibles, old letters, and family stories, in a steady stream that is still growing. Of course, this curiosity about ancestors has sometimes been difficult to satisfy, particularly as immigrant generations pass away. Nonetheless, even though very few people have uncovered unknown ties to Dante or the Medici, a great many have found that discovering more about their forebears is an unexpectedly rewarding experience.

Judge for yourself. With the following information about the sources available for your search, and genealogical chart for inspiration, you can begin to record your own family tree and to retrace the paths your ancestors took to the United States.

First write down the names of your family, going back as far as you can. Then, chart in hand, start talking to your relatives. Their memories may be your chief link with the past. Get the name of the town or region from which your family came. If the names can't be remembered, sometimes a special geographical feature like a river or a mountain may be the key to locating a small village on the map. Ask for the dates your family arrived in America, the names of relatives with whom they traveled, and the names of those left behind.

If you have no relative who can recall needed names, places, and dates, look into church records, which are often more useful than civic documents in tracking down immigrants' vital statistics. Italians who were new in America often neglected to register births with the state—since they lived in isolated enclaves, spoke little English, and were usually attended in childbirth by neighborhood midwives rather than doctors—but they rarely failed to have their babies baptized. (Marriages, on the other hand, were generally registered with both church and state.) Unfortunately, most churches do not keep central indexes of their records, and the Roman Catholic church—the most likely source of information on Italian immigrants—presents a few special challenges. Historically, Catholic church records have been kept in Latin. By church law, only priests can search the records and issue certificates—not photocopies—of church-recorded events. The main problem, in any case, is finding the right church. If you are not sure what parish your ancestor belonged to, check the telephone book for church names that sound Italian—St. Anthony's or St. Joseph's, for instance.

The more extensive list of civil sources includes records of immigration, naturalization, birth, death, marriage, and divorce, as well as ships' passenger lists. Through the years, changes in census laws have resulted in more leads for Americans investigating their family origins. In 1850, the census listed the name of every individual in each household, and by 1880, the adults' birthplaces and occupations were also included. The 1870 census indicates whether males over twenty-one years of age were U.S. citizens, information that provides another piece of your puzzle. If you discover that a member of your family is listed as a citizen, the next step is to look for his naturalization papers.

When your ancestor became an American citizen, the papers filed listed his place and date of birth, the place and date of his U.S. arrival and his address. Occasionally, they also mentioned the name of the ship he arrived on and his occupation. You can obtain a record of a naturalization *after* September 27, 1906, by applying to any local office of the U.S. Immigration and Naturalization Service or by writing to the national office in

Italian boy, Sicily (Photo by Pamela Parlapiano)

Italian children, Sicily (Photo by Pamela Parlapiano)

Washington, D.C. Before 1906, naturalization records were issued by local courts and not kept in duplicate in the immigration service's central files. A WPA project that undertook the sorting out of early records only managed to finish copying and indexing those of Maine, Massachusetts, New Hampshire, and Rhode Island. This work is filed in the National Archives in Washington.

In order to search ships' passenger lists, it helps to know the name of the port and the date of arrival of your ancestor, as well as the name of the ship. Even if you only know the region of origin and the approximate date of arrival, you can check lists of ship arrivals which tell where each ship sailed from.

After 1893, ships' passenger lists began to include the immigrant's last address in his or her country of origin, port of arrival in the U.S., and final destination in this country. In addition, they noted the name, address, and relationship to the immigrant of any relative in this country. By 1906, federal law also required a description of the passenger and notation of his or her birthplace. Post-1907 records leave more clues for the genealogical investigator: from this year, the name and address of the immigrant's nearest relative in his native country were included. However, there is a restriction on ship passenger lists: records and indexes are only opened to the public after fifty years.

Knowing that all these sources exist isn't very helpful, of course, unless you know how to obtain access to them. Check through the reference books listed below, or write to the U.S. National Archives in Washington for brochures.

Another major source of information is the Church of Jesus Christ of Latter-day Saints, which, for theological reasons, has assembled the world's best collection of genealogical material. Church branches, located in most major cities, have excellent reference collections that are open to the general public. For a fee, they will send to the central library in Salt Lake City for microfilmed records, not only from the United States, but also from the many countries whose sources the Mormons have copied and indexed. In addition, the Mormon libraries also provide names of certified private researchers you can hire to do the necessary research.

Once you have traced your family back to a particular Italian town, you may be able to go back up to 450 years more with the help of the *Handy Guide to Italian Genealogical Records* by Phyllis Pastore Preece and Floren Stocks Preece. The book contains a Mormon monograph on Italian sources, plus a brief history of Italy and a map to help you get your bearings. There are useful tips (for example, you might not have guessed that records in the Piedmont region were generally kept in French), explanations of the thirteen major genealogical sources in Italy, and advice on how to gain access to them. You can explore death and burial certificates (kept since 1600), the *catasti* (census or tax-assessment records) of the papal states (maintained since the fourteenth century), and marriage records (preserved since about 1545). Because Italy was unified only recently in comparison to other countries—even the United States—records are often scattered, and tracing your family tree can be complicated. One Italian-American woman, who did manage to chart her lineage to the 1880s, noted that she'd had a much harder time doing it than her Anglo-Saxon husband, whose family records were on file in England and New England.

There are several ways to tackle Italian source material. You can write, in Italian, to the registry office *(Ufficio Anagrafe)* of your family's hometown in Italy, or to the parish priest there. If you are not sure where your family's town is located, write to the Italian Government Travel Office or to Italian state archives.

Even if you don't manage to trace your genealogy back to the Medici, you may be able to reconstruct enough of your family's history to preserve for future generations a richer sense of who they are.

*Jean Grasso Fitzpatrick and Priscilla G. de Angelis*

# Tracing Your Family Tree

The following guide to books, government agencies (both here and in Italy), and commercial researchers will start you off on your search. Be sure to enclose a stamped, self-addressed envelope (or, when writing to Italy, international postal coupons) with all inquiries. If you apply to Italian sources for information, write in Italian.

## Sources in the U.S.

National Archives, General Services Administration, NATS, Washington DC 20408

Immigration and Naturalization Service, Washington DC 20536

Italian Government Travel Office
630 Fifth Avenue
New York, NY 10020
212-245-4822

### REGIONAL ARCHIVES

Address inquiries at each address to:
Chief, Archives Branch
Federal Archives & Records Center, GSA

**New England:**
380 Trapelo Road
Waltham, MA 02154

**New York, New Jersey, Puerto Rico, the Virgin Islands:**
Building 22-MOT Bayonne
Bayonne, NJ 07002

**Delaware and Pennsylvania,** and for microfilm loan for the **District of Columbia, Maryland, Virginia, & West Virginia:**
5000 Wissahickon Avenue
Philadelphia, PA 19144

**Alabama, Florida, Georgia, Kentucky, Mississippi, North Carolina, South Carolina, & Tennessee:**
1557 St. Joseph Avenue
East Point, GA 30344

**Illinois, Indiana, Michigan, Minnesota, Ohio, & Wisconsin:**
7358 South Pulaski Road
Chicago, IL 60629

**Iowa, Kansas, Missouri, & Nebraska:**
2306 East Bannister Road
Kansas City, MO 64131

**Arkansas, Louisiana, New Mexico, Oklahoma, & Texas:**
4900 Hemphill Street (building address)
P.O. Box 6216 (mailing address)
Fort Worth, TX 76115

**Colorado, Montana, North Dakota, Utah, & Wyoming:**
Building 48, Denver Federal Center
Denver, CO 80225

**Northern and central California, Hawaii, Nevada** (except Clark County), **& the Pacific Ocean area:**
1000 Commodore Drive
San Bruno, CA 94066

**Arizona, Southern California, & Clark County, Nevada:**
24000 Avila Road
Laguna Niguel, CA 92677

**Alaska, Idaho, Oregon, & Washington:**
6125 Sand Point Way NE
Seattle, WA 98115

## Sources in Italy

Istituto Centrale di Statistica
Via Cesare Balbo, 16
000144 Rome

### STATE ARCHIVES

Archivio Centrale dello Stato
Piazzale degli Archivi
000144 Rome

Archivio di Stato
Piazza de' Celestini 4
40123 Bologna

Archivio di Stato di Firenze
Piazzale degli Uffizi
50122 Florence

Archivio di Stato di Risorgimento
Via S. Egidio 21
50122 Florence

Archivio di Stato
Piazza Guidiccioni 8
55100 Lucca

Archivio di Stato
80135 Naples

Archivio di Stato di Pisa
Lungarno Mediceo 30
56100 Pisa

Archivio di Stato di Roma
Corso Rinascimento 40
00186 Rome

Archivio di Stato di Trieste
Via XXX Ottobre 7
34122 Trieste

Archivio di Stato di Venezia
Campo di Frari 3002
30125 Venice

## Commercial Researchers

Istituto Araldico Coccia
Borgo Santa Croce, 6
Palazzo Antinori
Casella Postale 413
Florence

Istituto Araldico Genealogico Italiano
Via Torta, 14
Florence

Accademia Internazionale Araldica
Casella Postale AD 2135
00100 Rome

Istituto Storico Araldico Genealogico
Internazionale
Via Pio VIII, 5
00165 Rome

Trafford R. Cole
Via Giolitti 21
35100 Padua

For additional names of commercial researchers, write to the Italian research director of the Latter-Day Saints' Genealogical Society:
Keith Rose
146 E. 100 South
American Fork, Utah 84003

## Books

Phyllis Pastore Preece and Floren Stocks Preece, *Handy Guide to Italian Genealogical Records,* and James C. Neagles, *Locating Your Immigrant Ancestor—A Guide to Naturalization Records;* both from The Everton Publishers, P.O. Box 368, Logan, Utah 84321.

Timothy Field Beard with Denise Nemong, *How to Find Your Family Roots* (McGraw-Hill, 1977).

Genealogical Society of the Church of Jesus Christ of Latter-Day Saints, *Major Genealogical Record Sources for Italy* (50 E. North Temple, Salt Lake City, Utah 84150).

*Where to Write for Birth and Death Records, Where to Write for Marriage Records,* and *Where to Write for Divorce Records,* Superintendent of Documents, Government Bookstore, 26 Federal Plaza, New York, NY 10007 (70¢ per booklet).

Gilbert Doane, *Searching for Your Ancestors* (University of Minnesota Press, 1973).

# Italian-American Cultural Organizations

*America-Italy Society, Inc.* 667 Madison Ave., New York, N.Y. 10021 (212) 838-1560.

A cultural link between Italy and the United States, the society offers courses in Italian literature, language, and cooking and sponsors lectures, films, concerts, and social events.

*American Association of Teachers of Italian* Department of Italian, Rutgers College, New Brunswick, N.J. 08903 (201) 247-1766.

Founded in 1923, the AATI publishes a quarterly newsletter and the literary magazine.

*American Committee on Italian Migration* 373 Fifth Ave., New York, N.Y. 10016 (212) 679-4650.

This nonprofit organization's purposes are the promotion of fair U.S. immigration policies and assistance to Italian immigrants in their problems of resettlement and assimilation.

*American Italian Historical Association* 209 Flagg Place, Staten Island, N.Y. 10304 (718) 351-8800.

The association collects, preserves, studies, and popularizes materials that shed light on the American-Italian past in the United States and Canada and maintains archives.

*Casa Italiana of Columbia University* Center for Italian Studies, 1161 Amsterdam Ave., New York, N.Y. 10027 (212) 280-2306.

The casa is a resource on Italian culture for the university and the broader community. It sponsors cultural events, lectures, and exhibits.

*Center for Migration Studies* 209 Flagg Place, Staten Island, N.Y. 10304 (718) 351-8800.

The center is an educational, nonprofit institute founded in 1964 to encourage and facilitate the study of sociological, demographic, historical, economic, legislative, and pastoral aspects of human migration and refugee movements. Publishes *International Migration Review* and *Migration Today Magazine.*

*Commission for Social Justice, Order Sons of Italy in America* 138 Woodfield Road, West Hempstead, N.Y. 11552 (516) 538-0800.

The anti-defamation arm of the OSIA works actively to insure equal concern, treatment, and respect for all Italian-Americans and other ethnic groups in employment and media.

*Immigration History Research Center of the University of Minnesota* 826 Berry St., St. Paul, Minn. 55114 (612) 373-5581.

The center collects publications and conducts research on the history of Italian immigration, settlement, and adjustment in North America.

*Italian American Cultural Society* 19800 Frazho Road, St. Clair Shores, Mich. 48081 (313) 772-7080.

Founded 1957, the society's aim is to preserve Italian background and publicize Italian-American contributions to the United States and the world.

*Italian American Librarians Caucus* 6 Peter Cooper Road #11G, New York, N.Y. 10010 (212) 228-8438.

The caucus provides guidelines and studies on Italian and Italian-American materials and populations particularly relevant to libraries and information centers.

*Italian-American Media Institute* 1019 19th St. N.W., Suite 800, Washington, D.C. 20036 (202) 293-1713.

The institute is a project of the National Italian American Foundation and conducts research and training for the purpose of fostering a positive image of Italian-Americans in the mass media.

*Italian American War Veterans of U.S.* 4645 Oberlin Ave., Lorain, Ohio 44052 (216) 282-3220 and 390 South Leonard, Waterbury, Conn. 06705.

The veterans publish the ITAM Torch Quarterly and the National Directory (annually). They hold a convention yearly in Washington, D.C.

*National Italian American Foundation* 1019 19th St. N.W., Suite 800, Washington, D.C. 20036 (202) 293-1713.

Founded in 1975, the foundation's activities are research and education concerning art, culture, sciences, and social history, seminars, regional meetings, lecture series, studies, and cultural events. It compiles statistics, presents awards, and publishes the Washington Newsletter (monthly).

*Order of the Sons of Italy in America* 2007 E St. N.W., Washington, D.C. 20036 (202) 547-2900.

Founded in 1905 as a fraternal organization, the OSIA promotes cultural and social activities through two hundred chapters throughout the United States. It sponsors education and anti-defamation projects as well as charitable and social services.

*UNICO National* 72 Burroughs Place, Bloomfield, N.J. 07003 (201) 748-9144.

UNICO was founded in 1922 to encourage Italian-Americans to participate actively in promoting their cultural heritage within the general community. Through its local chapters it conducts a wide range of activities in awarding scholarships, fighting defamation, and conducting a variety of health and social service programs. It has a membership of over ten thousand.

For a more extensive list of Italian-American organizations in the United States you may want to consult *The National Directory of Research Centers, Repositories and Organizations of Italian Culture in the United States,* edited by S.M. Tomasi (Torino: Giovanni Agnelli Foundation, 1980).

Available in the Center on Migration Studies, 209 Flagg Place, Staten Island, New York 10304.

# Selected Bibliography

Abelson, Ann. *The Little Conquerors.* New York: Random House, 1960.
   A novel of an Italian-American family, headed by a strong, matriarchal figure, fighting their way up in a New England town.
Amfitheatrof, Eric. *The Children of Columbus.* Boston: Little, Brown, 1973.
   A well-written, popular history that stretches from Columbus to the 1970s and includes sources and references.
Barolini, Helen. *The Dream Book.* New York: Schocken, 1985.
   An anthology of the writings of more than fifty women of Italian-American background with an introduction explaining the historical and social context of their long "silence."
Cordasco, Francesco. *Studies in Italian American Social History.* Totowa, N.J.: Rowman & Littlefield, 1975.
   A collection of essays, including Valentine Rossilli Winsey's compilation of interviews, "The Italian Immigrant Women Who Arrived in the United States before World War I."
Caroli, Betty Boyd, Robert Harney, and Lydio F. Tomasi. *The Italian Immigrant Woman in North America.* Staten Island, N.Y.: American Italian Historical Association, 1977.
   An important research collection covering all aspects of Italian-American women's lives from old-country origins to present-day problems.
Covello, Leonard. *The Social Background of the Italo-American School Child,* edited and with an introduction by F. Cordasco. Totowa, N.J.: Rowman & Littlefield, 1972.
   A classic by a much revered figure among Italian-American educators, it throws light on Italian-American social history.
D'Ambrosio, Richard. *No Language but a Cry.* Garden City, N.Y.: Doubleday, 1970.
   A novel embodying psychological aspects of a young girl's struggle against neglect.
De Capite, Michael. *Maria.* New York: John Day, 1943.
   A penetrating novel centered on the final triumph of the main character, Maria, to overcome slum life and two difficult marriages.
De Conde, Alexander. *Half Bitter, Half Sweet.* New York: Scribner's, 1971.
   A good book on Italian-American history, with attention to relations between the United States and Italy.
Di Donato, Pietro. *Christ in Concrete.* Indianapolis: Bobbs-Merrill, 1939.
   An autobiographical novel with a striking portrait of the widowed mother and family life during Depression years.
———. *Immigrant Saint.* New York: McGraw-Hill, 1960. The biography of Mother Cabrini, who worked among the poor, founded hospitals, and was canonized.
Ets, Marie Hall. *Rosa: The Life of an Italian Immigrant.* Minneapolis: University of Minnesota Press, 1970.
   An important oral history document: the vivid and compelling words of Rosa recount her life and hardships and her triumphant survival.
Fante, John. *Brotherhood of the Grape.* Boston: Houghton-Mifflin, 1977.
   An important novelist depicts the tensions in an Italian-American marriage and evokes a memorable portrait of a long-suffering wife.
Forgione, Louis. *The River Between.* New York: Arno Press, 1975.
   A realistic novel depicting the passions of a troubled family relationship, focusing on a woman and her father-in-law.
Gambino, Richard. *Blood of My Blood.* Garden City, N.Y.: Doubleday, 1974.
   An excellent sociological study of the dilemma of being Italian-American.
Gans, Herbert J. *The Urban Villagers.* New York: Free Press, 1962.
   Italian-American culture within a working-class context in Boston's West End with some valuable insights on women.
Green, Rose Basile. *The Italian-American Novel.* Rutherford, N.J.: Fairleigh Dickinson University Press, 1974.
   A critical study of Italian-American literature as a documentation of the interaction of two cultures. A wide-ranging analysis of authors.

*Images: A Pictorial History of Italian Americans.* Staten Island, N.Y.: Center for Migration Studies, 1981.
    Photographs and documentation exploring three centuries of the Italian presence in America.

Iorizzo, Luciano, and Salvatore Mandello. *The Italian-Americans.* New York: Twayne, 1971.
    A survey that seeks, through original research, to integrate the story of Italian-Americans with American history.

Johnson, Colleen Leary. *Growing Up and Growing Old in Italian American Families.* New Brunswick, N.J.: Rutgers University Press, 1985.
    How Italian Americans view the life cycle.

Krause, Corinne. *Grandmothers, Mothers, and Daughters.* New York: American Jewish Committee, 1978.
    An oral history study of "ethnicity, mental health, and continuity of three generations of Jewish, Italian, and Slavic American women."

Lagumina, Salvatore J. *The Immigrants Speak.* Staten Island, N.Y.: Center for Migration Studies, 1979.
    A volume of oral history in which the immigrants speak for themselves on identity and assimilation. Includes the reminiscence of journalist Clara Corica Grillo.

Lapolla, Garibaldi M. *The Fire in the Flesh.* New York: Arno, 1975.
    A novel of a young Italian girl who uses her beauty in a quest for power and wealth in America. A provocative treatment.

Miller, Arthur. *A View from the Bridge.* New York: Bantam, 1972.
    A play by a famous American dramatist concerning sexual and familial tensions in an Italian-American setting in Brooklyn.

Morrison, Joan, and Charlotte Fox Zabusky. *American Mosaic.* New York: Dutton, 1980.
    Interviews with immigrants who arrived in the United States from 1906 to 1978, including the stories of two Italian-American women.

Neidle, Cecyle. *America's Immigrant Women.* New York: Hippocrene Books, 1975.
    A chronicle of significant contributions of immigrant women to the foundation and development of the American nation.

Pagano, Jo. *Golden Wedding.* New York: Arno, 1975.
    A novel encompassing a half century in the story of the Simones, chronicling a family from its start to a golden wedding anniversary.

Papaleo, Joseph. *Out of Place.* Boston: Little, Brown, 1970.
    A gifted novelist writes of the problems of assimilation and particularly those of Italian-American women.

Peragallo, Olga. *Italian-American Authors and Their Contribution to American Literature.* New York: Vanni, 1949.
    A pioneer in the field of literary bibliography, Peragallo compiled the first survey, including eleven women authors.

Puzo, Mario. *The Fortunate Pilgrim.* New York: Atheneum, 1964.
    In his finest novel, Puzo depicts the story of Lucia Santa, a formidable Italian immigrant, as she struggles for her family's survival in New York's Hell's Kitchen in the 1930s.

Rolle, Andrew. *The Italian Americans, Troubled Roots.* New York: Free Press, 1980.
    An important work of psychohistory that discloses the conflict in the lives of Italian-American women.

Scarpaci, Jean, ed. *The Interaction of Italians and Jews in America.* Staten Island, N.Y.: American Italian Historical Association, 1974.
    The proceedings of the association's annual conference.

Tomasi, Lydio. *The Italian American Family.* Staten Island, N.Y.: Center for Migration Studies, 1972.
    A booklet examining the interplay between individual, transplanted family, and society in the Southern Italian's process of adjustment to urban America.

Wertheimer, Barbara. *We Were There.* New York: Pantheon, 1977.
    The story of working women in America, including information on women in the trade union movement. Annotated bibliography.

Yans-McLaughlin, Virginia. *Family and Community, Italian Immigrants in Buffalo, 1880–1930.* Ithaca, N.Y.: Cornell University Press, 1977.
    A scholarly presentation using family as a focal point in a specific time and place to show the process of immigrant adjustment in America.